Music Education with Digital Technology

Also available from Continuum

Music Development and Learning, David Hargreaves and Adrian North

Art Education 11–18, 2nd Edition, Richard Hickman

Music Education with Digital Technology

Edited by John Finney and Pamela Burnard

Education and Digital Technology

continuum

Continuum International Publishing Group
The Tower Building
11 York Road
London
SE1 7NX

80 Maiden Lane, Suite 704
New York, NY 10038

www.continuumbooks.com

British Library Cataloguing-in-Publication Data
A catalogue record for this book is available from the British Library.

ISBN: 0-8264-9414-5 (hardcover)

Library of Congress Cataloging-in-Publication Data
To come

Typeset by Data Standards Ltd, Frome, Somerset, UK.
Printed and bound in Great Britain by Athenaeum Press., Gateshead, Tyne & Wear

Contents

Series Foreword: Education and Technology

Series editors: Anthony Adams and Sue Brindley

It is fitting that the first book in this new series on teaching with digital technologies makes as its first and explicit claim that it is concerned with 'change and innovation in teaching'. This might be the claim we want to make about the entire series. We are concerned, as Series Editors, with bringing about opportunities to engage with fresh perspectives on teaching with digital technologies. Our guiding principles for the series are to allow an exploration of the exciting potentialities of working with digital technologies and simultaneously to allow us to use the lens of digital technologies to revisit and perhaps rethink approaches to teaching and learning more generally.

Digital technologies beckon a renaissance in teaching and learning: a reframing of a theory of knowledge which challenges accepted thinking and pedagogies in the field. In this sense, no one volume in this series will be about classroom approaches, though this will certainly be a major strand of each book. Further, an equal (though perhaps potentially more long-term) aim is that each book will stimulate deeper thinking in the field and will therefore contribute to the development of practitioner professional knowledge (and therefore the ongoing development of professional autonomy) through research.

In this volume on music education, Burnard and Finney invite us to explore the ways in which music education is responding to, and indeed driving, new thinking about pedagogy; about student ownership of knowledge; about creativity in teaching and in learning. The volume is informed throughout by three research perspectives: practitioner research; construction of case studies framed by a wider research perspective; and research as a catalyst for change – in practice, policy and teacher professionalism.

The first section concerns itself with the changing identities of teachers. All change requires adaptation, but Burnard and Finney are also keen to signal that effective use of digital technologies is rooted in continuity of good practice: 'Teaching music in the digital age will require thoughtful and reflective teachers'. Their concern in this section is to capture the ways in which new generations of music educators explore and define how effective learning should happen in the digital-rich classroom. We see here the representation in action of teacher as researcher – and in this case, the perspective of the new teacher, capturing, analysing and responding to classroom-focused findings. We see how these new teachers define and discuss the ways in which their pedagogical repertoire is enhanced through the use of digital technologies in music teaching.

The second section explores through case studies the wider perspective of responses to the use of digital technologies in the music classroom, and takes us specifically into the experiences of students and composition. The case study approach allows us to understand not only the classroom approaches taken, but also crucially the responses of students within those classrooms. Case study proves a powerful teacher mechanism for enhancing understanding of learning in the music classroom.

The third section explores strategies for change. Offered here are, in Burnard and Finney's words, 'sets of dynamic strategies to explore how music teachers' knowledge of technologies can be embodied in a relationship with music'. Incorporating both UK and international perspectives, this section challenges us to consider how and why we teach as we do and the place of digital technologies in that conceptual framework.

This volume has been designed to make a major contribution to the debates about how students interact with and make best use of technology in music. However, in their final statement the authors sum up the reasons why enterprises such as the production of this volume, and your reading of it are of such importance:

> recognition, research and sharing of good practice by teachers ... is fundamental if we are to develop the best teaching and learning in our music classrooms today.

As Series Editors, we can think of no better motif for the series on teaching and learning with digital technologies than the significance of recognition, research and sharing of good practice. We recommend this volume to you.

Sue Brindley
Anthony Adams

Biographies

Anthony Adams was appointed as a lecturer in English Education at the University of Cambridge in 1972, after a career in secondary schools and as an Inspector in a Local Education Authority. He was also, until July 2007, Director of Studies in Education at Trinity Hall, Cambridge, and a Fellow of Wolfson College. He has a wide experience of publishing, both of his own books and as an editor, and lectures internationally on language awareness and digital technologies

Sue Brindley is a Senior Lecturer at the University of Cambridge Faculty of Education. She coordinates the development of blended learning in the Faculty and the MEd in Researching Practice. She previously worked as Professional Officer at QCA and a lecturer at the Open University. She taught for many years in secondary schools in the East End of London where she was a Deputy Head and Acting Head.

Acknowledgements

We would like to thank Kiare Ladner for her hard work, efficiency and support in attending to editorial and formatting detail. We are also grateful to university lecturers Magne Espeland and Martin Fautley, and secondary school music teachers Laura Scott, Jenny Francis, Roger Green and John Arkel for reading and commenting on chapters. Finally, we are indebted to the support and collegiality of Sue Brindley and Tony Adams for encouraging us to pursue the project.

Introduction

This is a book about change and innovation in music teaching. It comes at a time when music education, schooling and learning are being redefined. Although the school remains the central focus of music educators, its position within a much wider sphere of musical education is challenging thought about present and future scenarios. Are schools and their music really as slow to respond to change as is frequently argued?

Headley Beare, writing from Melbourne, Australia challenges the myth of the unchanging school (2003). Despite the impression that schools do not change very much, Beare argues that we are at a time when structural and framework changes to schooling are in progress and adapting to a new world order. Beare reminds us that there are

> new ways of viewing knowledge, new ways of conceiving of planetary systems, new patterns of interactions across the world of work, new approaches to birth control, child-bearing and child rearing, and powerful new information technology which not only speeds up access to the volume of information, but in many ways supersedes print materials and the traditional techniques of publishing (2003 p. 2).

The school can now be accessed from home, home accessed from school, and the rest of the world from both. There are indications that the nine-to-five factory day is being replaced by a more flexible arrangement and that learning may take place in multiple, diverse environments. While state-managed curricula intensify, with attention to ever more precise outcomes, standards and standardization, in lively counterpoint runs a call for the re-modelling of schooling. A revolution is taking place with the demands for creativity, innovation, fresh models of learning and the melting down of traditional school subjects into a wash of generic skills. And at the centre of this revolution, sometimes referred to as the third industrial revolution, is Information and Communication Technology (ICT).

The combination of music and ICT, or what is now preferred in official talk within the United Kingdom as music technologies, has come to be viewed by governments and their managing agencies as a primary catalyst for change. Indeed, technologies are considered to be the drivers of change, inviting frontier thinking and boundary breaking. Through technologies, present practices can be reviewed and re-contextualized – or more interestingly, transformation and re-envisioning of the future can take place.

Music has long been at the forefront of technological advancement, with music educators harnessing its potential long before the advent of digital technology.

Technology/instruments are the very tools that mediate in the reception and consumption of music, along with its making and production. They are the media through which musical impulses come to be projected and ingested, offering music teachers and the young people they are teaching unprecedented scope for democratic engagement in making music. Access to music technologies brings the potential to ensure self-realization and the realization of social solidarities and group identities. It can link local communities with the global community, making claims on both the vitality of neighbourhood and a much wider interconnectedness. Music and music learning is at ease in the digital age. Yet if this is so, then why is there a gulf between what needs to be done in music teaching and the resources available to do it?

While schools are changing and the system of regularized schooling may be in the throes of radical revision, students, along with society, are changing even more rapidly. Young people's fluency of access to music, and their capacity to exercise finely grained judgements about the way they choose to use it, create ever greater challenges for the music educator at the beginning of the new century. By the early years of secondary school, young people demonstrate a capacity to design their own music curricula and musical educational programme, as well as to question the authority of music in school. Accorded full human rights and entitlements, these young people are quick to show social maturity and an insatiable search for autonomy. Music and its technologies feed their quest. ICT becomes the medium through which their social maturity can be harnessed and matched by intellectual challenge. But if this is to represent more than the seductive voice of better futures over-dubbing dismal and disappointing pasts, then there are challenging questions to be tackled too. What is this change for? What will be improved? How will worthwhile human values inherent in the act of making music – such as the experience of timelessness, reflection, mutuality, empathy and endurance – be preserved and sustained in a digital age?

Introducing Part I: Changing Identities

Teaching music in the digital age will require thoughtful and reflective teachers. In Part I of the book we gain the perspectives of a new generation of music teachers and at the same time hear the voices of their students. By way of providing a United Kingdom context for these voices, John Finney's opening **Chapter 1** sets out to vividly represent a social reality in one secondary school, while focusing on the identity project of a student working 'on the edge' of schooling. The student, PJ, is without music educational credentials. No institution has conferred legitimacy on his achievements. His situation serves to illustrate the complex interplay between the structures that continue to distribute success unequally and the student's search for agency and autonomy. If identity is best thought about in terms of that meeting place between who a young person wants to be and what the world allows him to be, then the case of PJ and his evolving digital musical mind may be particularly illuminating.

John Finney's quasi-ethnographic approach is complemented by Hannah Quinn's self-narrative style in **Chapter 2**. She tells the story of coming to shape an identity through the discovery of electronic music, as she calls the music that was to prove so significant in her musical life history. Hannah reflects on a vividly remembered sense of liberation that she experienced in becoming an electronic musician and the ways in which this has led her to review her priorities as a developing secondary school music teacher. Hannah's deeply communicated trust in the creative capabilities of her students sits alongside a growing mistrust of the agencies, both national and local, that set in place all that constrains her students' creativity.

In **Chapter 3** Louise Cooper, writing as a trainee music teacher, creates a well-bounded case to explore gender issues and ICT. Louise's unit of analysis is three classes of students, aged 13–14, to whom she taught music technology alongside their non-music technology lessons. A helpful triangulation of data, some of which is rich and thick, leads to a set of propositions waiting to be tested by other teachers. But unlike Hannah, Louise has no electronic musical identity and remains circumspect about the potential of technology to provide for a comprehensive musical education.

Serena Croft in **Chapter 4** takes a reflective stance too, although her concern is with the changing motivations of her students as ICT became a central resource for their development as composers. Looking back on the programme of action research in her classroom, Serena finds that Csikszentmihalyi's theory of Flow provides a helpful way of understanding the levels of commitment evidenced in her students' work. Beyond this, Serena develops a theoretical model through which she is able to regulate her own well-being and professional development as she makes sense of changing professional circumstances.

The case of Alex Baxter in **Chapter 5** reveals a resourceful novice music teacher tackling the problem of survival in his first year of teaching. Alex invokes a programme of action research through which he both reaffirms a musical identity of his own and attunes to the burgeoning musical identities of his students. There is transformation in student engagement as the students' most personal possession becomes the instrument through which new musical identities are celebrated.

The first part of the book sees teachers, in the role of practitioner-researchers, developing theoretical insight and learning to view music teaching differently. Digital technology is evidently moving the minds of teachers and students alike.

Introducing Part II: Researching Digital Classrooms

In Part II, we gain from the perspectives of researchers who offer many ideas for fuelling the change process in teacher practice. The authors share the specifics of their own research through reports, ranging from case study research constructed around individual cases to generalizations across cases of learners' experiences in techno-logically mediated musical settings. There are representations of collaboration and collaborative musical events, and persons within those events, using digital media. Each chapter illustrates what we can learn from research, concerning both the potential of technology to enhance music teaching and learning, and the potential of research to fuel the change process in teacher practice.

Michael Challis addresses issues in **Chapter 6** that are drawn from a study investigating learners' musical identity and the motivation of boys to take up DJ culture. Mike uses a case study approach to look at how students learn to develop their compositional skills. The process begins with listening to other people's music on vinyl and learning to manipulate it using turntables. It proceeds to using drum machines, synthesizers, samplers and loop players to create rhythm, bass line and thematic elements, culminating in the creation of a complete track. Finally loops of original material are used to incorporate the computer into a complete live performance.

Research from Ireland is reported by Kevin Jennings in **Chapter 7**, whose illuminating case study collects, records and analyses data to further our understanding of young people composing music with computer tools. Kevin reports on an investigation into the design and development of creative music learning software which makes use of novel computer-based graphical representations of musical information for student composing. He affirms the importance of building an understanding of teachers and teaching with technology which bridge the research–practice divide. Rethinking how to compose with computers as mediators is taken up as a question that requires reflection by teachers at each step along the way. This is a study which illuminates complex issues at work and penetrates the varying conditions of musical notation when children compose music with computers.

Perspectives from Australia are offered by Andrew Brown and Steve Dillon in **Chapter 8**. Their research explores the potential for using computers, linked via a network, as instruments for collaborative musical improvisation. Andrew and Steve remind us of what teachers can learn from how students experience collaborative music making, namely ensemble playing and group improvisation. They use the notion of musicianship to define the computer as instrument. A new use of music technology arises through the development of case study research within virtual and present collaborative learning spaces, which have the potential to fuel the change process for teachers.

The potential of e-learning environments to provide collaborative and supportive learning spaces is corroborated in **Chapter 9** by Frederick Seddon. Writing from Italy, Frederick uncovers insights about opportunities for computer-based collaborative composition. He introduces key considerations to be made in an on-line classroom and the benefits of interactive e-learning, not only within and between schools but also in terms of group composing in global classrooms. The use of synchronous communication (based on real-time interaction) and asynchronous communication (based on delayed interaction) are addressed as effective forms of music learning.

Teresa Dillon in **Chapter 10** focuses on the study and principles of collaborative music technology practices. Teresa addresses the use of existing technologies in the classroom and how to better embed these existing technologies within the secondary music curriculum. Drawing on case study examples carried out on the use of keyboard and eJay computer-sampling software, Teresa reports on research that addresses a range of musical, creative and collaborative practices supported by music technology. The insights from this research have the potential to fuel the change process for teachers in the ways we plan for and use electronic keyboards in music classrooms. The starting points and themes for supporting teacher development and student learning cover a whole range of digital technology.

What is common across all of these research reports is the extent to which research uncovers new ways of thinking about classroom practice. Illustrative examples range from student-led discussions, peer assistance, self-evaluation and student-centred analysis, to how a teacher might develop an online pedagogy, scaffold a task, and provide the necessary resources and strategies for guiding the student's discovery and construction of new knowledge. The findings converge on the notion of the music classrooms as a learning community in which members share resources in both virtual and actual collaborative learning environments. This allows synchronous, collaborative improvisation and composition over long distances, develops networks, and involves a willingness to engage in high levels of social interaction in the construction of knowledge. The microworlds evidenced from findings on 'environment' and 'community' make clear that there are some key aspects of classroom practice that need careful consideration and perhaps redefinition. The articulation of new models of successful classroom practice, and some rethinking of the traditional models of pedagogy and related strategies, follow.

Introducing Part III: Strategies for Change

In Part III of the book we gain from the perspectives of researchers who offer ways of changing practice, policy and teacher professionalism. In these chapters, authors are less concerned with raising questions than offering sets of dynamic strategies to explore how music teachers' knowledge of technologies can become embodied in a relationship with music. This section examines strategies for exemplar practice that make for smart working and creative use of technology at the centre of the curricula. How can we use digital technology to help us to realize the inextricable connection between what we teach, how we teach it and how we train teachers to teach it?

Perspectives and strategies developed from the USA are presented by Alex Ruthmann in **Chapter 11**, which provides valuable ways for music educators to engage and extend students' learning using online technologies. Alex carefully considers the use of major online collaborative tools, which include blogs, podcasts and wikis. There is no doubt about the benefits of introducing students to these devices as a natural part of the students' creative and learning processes and as a means to gain a greater understanding of their work. Alex offers up descriptions rather than prescriptions for increased collaboration and reflective practices, shared both within and beyond formal school settings. Opportunities for teachers to develop expressions of practice which simultaneously develop the skill of reflective practice are suggested.

In **Chapter 12**, Jonathan Savage seeks to develop a theory to illustrate two models of musical practice using ICT within the music classroom. These models penetrate the varying conditions of musical practice with ICT, founded on the comparison of case with case. Jonathan introduces the powerful idea that the music technology classroom is rich in opportunities to try different approaches to teaching, and to learn from the experience of students in particular. One approach is 'extrinsic' to the technology itself and the other is 'intrinsic' in that it imbeds the exploration and engagement with sound itself. The metaphor of 'doorways' to musical encounters with ICT is introduced as specific pedagogical strategies for changing teacher practice. This chapter has much to teach us about how technology can play a creative role in music teaching and be used as a tool to create a more inclusive music curriculum.

Ambrose Field in **Chapter 13** builds on the 'intrinsic' argument of Jonathan Savage and makes a powerful case for starting inside the technological medium itself. In this way, new forms of musical expression become possible and new definitions of contemporary musical culture emerge. Many existing approaches to the teaching of music technology are rendered obsolete and particularly so at examination level.

Chapter 14 is written by Richard Hodges, as a teacher designing higher education programmes, in response to demands from young people inspired by the relationships between popular music and music technologies. Richard argues for the rethinking of what is accredited musically and how it is accredited within the school system. If music in the school is concerned with 'wider participation' then the subject is in need of being thought about in a different way. Existing frameworks and specifications may be inappropriate if young people are to be equipped with skills and practical competencies as part of an invigorated vocational education.

Lessons from education-reform experiences of Australia, Singapore and Hong Kong are offered by Samuel Leong in **Chapter 15**. Samuel cogently argues why the impact of reform has transformed schools and their practices with varying levels of success. He offers a vision for leadership 'that dares to replace piecemeal solutions lacking in symbiotic impact and sustainability with a more comprehensive approach to seeking, implementing and enforcing solutions'. The lessons that follow are compelling. They provide testimony to the advantages of locating teachers in the context of imposed change, while taking into account the influences of their beliefs on their practice.

In **Chapter 16**, Pamela Burnard argues why we need to rethink how music teachers can become more active agents of change in music education. Pamela's chapter calls for music teachers to enter into the educational debate on music technology, presupposing that researching practice is now an expectation and an available option to teachers. In this way, the questions raised in Part I are restated in the final chapter, with the imperative of placing music teachers at the front and centre of the research process.

Each of these authors makes it clear that teaching music in the digital age requires a view of learning, of the place of the learners (which includes the teacher as learner and as researcher) and of what counts as worthwhile learning which can be understood and effectively implemented in the context of contemporary music education.

The perspectives shared in the book present a unique international view and open the doors to further understanding of the complexities of teaching music in the digital age. The contributors from America, England, Ireland, Italy, China and Australia highlight the need to look for learning across and beyond the walls of classrooms and schools. Their contributions emphasize the teacher's role in educational change and provide a comprehensive view of how students interact with and utilize technology in music learning. Such recognition, research and sharing of good practice by teachers as practitioner-researchers is fundamental to developing the best teaching and learning pedagogy in our music classrooms today.

References

Beare, H. (2003) *Creating the Future School.* London and New York: Routledge Falmer.

Part I: Changing Identities

Chapter 1

Music Education as Identity Project in a World of Electronic Desires

John Finney

Jennie is in Year 9 at secondary school in the east of England. She is continually irritated by her ICT lessons at Lode Village College:

> *The teacher is slower than me. He's doing something and he doesn't know how to do it and I just want to shout out what to click on. To me it just seems like common sense.*

Jennie's father introduced her to the computer at the age of two and to word processing when she was five. With a little help, she easily picked up the music program Finale Notepad and uses it to compose meandering songs on her computer when she has time to spare. Sunday evening sees her attending to the downloading of a new ring tone. The bus journeys to and from school in the week ahead require contemplation and preparation, since these are important impression management times and times of tacit social-musical exchange. She says:

> *We'll be sitting on the bus when you hear a ring tone floating down the aisle, so when we get home that night, I'd remember it and type it into the search box, and get it on my phone and play it on the bus the next day. There's a bit of competition to see who has the loudest.*

Jennie's repertoire of ring tones will have been sifted and sorted by the end of the week and, like her contemporaries, electronic music will have pervaded both her private and public life. For Jennie, music education is a segmented business: a bit takes place in school but much more outside, with a great deal of dedication to her euphonium-playing in the village brass band as well as to the music of a local radio station (in which her listening taste coincides with that of her mother).

Moving from the shifting reality of Jennie's social world to a world of academic rhetoric, the question 'Where is music education?' is asked by Sloboda (2001) as he exposes the challenge facing those responsible for providing a music education. With this comes a direct challenge to school music teachers:

> Classroom music, as currently conceptualized and organized, may be an inappropriate vehicle for mass music education in 21st-century Britain. Hints of effective parameters of a more effective music education environment may well

be found within the somewhat anarchic mixed economy of out-of-school music provision in this country. (Sloboda 2001, p. 243)

Sloboda notes seven cultural trends that prompt a revision of established ways of thinking about a musical education. Multiculturalism, Youth Culture, Feminism, Secularism, Niche Cultures, Postmodernism and Electronic Communication, in Sloboda's view, conspire to restructure our musical social reality at the beginning of a new century. In the case of Electronic Communication, Sloboda points out that institutions such as schools no longer provide a privileged route to access. Indeed, it is likely to be the case that schools are seriously underprivileged in this respect, and that both technological resources and 'know how' lag behind what is available out of school.

A study of young people's music in and out of school (Lamont *et al.* 2003) showed, perhaps unsurprisingly, a more robust commitment by young people to music out of school than in school. The researchers conclude:

> The current challenge for school music is to maximise the experience of *all* pupils during the statutory period, and to help those who show an additional interest in music beyond the classroom to develop that, recognising the value of their own contributions, developing their individual skills through valuable social, cultural, and primarily musical experiences and activities, and providing the confidence to partake in musical activities in whatever personal or social context they choose. (*Ibid.* p. 240)

In the light of this fresh plea for a more inclusive approach, with its call for greater mutuality between formal and informal ways of engaging with music (see also Swanwick 1999, Green 2001), I would like first to establish a way of thinking about where a music education takes place in order to better understand young people's engagement with music in and out of school. By way of illustration, I will then describe the musical education of a young person with quite a different socio-musical profile from Jennie but who is attending the same school. Unlike the work of Lamont *et al.*, my concern will be with the way social structures bear upon young people's musical lives in and out of school – the way power and control operate to create the boundaries that both empower and disable young people in their search for a musical education. This, in turn, will lead to a better understanding of the social strategies devised by young people in order to gain distinction and status through music.

In following such an approach, I acknowledge the work of Bourdieu (2004) and Bernstein (2000) who in their different ways enable an enormously rich description of schooling, culture and society. Throughout the chapter, I make the assumption that young people today are members of a 'computerized generation' (Lyotard 1984) and that their musical thinking is infused with digital imagery. I begin by way of an explanatory note.

Where *is* Music Education?

School is charged with the responsibility for socializing young people into ways of being and thinking that are believed to be appropriate for their future roles in society. This requires that they develop patterns of behaviour acceptable to the institutional life of the school. Thus, the school sets in place formal learning environments and musical learning becomes part of a series of experiences that are regulated and ritualized, in which student choice and autonomy are to a greater or lesser extent restricted. The validity of these experiences is measured in terms of outcomes, levels of attainment and examination success; criteria for success are externally imposed.

Music is no different to other subjects in this respect and relies upon this framework of accountability for its status and place in the curriculum. The regularities, rituals and formalities that circumscribe school music create boundaries between the exercise of free and unfettered musical impulse and the channelling of these into musical contexts and conditions. These are determined by the teacher, and sanctioned by the school and those agencies charged with monitoring its effectiveness and its efficiency.

At the same time, within the school there may be another curriculum, a curriculum 'on the edge' as it were. This has sometimes been referred to as the open curriculum: one where content and style are determined by the students themselves, where interests and concerns, fantasies and ambitions are given space to grow. Students may seek to take advantage of resources and space where they can find autonomy over the musical decisions made. Their engagement with this informal curriculum, possible only in negotiation with the music teacher, may be casual, spontaneous and irregular or indeed regular and far from casual.

The pattern of the formal and informal curriculum, the regulated and unregulated, is replicated out of school: students may themselves find commitment to a formal musical learning environment in which there are regularities and rituals similar to those in school, where content and style are in the hands of others, and where choice and autonomy are constrained. Just as school may find space for the informal, the unregulated, so out of school there will exist an informal musical education where autonomy is sought and found. A distinctive aspect of these informalities will be a realm of privacy: music learning takes place in solitude, is contemplative in character and work may or may not be held back from future publication. I will call this the private curriculum.

Table 1.1 clarifies these distinctions, adding another curriculum that I have created: the ring tone curriculum. The ring tone of the mobile phone represents the most vibrant symbol of young peoples' conscious and unconscious engagement with music. It is an expression of personal and social identity – an emblem of existence, a public presentation of who they wish to be seen as – foregrounding their engagement with music and, of course, digital technology.

Table 1.1 Locations of music education

In School		Ring tone Curriculum	Out of School		
Formal Regulated Ritualized	Informal Unregulated Spontaneous		Formal Regulated Ritualized	Informal Unregulated Spontaneous	Private Undisclosed Contemplative

Where *is* music education? The answer is complex: all around, in and out of school. It is regular, ritualized, spontaneous, irregular and pervaded by ICT. The learning is both intentional and unintentional, formal and informal, casual, frequently private and variously directed by self and others. I make use of an instance of music education by way of illustration.

Music at Lode Village College

I arrive a few minutes before the lunch break and time my entrance to the music block so as to join those arriving from other parts of the school to take part in music at lunchtime, a profitable time for the ethnographic researcher to be 'hanging around'. I will be spending the next sixth months 'hanging around', talking casually and conversationally to students and in a more structured way to their music teacher. As my enquiry develops I come to engage with one pupil in particular.

As I approach the entrance to the music department, Year 7 pupils Alex, Sarah and Jessica arrive to complete the urgent business of the composition of their song, 'Where have all the answers gone?' This song sets out to deal with 'the blur' that is Year 7 in their new school. Its lyrics have already been created through their mobile phone conferencing the previous evening. The impulse is strong. The song must be sung. Jessica explains:

> *You ask questions but never really get the answer. It's the same at home. You ask if a friend can come round and there isn't a straight answer. I wouldn't mind if they said, 'I don't like that person, don't think they're suitable.' But they don't.*

Alex, Sarah and Jessica, like other pupils in the school at Key Stage 3, receive an hour-long music lesson each week. By Key Stage 4, music is well established and 25 per cent of each cohort opt into the examination course in music, three times the national uptake. Examination groups include students who have enjoyed a good number of years of formal instrumental instruction, those graduating from more informal engagement with music in and out of school, and those developing musical skill through the formalities of their school music curriculum.

Alex, Sarah and Jessica have booked the use of one of the department's three practice rooms and work through the 50-minute lunch break. In the main music room, three Year 11 students (two male guitarists and a female vocalist) rehearse their performance for the next day's whole-school assembly. In the second music room, smaller in size, the music teacher rehearses the choir. I join PJ, a Year 11 student, in the recording studio as he begins work on one of his hip hop productions. Scalic warm-ups seep through as I learn to become a part of the private world of PJ's musical ambition.

The Music Teacher's Perspective

Anne, the music teacher rehearsing the choir, has been teaching in the school for the past ten years and has been a teacher for 18 years altogether. She is highly regarded by the school community and much respected by her students. Comments from her students – 'she is good fun but still gets the work done'; 'you can talk to her about anything, not just music'; 'firm and supportive'; and 'prepared to put in time for us' – tell of a teacher dedicated to forming relationships and finding ways of engaging her students in music. Anne thinks of the music block as a resource available for all.

There is two-way traffic in the music department at the end of the school day, as well as at the end of morning lessons. Students come to find a space where they can be musical in the way they want to be. They are taught that the music department is theirs to make use of: a place to extend work begun in class, a place to initiate work of their own, a place where those receiving instrumental lessons are expected to refine ensemble skills, a place where all are free to share enthusiasms, and a place where wayward impulses may get translated into musical realities. Anne views the hour-long weekly music lesson as the place where it all begins:

> *Students are told in Year 7 that this is their department to take advantage of. Students use the department at lunchtimes to make music, share their listening passions, create spontaneous performances for friends as well as highly organized and planned activities. Boys tend to want to organize themselves. At times the demand is overwhelming and the diversity and complexity of operations becomes unsustainable. When this happens I call for a two week break and lock myself and colleagues in the department and eat cake. At the end of the day the secret is making sure that the Key Stage 3 curriculum is as accessible as possible. The only place you can really capture the kids, make sure how they feel about music, is in lessons. Once they feel they are good at music, and it doesn't matter at what level or what ability they have, but once they feel they are good at music, they will then trust you enough to actually take up the offer to come to lunchtime or after school, and take up the offer of extra-curricular music lessons. The curriculum has got to be right and it does have to be successful for both genders and all abilities.*

I am intrigued as to what Anne means by the phrase 'all abilities'. Is she referring to musical abilities? How might one think about musical ability? Does Anne mean musical achievement, indications of musical aptitude or simply an enthusiasm and motivation to do music – or is this a matter of cognitive ability scores?

In response to my probing, Anne immediately talks of a 'labelling school' with a push for exam results and of working with predictive data in order to take students beyond normal expectations. She is clearly uneasy about working with data based on the measurement of a limited range of cognitive attributes, but speaks of those with low ability in music, those better in music and of those who are 'gifted and talented'. She tells of how, by the end of Year 7, she begins to identify students with musical potential and seeks to enhance their musical experiences. This might mean being invited on a special musical trip to a London show or taking part in a special workshop.

At the same time, Anne puts on her 'inclusion hat' as she identifies those she believes to be underachieving. A recent Senegalese drumming day, for example, involved a large number of Year 9 underachieving boys. Anne believes the music department is making a tangible contribution to her school's improvement agenda and that she is able to work with external pressures to create a meaningful curriculum, managing local and national initiatives as well as what she considers to be parental expectations.

Anne also takes care to listen to her students: an informal consultation is carried out as part of her ongoing 'getting to know you' conversations, which aim to build trust, cooperation and collaboration. A phrase frequently used in discussions with Anne is 'the circle of trust' that she seeks to forge with her students. This circle is thought of as ever-expanding so as to create a whole-school community of music making that even embraces the wider community located in a semi-rural area close to the city.

I ask Anne to introduce me to four students who are engaged with music through digital sequencing programs, in or out of school. I talk to Jennie in Year 9 (whom I introduced at the beginning of the chapter), Nick in Year 11, Steve in Year 9 and PJ in Year 11, with varying degrees of regularity over a six-month period. I track their perceptions of themselves as consumers and producers of music, learning about some of the ways in which they are shaping their musical identities. In this way I aim to shed light on and, to some extent, to unravel the complexities of these young peoples' engagement with music, as well as the part played by information and communication technology.

My consultants, Jennie, Nick, Steve and PJ, tell me of their various music curricula ranging across the regulated and unregulated, in and out of school. They tell me about their contemplative and private work and describe their ring tone work. (In Years 8 and 9 their commitment to ring tones is fluid, though it becomes more stable, subtle and cynical in Years 10 and 11.) Table 1.2 shows how Jennie, Nick, Steve and PJ map onto our model.

Table 1.2 Locations of music education – the students

In School		Ring tone Curriculum	Out of School		
Formal	Informal		Formal	Informal	Private
Regulated Ritualized	Unregulated Spontaneous		Regulated Ritualized	Unregulated Spontaneous	Undisclosed Contemplative
Jennie Nick Steve	Nick PJ	Jennie Nick Steve PJ	Jennie	Jennie Nick Steve PJ	Jennie Nick Steve PJ

Jennie's preoccupations, as we know, are with the local village brass band and private computerized song compositions of overwhelming significance. Though Steve makes casual and indifferent use of a sequencing program at home, in contrast his father dedicates long periods of leisure time to computer composition. Nick composes 'silly songs', counterpointing his conscientiously refined GCSE compositions on his home music studio. Yet, as I learn more, I become particularly intrigued by the unregulated music curriculum of PJ. Unlike Nick in Year 11, PJ has not followed the GCSE music course. Rather, he has created an independent learning programme of his own that is reliant on the use of the music department's recording studio. It is the identity project of PJ that I examine further in this chapter.

The Case of PJ

PJ opted out of the regulations of school music at the end of Year 9. He has a long standing Dizzee Rascal ring tone and well-focused musical ambition. In preparation for his future as a rap artist, PJ first seeks to master the skills required of a rap producer. This involves making tracks to which the rap artist can respond. In producing tracks for imagined artists, a highly nuanced level of analytical listening, a sharpening of personal taste and a strengthening identification with a particular taste community are required. The distinctions between British and American hip hop are elaborated upon at length, their cultural messaging well known. PJ enjoys instructing me in the inner workings of hip hop: he tells of the subtle blending of simplicities and complexities and of those elements critical to insider idiomatic and stylistic meanings.

PJ's programme of self-education is well developed. He knows how he does music. He works with self-made targets and is ruthless in meeting them. Indeed, failing to meet his own deadlines is a source of anxiety and frustration.

Making tracks involves the appropriation and transformation of material and ideas gleaned through listening. This is rarely a direct process of listening and copying. Rather, PJ describes it as:

> *You listen to the music and think, oh that's really good, you know. Oh, I wish I could do that. There's a sense of jealousy in that. So I pause the music and just sit in silence for a bit, have silent thoughts and then, I don't know how it happens but something would come to me by thinking in my head, I just feel like, that sounds good, that sounds really good. I have to go then and there otherwise I would forget it and I would regret it, not putting it down. So yeah, go straight to my guitar, put it in the form of a guitar, the blues scale and all that, make a recording of it, take it to school and play that and try to put it on the keyboard. I get there in the end.*

What PJ arrives at is different, original and his own to mould (with the help of 'Reason', the sequencing program available in the music department's recording studio). For PJ, this is creativity, individuality and distinction. The interface between PJ's out-of-school private curriculum and the school's 'on the edge' curriculum is encouraged by his music teacher, who arranges periodic technical support from a former student and now producer for his own rock band. His music teacher's role remains that of facilitator and PJ's productions remain undisclosed to his music teacher. There is a history to this.

At option time in Year 9, PJ felt convinced that his music teacher didn't like him. Physical education promised a higher grade than music and although he remembers always wanting to make music, he had never wanted to compare himself to others. He knew that his particular style would come under scrutiny if he were to be subject to the regulations of the GCSE course and that there would be a requirement to conform to criteria beyond his control. He likes his style and is wary of outsiders, saying:

> *Tweaking to make it better, I don't like that. It doesn't become mine any more. I like to be myself. I have my own style, individual style.*

PJ is also aware, however, that he is working within stylistic conventions, with a community waiting to validate his musical productions. His moves towards public ratification are cautious and I seem to be helping a little in this. He appears to welcome my interest, empathetic style and the congruence I show between his creative process and my own as I begin to tell him about how I do music. I note that PJ, in due course, moves from talking about himself as a 'producer' to referring to himself as a 'composer'!

Anne recalls PJ featuring amongst the underachieving Year 9 boys, as well as his fading commitment to the guitar lessons specially arranged at the request of his father. PJ had become a difficult member of the Year 9 class. He lacked focus and presented strong and uncompromising ideas that others found difficult to work with in group work. Unsurprisingly, he became a passive class member by the end of Year 9, with a negative reputation developing within the school. Anne explains:

> *When he was in the classroom the peer group made it difficult for him to achieve and made it much cooler for him to just sit there and do very little, or do the least he could do. And he was underachieving all the time. So, of course, I used to nag him and say, 'come on PJ, you can do better than this, what about trying this with the music, or adding this or adding that.' And, of course I needed to gently cajole him into attending his guitar lessons. However, our relationship changed in Year 10 when much to my surprise he auditioned for the school show,* West Side Story, *and what a voice! After the show he asked if he could come in at lunchtime to make his music. Interestingly, he now wants to do music technology as a post-16 subject at the sixth form college.*

PJ is thoughtful about his personal journey and the task of overcoming what he refers to as 'the silent killer', the pressure to conform to dominant peer cultures. PJ recalls the unease felt in the process of determining his own musical pathway:

> *I felt restricted, because you're mates with these people. You can't say you like what you really do too much, because they don't like it. I would go home feeling so suppressed. And I wouldn't know why. I'm not saying that my friends are bad people or anything like that, but it was my friends who were stopping me from actually really getting into music. I learnt to be not too enthusiastic about it.*

PJ recalls school music lessons with satisfaction and believes he got something important from these, and in particular his occasional guitar lessons:

> *I learnt about BB Mac and people like that. And I really got interested in them. And I constantly wondered what inspired them to do what they did, and to make them great, or gave them the determination to do that. And how could I get it, you know. And still to this day I don't know, but it's something that keeps me going because I want to find out what inspired them. I want what hit them to hit me, yeah. I didn't start getting into music until I was twelve. I picked up the guitar a bit and when I came here and they had a studio and I thought, great. And it was only last year that I got a full tutorial on it. So if I had started on it when I was in Year 9 I suppose I would have had a lot more work than I do now. But it was just a case of my being shy and not asking, not getting what I want immediately. I still suffer from that now, so you know, it is something I learn.*

PJ is thoughtful and to an extent rueful about his lack of music theory. Although he is aware that his lone musical programme has left him without the knowledge that he believes he needs in order to fulfil his musical ambition, his mastery of the art of self-instruction reassures him that this can be overcome. As Year 11 comes to an end he is voted the most popular pupil in the school. But PJ is learning to live not with the acceptance of this, but with a devastating rejection. He has been refused a place to study A Level Music Technology at Sixth Form College. PJ turns to another post-16 possibility in order to return to a regulated music curriculum.

Discussion

As I grew to know the musical work of Jennie, Nick, Steve and PJ, a model emerged explaining where music education might be and how it might be viewed as having some coherence. I came to see that the much used distinction between the formal and the informal could be more usefully replaced by making the distinction between the regulated and unregulated, and that the distinction between private work and publicly presented work was significant. These distinctions helped me to better understand the structures that exercise power and control over the musical education of young people, and which they react and respond to in order to achieve status and control over their lives. In the case of PJ, the dissonance between what the regulated school curriculum had to offer and what he needed was too great to resolve, despite the best efforts of his music teacher to create a fluid boundary between music in and out of school.

PJ's formal musical educational project had involved experiencing the statutory music curriculum as represented by Key Stage 3 music lessons, sporadic attendance at guitar lessons and a vocal performance in the school production of *West Side Story*. These were regulated within the norms of secondary schooling. They furthered the aims and ethos of his school as it operated, both within a national agenda of school improvement and effectiveness, and within its own special character and set of values. PJ's decision not to pursue the regulations of an examination course in music at age 14 arose from a difficult Year 9 school experience. This labelled him as underachieving and, despite the best efforts of his music teacher, failed to convince him of his potential to succeed in conventional terms. PJ's musical ambition, however, was not closed off by his school. There was space to find a way back.

The music department of Lode Village College offered the possibility of an unregulated music curriculum, which allowed PJ to further his particular identity project. It enabled him to move into a well-established community of taste, leaving behind school and national musical educational norms while exposing himself to another set of externally imposed criteria. In this process, PJ came to manage a programme of self-regulated musical learning and to understand more about how and why he does music, and where a musical education could be found. His musical education has to date been in many places, some of which I have not documented here and which I know nothing about, including those within his family and network of hip hop. It would seem that learning within the regulated curriculum, experienced up to age 14, had not been insignificant for PJ, albeit that incidental rather than intentional learning took place. His deregulated (self-regulated) post-14 experience that followed provided for richness of learning and led to his desire to enrol for a regulated post-16 musical education.

Working 'on the Edge'

What are the outcomes of PJ's unregulated musical education? We might speculate on the achievement of a good degree of personal autonomy and the flourishing of creative capabilities, linked to learning how to learn and setting in train a lifelong pattern. As musical goals are met, so evidence of a respect for the musical and artistic work of others emerges. In addition, PJ has a charisma that makes him highly employable and this is not even taking into account his potential as a rap artist. In a great many respects, therefore, his unregulated curriculum has met and exceeded the expectations of our state-sponsored education system.

Of course, we might be wondering how it could be possible to accommodate PJ's personalized learning programme in an education system that insists on the accreditation of elaborated cognitive capacities, and whose power and authority depend upon the regulation and the maintenance of well-defined boundaries. In the case of music, these boundaries are in some part created by what sociologists have referred to as high status knowledge. In the case of music, this is knowledge that arbitrates in matters of taste. It defines what counts as music and what doesn't count as music, and determines who is and who is not the musician. It continues to privilege elaborated musical structures and insists on a particular approach to the decoding of musical works. It is this that regulates formal musical learning and celebrates orthodoxy rather than heresy in artistic work. In this way the performative culture of the school and the school system can be validated.

Teachers and students use different musical codes. Teachers tend to use elaborated codes derived from Western European 'elite' culture, whereas students use vernacular codes. ICT is crucial to this, since it is central to the students' code and to their musical consumption and production. For teachers, on the other hand, ICT is often alien to their code and can be a cause of anxiety and tension. This may lead them to evaluate the use of ICT-produced music negatively and to impose their own elaborated code – periodic phrasing, harmonic conventions, extended phrases, developmental variation and so on – on these pieces. In the case of public examinations, teachers know that examiners also operate within elaborated codes and will negatively assess work that does not conform to the norms of this code.

Students and teachers are therefore in danger of standing on opposite sides of a musical and linguistic chasm with few holding the key to unlock the other's code. The problem lies in the failure to communicate and lack of responsiveness between those formulating the official curriculum and those producing contemporary culture. In a world where many young people no longer recognize 'elite' culture as better than popular forms or more important to social success, the ring tone may grow as the most potent symbol of a young person's musical education. By doing music in the way he does, PJ stands as a potent symbol of how, where and why to do music. He is gaining access to what Bourdieu refers to as 'social capital' which, unlike 'cultural capital', is a matter of not what you know but who you know and who knows you (Thornton 1995). A further form of capital, referred to by Bourdieu as symbolic capital, is acquired too – this is concerned with the accumulation of prestige, celebrity status and honour (Bourdieu 2004; see also Jenkins 2003). It is about recognition. Phillips (2006) describes Bourdieu's explanations of how and why culture is produced in terms of existential crisis:

> once status is no longer safely embedded in social structure – once there has been the Reformation, the rise of capitalism, the French Revolution, and so on – recognition becomes the name of the game in a quite different way. More and more people have to find a place in the world instead of simply inheriting one. Prestige is up for grabs. The project of the modern, unmoored, displaced

individual is to find his value in the eyes of other people, and to resent this. (Phillips 2006, p. 273)

PJ's project is to attempt to turn resentment into enchantment by creating a music curriculum that is 'on the edge' of schooling, a place unlikely to be sponsored to any extent by the school system. While offering a social and psychological space for the adolescent seeking to find meaning and explore and shape identity through music, it remains beyond that which is assessed and accredited as part of the performative culture of the school. For PJ it is a private realm where a contented and relaxed sense of being alone allows for the discovery of what he really wants, irrespective of what others expect. Exploring this 'on the edge curriculum' might help to envisage a future form of schooling liberated from its current functions and performance requirements. For future generations of young people this could offer a valuable source of a 'personalized' musical education – one that would contribute to the conviviality of the school as a community of lifelong learners concerned with much more than what is offered by the official curriculum.

Conclusions

The music education of young people will continue to be in many places and the question remains: how is classroom music to be conceptualized and organized so that it can claim a central place in the project of mass musical education?

Pitts (2001) proposes that an answer lies in working towards a common understanding of what a music education might mean for key stakeholders: the student, the teacher and the policy-maker. However, even this is unlikely to resolve the question of what music and model of learning is ultimately legitimate in the face of competing perspectives within each stakeholdership. In addition, there exist many stakeholderships beyond the student, the teacher and the policy-maker; the music industry, the media and employers' association are but three significant examples. Culture exists to be contested and there is unlikely to be a moratorium in the struggle for legitimacy. Furthermore, the simply made distinction between formal and informal learning environments in music is analytically unhelpful, telling us little about states of regulation and lack of regulation which bear so heavily on young peoples' identity projects, their musical educational success and the acquisition of social and symbolic capital. The acquisition of social and symbolic capital will continue to be a major factor in determining the strategies adopted by young people in gaining access to a musical education.

'Young people live in a world of electronic desires where there are more choices than can be made and where time is fast.' (Willis 2001, p. 108) Indeed, it is doubtful whether young people make many choices at all. As we have seen in the case of PJ, however, young people will seek out agency in shaping their own musical education and the music educational practices of the future, wherever these may be located. At the same time we should not underestimate the ways in which structures constrain and distribute success in unequal fashion. The case of PJ is illustrative of this. Whether music technology can make for a more democratic future for music education remains to be seen.

Reflections

The case of PJ and his encounters with school music set out in this chapter serve to further the understanding of young people's identity projects. My motive has been to contribute to political and social change, and I am aware of political and value bias in the way I have gone about this. I have sought out certain kinds of data and chosen particular ways of collecting it. I have pressed the music teacher to the point of contradiction in order to expose the intractable ambiguities with which music teachers working within schools must live, in an age where public policy dominates practice and where professional autonomy is severely constrained. In a number of respects I now realize that I was never wholly truthful with those who participated in the research, whether students or music teacher. They did not know, for example, that I harboured a longstanding predilection for supporting those students who saw things differently, those who to me clearly were socially disadvantaged and who were predictably from working class backgrounds. PJ's story satisfied that bias well. I had taught many such students in a Basingstoke comprehensive school in the 1980s and witnessed how the structures of schooling contributed to their struggles, resistances and failures. My fairly recent reading of the work of Bernstein has helped me to understand all this better. What I find remarkable is that so little research within music education has a declared political bias, that so little research explicitly declares a concern for social justice, that so little research explicitly acknowledges the tensions that exist between structure and agency and that these tensions may well be largely irreducible. I do believe that research such as that undertaken here, for all its failings, can assist participants, the researcher and the researched, to better understand how they are placed in the world. It may help others to do likewise. I hope so. For my part I am grateful to PJ in particular for assisting me in that process.

References

Bernstein, B. (2000), *Pedagogy, Symbolic Control and Identity*. New York: Rowmann and Littlefield Publishers.

Bourdieu, P. (2004), *The Field of Cultural Production*. Cambridge: Polity Press.

Green, L. (2001), *How Popular Musicians Learn: A Way Ahead for Music Education*. Aldershot: Ashgate.

Jenkins, R. (2003), *Pierre Bourdieu*. London: Routledge.

Lamont, A., Hargreaves, D.J., Marshall, N. and Tarrant, M. (2003), 'Young people's music in and out of school'. *British Journal of Music Education*, 20(3), 229–42.

Lyotard, J.F. (1984), *The Postmodern Condition: A Report on Knowledge*. Minneapolis: University of Minnesota Press.

Phillips, A. (2006), *Side Effects*. London: Hamish Hamilton.

Pitts, P. (2001), 'Whose aesthetics? Public, professional and pupil perspectives of music education'. *Research Studies in Music Education*, 17, 54–60.

Sloboda, J. (2001), 'Emotion, functionality, and the everyday experience of music: where does music education fit?' *Music Education Research*, 3(2), 243–54.

Swanwick, K. (1999), *Teaching Music Musically*. London: Routledge.

Thornton, S. (1995), *Club Culture: Music, Media and Subcultural Capital*. Cambridge: Polity Press.

Willis, P. (2001), *The Ethnographic Imagination*. Cambridge: Polity Press.

Chapter 2

Perspectives from a New Generation Secondary School Music Teacher

Hannah Quinn

It is my hope, in my first years of teaching music in secondary school, to create relevant musical experiences through which students can discover what is of significance to them and form their own musical identities. The background to my teaching is my own musical education, which I consider to have been rich and varied, with the discovery of music technology right at its heart.

The chapter that follows is an autobiographical account of how I began to explore music, through ICT and beyond the bounds of my formal music educational experience. It tells of a medium that gave me access to a world of sound and which fuelled my desire to deepen and sustain my engagement with music. In due course, it was to bring me to my current profession, as a secondary school music teacher.

In the light of my own musical education, I wish to reflect on scenes from the classroom during my first year of teaching. I draw parallels between what I have observed from the ways in which my students have responded to my teaching and my own educational experiences. With this in mind, I consider how informal musical experiences impact on students, how music technology might help to revitalize our national music curriculum and how music can become ever more meaningful to students.

Musical Beginnings

When I was 5 years old, my mum sold the cooker for £50. With the money, she bought our first piano. My dad was extremely proud. He had never quite recovered from a childhood experience of chopping up the family piano for firewood, that same piano which his grandmother had played by ear so beautifully. I took up piano lessons immediately. My teacher was a kind and patient lady whose playing, as we approached her front door, sounded magnificently technical and virtuosic to my 5-year-old ears, and I was instantly inspired.

A few years later, enrolling at a local primary school with a thriving musical life led by Mrs Gibson, my school musical education began. I was able to start with learning the recorder, and later to learn the flute. In addition, there was a choir and an orchestra, which played arrangements that Mrs Gibson had painstakingly created.

I remember an epic arrangement of 'The Dam Busters March' in particular. At the end of each day, we would gather in the school hall and every week Mrs Gibson would have magically added another section for us to learn. I recall it as a painfully slow business, but its majestic infamous tune was something of an achievement for a primary school.

As my standing as a pianist was recognized, I came to be assigned the prestigious task of playing the school hymn for assemblies. This involved playing the grand piano in the hall, something which gave me a huge and lasting confidence as a performer. My memories of playing 'Autumn Days' alongside 400 peers still float through my mind whenever I have something nerve-racking to do.

Graduation to secondary school at the age of 11 provided further opportunities for musical exploration. Viola lessons with the peripatetic string teacher proved to be more challenging than I had imagined. Although I was hopeless, I stuck it out for a year, carrying the school's instrument around in an old pillowcase. I had also started playing the trombone in the local brass band, and this I loved. The good people who organized the band created a junior band through which beginners could learn from more senior instrumentalists. We could borrow instruments, which made it possible to join straight away. My two years in the band provided plenty of fun and even included a tour of Germany.

I moved to an independent school at the age of 12, commuting daily by train to Cambridge. Walking into the music department for the first time, I was impressed: this was a serious department with proper classrooms and hundreds of practice rooms, a far cry from the temporary spaces of my previous school where music had seemed to happen almost ethereally, without a real centre or home. At my new school music had high status, with highflying performers, many of whom were junior exhibitioners at music colleges in London where they went for instruction on Saturdays, and highly qualified instrument teachers, who came and went during school hours throughout the week. Although the extra-curricular programme catered for everyone's musical development in one way or another, music felt academic. I began to take my piano and flute playing seriously and started ticking off my ABRSM-graded exams.

Disenchantment

I remember very little about my GCSE examination course in music. In part it was overshadowed by other musical activities and all the musical learning that was taking place outside of the classroom, but in part I also was starting to feel a little ... well ... like there should be something more. With two Grade 8s under my belt – a competent performer whose horizons seemed to have been met – I had lost the will to continue learning to read more and more complicated notation and to practise for increasing lengths of time each day in an effort to produce the perfect performance. It was a soul-searching time, a time of confusion, a time wanting to be somebody and living with the fear of being nobody. Perhaps, above all, I desired to be released from the pressure to 'perform' and meet the expectations of others.

I was seriously reviewing the situation. I had a strong musical identity within school and within myself, which was important to me. Yet, I felt that I had stopped exploring who I was and who I might become musically. Was the world of classical performance to be the only avenue to pursue? Possibly I was simply bored and needed something to set the subject on fire again – a new motivation.

As part of the GCSE course, composition was required. I had never studied composition nor had I had tuition on how to compose music. The musical education of my teachers had presumably excluded this aspect of the curriculum, theirs being a performance-analytical tradition. Consequently, I produced what was necessary to meet examination requirements with little guidance and no teaching. I look back with regret for allowing my composition coursework to become a last minute business and something that *had* to be done.

Although I 'messed around' with improvisations on the piano, the memory within my hands always resulted in something vaguely classical sounding. I wasn't satisfied, for I craved something that sounded contemporary, something right at the cutting edge of modernity, something that was in some way futuristic. Returning to genres past was cheating. It was not even composing but something else altogether.

I wonder now whether many of our students feel similarly when we ask them to write a Bach chorale, a piece of Serialism, or even a 12-bar blues, that source of the most overdone and unoriginal of chord progressions! My more mature self understands the possibilities of learning techniques from other composers, as well as synthesizing and tapping into the ingenuity of young people's novel ideas and exploratory techniques. This leads me to wondering whether the GCSE syllabus, with its ever-narrowing criteria for success, is constraining my students' creativity.

As a musician passionate about music in many manifestations, the training I received in classical performance and the formalities of school examination did not begin to encompass all that captivated me. My younger self had participated in the formative experiences of music making across expressions and genres, from playing gamelan at London's South Bank Centre, to listening to popular music with friends, to listening in bewilderment to jazz musicians and wondering how to improvise. These were the musical experiences contemporary to me and therefore relevant but it seemed that my formal educators knew nothing of this. They didn't know me as a musician of many parts and of many motivations.

A New Direction

One of my older brother's friends loaned me a recording by Autechre. I had never heard of the group before but as I sat listening to *Amber*, a fairly ambient sounding album written just before the dawn of electronica, I knew that this was the kind of music I wanted to write. I had the sense of being born again: the music of Autechre encapsulated everything I felt. One piece that particularly reverberated with my teenage soul was a track by the Aphex Twin. The artist had created electronic instruments that sounded organic and physical. Against these melting sounds were contrasted thick and angular break beats, and I recall thinking that some of these sounded distinctly industrial. The constantly changing metre provided opportunities for the layered sound to shift and change too. It was like nothing I had heard before. While my musical identity was resonating with the ambient and electronic sounds of Autechre, I perceived the musical identities of my peers to be resounding with the likes of the Manic Street Preachers, David Bowie and Whitney Houston. As I developed a bond with Autechre, Aphex Twin, Future Sound of London, Squarepusher and all that came from the Warp or Reflex record label, I sensed that I was finding a niche. This had become my world.

With the help of a Saturday job and some serious saving, I eventually bought myself an Atari ST computer and an EMU Proteus keyboard. As I began experimenting with creating electronic pieces on early versions of Cubase, I realized that I was entering an entirely new musical world. With my simple MIDI set-up, I could create up to 16 channels of sound. My keyboard had two real-time MIDI controllers so that I could record effects in real time over the top of the tracks. Hours and hours passed, on occasion with night turning into day, while I sat alone trying to get to grips with the finer subtleties of MIDI.

I was very happy. It felt as if I had the entire world of sound at my fingertips; a world of sound that was modern, contemporary and somehow futuristic. It was, of course, early days in my life as a composer, and the pieces I created had a strangeness to them since I didn't know how to create the convincing sounds that my musical idols were producing. Nevertheless, I took pride in the originality of my work and its particularly angular sound, which I recognize in pieces I write today. My compositions were handed around among my musician friends, and one was even used as a part in a piece for a tape and jazz quartet.

My 16–18 A-level years passed bearing a love for jazz and a rediscovery of the piano through great jazz pianists such as McCoy Tyner and Keith Jarrett. I did learn to write a Bach chorale, and hated it. I also learnt how to analyse and annotate scores, compare pieces of music and notate music through aural dictation. I didn't hate that quite as much but I do now ponder the value of perpetuating the practice. How is it that I am able to arrange pop and rock music by ear for my students? Should I be indebted to the aural training I received or did it have more to do with my wider range of musical experiences (trying to recognize Tyner's chord spacings and additions in an otherwise ordinary jazz standard)? Whatever the answer, my final years of school saw me still deeply in love with electronic music. I was becoming an electronic musician and that seemed to be the greater part of me. Perhaps it was something to do with the solitary hours which I had spent writing bits and pieces, the individual engaged with a computer, which allowed that deep relationship to develop. While I seem to have learned to enjoy both working alone and with others, my bedroom studio was a place of solitude, a private world where I was able to take things at my own pace, a place to both lose and find myself.

Moving On

There was no other option for me but to study music technology at university. Any possibilities of a performance-based degree had been wiped from my mind the moment I acquired my Atari computer. My school music teacher strongly advised me to find a place at a university where I would be taught how to record music in a highly professional manner but, although it was tempting, I knew that this kind of course was unlikely to unlock the mystery of the ways in which music is put together. Instead, after a visit to York University, I knew that I had found not only the right place but the right course. My interview, which allowed me to spend what seemed like ages talking to my future supervisor about the wonder of Brian Eno's 'generative music', convinced me.

York's music technology course was designed to teach students about the technical engineering dimension of digital musical instruments in the hope that they would go on to design and build the electronic musical instruments of the future. The highly imaginative people involved were a continual source of inspiration. Their work, rather than being an inwardly looking creative enterprise, sought to impact on the lives of the community, including those in prison and those without work.

In this environment I found some of the keys unlocking the mystery of music. I had not realized that mathematical models could be revealed so beautifully and applied so perfectly. They say mathematics and music go well together; I'm not sure why, but some moments in mathematics seemed deeply important to my 'quest'.

The musical studies involved Kabuki, improvised and non-notated music, music therapy and education, and electro-acoustic composition. Through composition studies, I began to understand how to give electronic music an organic and human feel, a trademark of the brilliant computer musicians who had inspired me so much. I also realized how advanced technology had become since the days of my Atari computer. There was talk about the birth of the 'bedroom studio', whereby everything that is needed for manipulating and processing sound could be held by a not particularly special personal computer.

Although I enjoyed my degree, as it turned out I wasn't destined to be an electronic engineer. I learnt a great deal but missed being musical every day. After finishing my studies, I worked as a part-time course tutor for the Workers Education Association, running a community choir and music-technology composition sessions. Along with this came the realization that I loved teaching, and teaching music in particular. The music technology sessions were organized for males who had fallen into the 'disenchantment bracket of society'. When my day job was done, I would pile enough equipment for two or three PC studios into my car and drive 30 miles to a small village in North Yorkshire. We would learn basic manipulation techniques and then my students were free to put their energies into their own creations. They were highly motivated and produced professional-sounding tracks. This was satisfying teaching.

While I liked working with adults, because I barely felt like one myself I decided to train to teach music to children of secondary school age. As I was to find, making music with children is not only deeply satisfying in itself but also serves to stimulate and feed one's own developing musicality. I quickly realized that in order to support young people's music making, an interactive and responsive approach to their musical utterances is needed – one that allows them to discover things for themselves while being prepared for anything they might potentially realize. I found myself wanting to work with 'what comes up' – the desire that may be at the heart of my creative journeying as a music teacher and musician.

Scenes from the Classroom

During my first year of teaching, the classroom environment was loud, challenging, diverse and hectic, as to be expected in a large community school. I spent most of the year trying to win over the students with diverse and accessible music-making activities. Finally they began coming to class full of expectation, although this certainly was not the case at the beginning of the school year, or even by the end of the first term.

When I arrived for the first week of my music teaching career, the department was in a temporary location. On occasion, I even found myself teaching in a corridor, added to which resources were lacking. Yet, despite some disastrous teaching leading to serious reflection and doubt, through a steady affirmation of my students' musical utterances our lessons became more cohesive. While the lessons were 'high-octane', they had purpose and appeared to have become, in some sense, special for myself and for my students.

There were times when it felt as though too great an expectation had been created: it was too much to expect that we could achieve what we had achieved the week before, or the week before that. During these times I maintained the faith that there would be a moment of intrigue at some point in each lesson to cherish and savour. If sufficient such moments could be experienced throughout the year, then I might have succeeded in sharing with my classes some of the wonder and curiosity that I had felt at their age. There is one particularly satisfying time that stands out in my memory. I wish to share it with the reader by describing the Year 8 music lessons spanning two weeks at the end of the school year.

In an act of freeing myself and my students from the planned curriculum, I had decided that the final two weeks of term would be dictated entirely by the students. The most popular choice of activity for the boys, and for most of the girls, was playing guitars and drums. The remainder of the girls wanted to sing.

The music department had two very old, forlorn and stringless guitars. Unsurprisingly, learning to play the guitar hadn't featured in our department's official schemes of learning, nor was it a skill I possessed. Fortunately, however, a Year 10 boy who was shadowing me over these weeks (as 'work experience', since he had aspirations to become a music teacher) could play wonderfully well both by ear and from tab-notation. I felt confident that Marcus would be able to share with us some of what he could do, and with growing enthusiasm for our project, staff and students found ways of gathering together the instruments we needed.

Marcus began the first session by demonstrating on an acoustic guitar, an electric guitar and an electric bass guitar. His listeners were engrossed. The opportunity to absorb music from a student who had a high musical profile within the music department, and who was also clearly well respected among his peers, was obviously a credible experience for these students. They eagerly asked him questions and were a superb audience to his playing. Quickly they became fired up and motivated to learn together on the instruments.

Elaine (the department's teaching assistant), Marcus and I had selected songs that used simple chords. As an introduction to the class's music making, we sang these songs, giving the students a feel for the music. Then, since the students were confident singers (a skill I had relentlessly pursued from the beginning of the year), we provided a lively accompaniment to their singing on guitar, bass and drums, modelling what we expected them to be able to do by the end of our project. With the prospect of a long summer holiday looming, the classes were in fine voice.

The next step involved learning how to play the chords. There were one or two students in each class who could already play, and these students naturally took on the roles of the teachers. With Marcus leading the way, and with the encouragement and guidance of their skilled peers, they persevered with the task and quick progress was made. By the end of the first lesson, there was much satisfaction amongst the students and they left rather more excited than when they had arrived.

The next week, after revising the chord fingerings, students were selected to use the electric bass to play along with the chord progression. As an individual mastered this, he/she would teach another, who in turn would pass on what had been learnt. In creating a learning community, we used the same approach to enable the students to play the drums. Before long, the whole class was making music together. They were determined to make their class band sound good and the final performance was credible. The students were pleased with themselves and were not slow to let me know this.

Using students as a central resource in the classroom was having a powerful impact on my thinking as a beginning teacher and helped to place school music-making in perspective. By freeing ourselves from the planned curriculum, we had invited in the talents and interests at the heart of the students' musical experiences out of school.

Unlike my own fragmented musical education, this showed promise as a more coherent way of proceeding.

Assessment for Learning

The two weeks of music lessons described above achieved musical outcomes which would more than adequately encapsulate strands of the National Curriculum for Music. Most students had acquired useful technical skill and produced a musical performance within two hours of work. The students were engaged in learning through a musical experience which they considered relevant and meaningful. The student leaders were largely responsible for providing the intrinsic motivation so clearly visible in the commitment of the students. Although it had been an informal and impromptu end-of-term project, it had been a success as a mini scheme of learning. I could have assessed the students according to the National Curriculum Level Descriptors, as my school expected me to do at the end of every unit of work. So why didn't I assess the students in this way and how was this short scheme different to the schemes that had been taught throughout the year?

Assessment for Learning (AfL) is a powerful theoretical tool. At its heart is the aim of helping learners in their learning and in their achievement of worthy goals, with the conviction that students will master the art of learning and become lifelong learners. My school was driving hard to integrate Assessment for Learning into all lessons with the aid of 'student-friendly' use of the National Curriculum Level Descriptors. This was to enable students to know their learning goals and in doing so to come to understand how it was possible to continually improve their performance.

In order to make these levels work within the limitation of one hour a week, there was a constant need to remind students what this language of description meant, to constantly show how the language of the Levels could be translated into musical values. In short, the phrases of the National Curriculum in Music Level Descriptors were to underpin everything that went on in the classroom. As a music teacher whose purpose it was to engage students musically, this language game, I had concluded, served to hinder that process. The official way appeared to me to be cumbersome and intrusive. This was not how I had learnt and not how I believed my students would learn.

How Electronic Musicians Learn

I had no idea that the two weeks of guitar and drum lessons would enable the students to achieve so much. As a young person, and as an electronic musician, I was able to discover music that was free from traditional forms and structures, free from time and key signatures, a music that appeared out of bounds. I was able to compose without definitions or restrictions and experiment with soundscapes rather than stereotypical textures. I had discovered what Carl Rogers so aptly described as a 'freedom to learn'.

As a competent classically trained musician I had, and still have, the opportunity to be creative within the classical medium – but I am left wondering about how students without the kind of privileged background that I had can be expected to use classical traditions creatively. Many of the schemes of learning devised for the first three years of secondary school are in danger of becoming less and less artistic as we strive to pass on the beacon of traditional knowledge to a generation for whom rondo, the concerto and phrase lengths have little relevance or meaning. Standardized curricula seeking standardized outcomes are likely to be disturbing to the creative professional musician.

It has been widely recognized that ICT should be embedded within all subjects in the school curriculum and used as a tool to facilitate subject-specific demands. In music, while ICT can be used to help present scores and record music, it can also be used in its own right to create music which can only be made through electronic means. It is this reality that had inspired me as a young person and that holds untold promise for students today.

Technology for Electronic Music

As our two-week band project demonstrated, music technology offers a way into music, specifically composition, which is potentially free from traditional constraints and makes the study of music more accessible to more students. Students come to school coded to make sense of the ways in which electronic music works and with bounding expertise in software manipulation. They are able to explore sonic textures through layering and multi-tracking, making musical decisions in the mixing of textures, creating of channel volumes and panning. Decisions are made as to how and when samples occur and orchestrations are achieved. Inexpensive wave-editing programs enable users to experiment with the cutting up of samples to create original sounds. These are then ready to be processed through sophisticated sound effects, which create interesting and unusual acoustical properties. Compositional techniques can be taught by music teachers, although it is recognized that other teachers may be able to teach them too. Additionally, students acquire techniques from each other, and take inspiration from producers and DJs to perfect their sound. Instantaneous aural feedback allows the students to create tangible sonic scrapbooks for manipulation, a much more workable method than pen and manuscript paper, and they are helped with the fixing of their compositional ideas. This new method of musical creation has created a new music, one quite unlike any before. The new music is concerned with bit-rates not time signatures, sample lengths rather than phrases and sound processors rather than textures.

ICT and the Unregulated Music Curriculum

Student musical utterances are profound and, in my experience, musical guidance and teaching needs to be immediately responsive to these sonic explorations. The idea of student self-assessment, fundamental to the Assessment for Learning model, is a valid one in that it allows students both to recognize their own skill level and to further refine their skills in order to improve. At the same time, most students have a musical background and education of some kind that provides them with sophisticated discriminatory skills. They will have a much stronger frame of reference with which to assess their musical achievements than that offered by phrases from the official descriptors. Every day I hear students consciously and unconsciously refining their own work and comparing it to music they enjoy and aspire to create. They are able to use their musical experiences to reflect on the projects they are working on, and it is in large part this wealth of experience which gives them guidance and the ability to make musical choices.

While the crisis of identity in adolescence is doubtlessly relieved by the existence of music, music can also become a determining influence in shaping a young person's future. My own experience with music technology gave me an energy and renewed desire to study music. It came at a time when my formal musical education appeared to be irrelevant, lacking in substance and uninspiring. Students are quick to acknowledge an emerging new music: we need to join them on this journey of discovery to find its meanings and rediscover a creative music curriculum.

Chapter 3

The Gender Factor: Teaching Composition in Music Technology Lessons to Boys and Girls in Year 9

Louise Cooper

Introduction

Much recent educational debate has centred on the discrepancies between boys' and girls' achievements. Girls consistently achieve higher results at both GCSE and A Level. In GCSE music, while there are now as many boys as girls, girls continue to outshine boys by 10 per cent in terms of the achievement of the highest grades. There are still more girls than boys who learn to play musical instruments, and it is claimed that music 'veers towards the feminine'; that it is constructed as a feminine subject (Coomber *et al.*, 1993; Green 1997). Some argue that within Western culture, structured in terms of a mind–body split, the appeal of music to the body predisposes it to be feminine (MacDonald *et al.*, 2002).

At the same time, research findings maintain that information technology is widely perceived as masculine. Boys are more likely to use computers for game-playing and programming, for example. Boys tend to use technology for creative, undisciplined purposes, while girls respond better to set tasks with clear parameters. According to Noble and Bradford, 'The computer gives the boys many of the things they like. It is practical and hands on; it gives instant results' (2000, p. 30).

As a trainee music teacher, I was presented with an opportunity to teach three mixed Year 9 classes in an Upper School for students aged 13–19. Interestingly, in addition to their weekly music lesson, the students were provided with a course in music technology. This took the form of two six-lesson units of work. In view of the ongoing debate about boys' and girls' achievement, I wanted to discover whether music technology lessons would prove inclusive for girls and boys alike. I was also interested in evaluating the quality of the musical outcomes and in making comparisons with regular music lessons. More generally, I was quizzical about the place of ICT in the music curriculum, particularly as I viewed myself as a relative novice in this area. As a beginning music teacher, I wanted to understand the ways in which music technology was transforming the scope and potential of music education, and to consider what part I might play in this transformation in the future.

Teaching Composition through Dance eJay and PowerPoint

The six-week project described in this chapter, led by myself and another trainee-teacher, involved the creation of music using Dance eJay for the purpose of accompanying a set of evocative images on PowerPoint. Dance eJay is representative of inexpensive music sequencing software that enables the manipulation of pre-packaged samples of sound. The program allows a student to compose with preset musical fragments. The user can select and build various textures of sound, according to taste, by layering the fragments. It is visually stimulating since the colour-coded fragments do not use notation but rather, in the form of musical building blocks, can be assembled on the screen in the way of Lego pieces. In this way, the program encourages construction in linear style. Star-banding on each fragment is the only concession to harmony and a more vertical mindset.

Each class was given a demonstration of the type of presentation to which their work would lead. They were then asked to organize themselves into groups of two or three, which led to single-sex groupings. The students selected their images from a set of PowerPoint folders that had been previously created. There were six topics from which to choose: Space, Landscapes, City Life, Natural World, Life Cycle and Machines. Once the group had decided on a topic, each member chose at least two contrasting images on which their individual composition would be based. The assessment criteria for their work was made into a PowerPoint presentation and saved so that it was available for the students to check at any time. Subsequent lessons were given over to individuals who were either composing their work or listening to and appraising others' work, both within their own group and within the class as a whole. The last lesson in the course involved each group sharing their presentation of images and music with the rest of the class.

On completion of the project, students from all three classes (76 in total and gender balanced) completed two questionnaires. The first set out to gain a perspective on the students' musical backgrounds and use of music technology outside the classroom. The second sought out attitudes towards the use of Dance eJay. The questionnaires were supported by evidence gleaned through a lunchtime meeting with seven students (four boys and three girls), which probed further views about music and music technology. The meeting was largely unstructured, though recorded and transcribed, allowing me to discern emerging themes and to follow students' perceptions. Further to this, I analysed the compositions of three boys and four girls. Finally, I was able to draw upon my participant observations by reviewing notes made as part of lesson evaluations. The analysis that follows is based on these interlocking sources of data. Following discussion of girls' and boys' approaches to composition, I conclude with a set of propositions for other music teachers to test.

How Good do the Students Perceive Themselves to be at Using Dance eJay?

Although the results of the questionnaire showed that both boys and girls felt positive about their ability to use Dance eJay, they also consistently showed that the boys were more emphatic about their confidence than the girls. While the percentage of girls and boys agreeing that they have always found Dance eJay easy to use remained similar, at 62.5 per cent and 60 per cent respectively, the percentage of those that strongly agreed with the statement differed, at 12.5 per cent and 30 per cent respectively. The additional confidence of boys was also reflected in the figures relating to how students viewed their achievements with the program. Here there was an even greater discrepancy between the boys and the girls: 70 per cent of boys strongly agreed that they found Dance eJay easy to use, compared to 31.25 per cent of girls. Exactly the same tendency showed itself in questions relating to the technical aspects of the program.

One explanation for boys' tendency to feel more confident about their technical fluency can be found by looking at the results of the question that enquired about the technical background of the students. Slightly more girls than boys had a computer at home – 93 per cent compared with 86 per cent – but the number of boys who used the computer for completing homework was much higher than that of the girls. Only 20 per cent of girls did most of their homework on a computer, compared to 36 per cent of boys. This evidence confirms the results of other research into this area (Coomber *et al.* 1993, p. 128).

The most significant results of the questionnaire arose from an analysis of the number of boys and girls that made use of the music technology club which their school offered on Friday lunchtimes. Of the girls, 93 per cent did not attend, with 7 per cent attending only infrequently. On the other hand, only 50 per cent of boys did not attend: 29 per cent attended regularly, a total of 21 per cent attended quite often or not very often in the focus group, and a far greater number of boys than girls attended infrequently. Similar reasons for not attending music technology were given by boys and girls. At no point was gender mentioned as a reason for not attending. The implication, therefore, is that girls do not necessarily feel intimidated by technology and nor do they perceive themselves to be less capable because of their gender. These results suggest that girls are simply less interested in using the technology than boys.

Music Technology and Perceived Stereotypes

Data collected from the focus group discussion revealed that gender was not a factor in successful use of music technology. The overwhelming response was that in order to be successful, a musical understanding was required. Only one student associated this with learning an instrument, as shown in the following boy and girl ('B' and 'G') responses.

Q: Do you think there is a certain type of person who is good at music technology?

G: I think there is a certain type of people. They have to be musically minded, experimental and be able to take criticism.

G: I think all people should be able to enjoy music tech, although only some people are good at it. Usually people who have a strong musical interest/ talent are good at it.

B: Anyone, but it takes a level of ingenuity and creativity to compose music. Although [you need] a basic understanding of music, you don't need to be good at music.

B: I think they have to have a basic understanding of music to do music technology.

B: Anyone.

B: Anyone can do it as long as they try.

B: Anyone, with the right amount of help.

G: I think all people are good at music technology and can do it. But people who play an instrument and read music usually end up doing it better than those who can't play or read music.

The students made the connection between musical people, creativity and a successful composition. They acknowledged the need for musical creativity within technology lessons, yet also said that the program was accessible to everyone.

Table 3.1 'I like using Dance eJay in music lessons'

	Agree	Strongly agree
Boys	20	80
Girls	50	37

If it is the case that girls are less interested in using technology, then these findings need to be questioned. Coomber suggests that lack of experience, confidence or opportunity, or even the expectations of teachers, are all factors that may contribute to such a situation, and concludes that girls must be given the opportunity to familiarize themselves with technology in a non-threatening environment (Coomber *et al.* 1993, p. 132). The research for this project, however, suggests that girls do not lack experience, confidence or opportunity and that the way in which the music technology lessons are carried out certainly establishes a non-threatening environment. Further research is therefore needed to investigate the underlying reasons for girls' attitudes.

Evaluating the Musical Worth of Dance eJay: Students' Perspectives

B: With Dance eJay you just need to try it out to see what sounds good so you don't need to worry about time and pitch or whatever.

What do the students themselves feel they gain from these lessons? How do they rate their efforts in composing? Some students felt that because they were not taught about pitch or time, their lessons did not have very much musical worth. It appears that they undervalued their musical achievements in these lessons. On the other hand, perhaps it is because the learning is not made as explicit as it is in regular classroom lessons that the students are hesitant in affirming musical value in these lessons.

There was very little 'technical' language in the starters or plenaries. Technical language was sometimes used on an individual basis between the teacher and the pupil, where it was possible to introduce the correct language in a casual context and to increase understanding with examples from the student's own work. Forging a stronger link between music and language would help to ensure that programs such as Dance eJay are used to maximum benefit:

B: You don't really learn as much as you would if you were learning in class.

Q: Why do you say that? (to same boy)

B: Cos it doesn't tell you all the different notes that you use and things and notey and technical things.

From a teacher's perspective, however, it was clear that some of the most creative work took place during these music lessons. It may be that the value system which has developed around music, not only in music technology lessons but in the whole music course, needs re-evaluation. Students have gained the impression that the outcome of a successful music education should be knowledge of 'notey and technical things' – and this is an issue that needs to be addressed.

In the pupils' opinion, one of the most prominent drawbacks to using the Dance eJay was being limited by a series of set sounds in a set style of music. After a while, this made the pupils frustrated because they could not produce the exact sound that they needed:

B: I think that Dance eJay is just for using dance music. It's programmed so that only dance music is available. If all styles were available it would be much better because a lot of modern music is a fusion of classical and Indie or something like that. It would sound much better if it could combine.

B: I think occasionally that music tech can get frustrating because you hear one piece of music and you think I like that and it would be good with this drum part and then you think it would be good with this but then you can't find the right tune to go with it.

B: ...I prefer to just use an instrument to using a computer because you can work on getting a melody out of it - getting a tune out.

Q: Do you find that you can't do that on computer programs? (to same boy)

B: Yes, cos it just takes longer and it's more limited.

According to the questionnaire, however, in contradiction to the last boy's comment, the overwhelming majority of students prefer composing on Dance eJay to composing on classroom instruments (Table 3.2).

Table 3.2 'I prefer to use Dance eJay to compose in music rather than composing using classroom instruments'

	Undecided	Agree	Strongly agree
Boys	20		80
Girls	37	12	50

Moreover, the boys were much more in favour of Dance eJay in comparison to classroom instruments than the girls. Given that many students feel insecure about music if they do not learn an instrument, this could be reflective of the fact that more girls than boys learn or have learnt an instrument: 73 per cent of girls compared with 50 per cent of boys. In fact, the boy who made the last comment was a very proficient instrumentalist on three different instruments. On the other hand, these results could also reveal that boys have a greater interest in technology than girls.

Comparing Music Technology Lessons with Regular Music Lessons

B: I'd prefer to work on a computer and on my own but when people listen to my mixes like on Dance eJay, I do kind of listen to what they're saying and just try it out and if it doesn't work then I'll take it out and also if I listen to other people's mixes if that sound quite good then I might try something like that for my next one.

On the whole, students were incredibly focused in their music technology lessons and even the most difficult students seemed compelled to work hard. A pupil on the verge of permanent exclusion, for example, managed to produce work of a better and more creative standard than that of most of his peers.

Although the school had the resources to allow one computer for every pupil, most students chose not to work in isolation. Amid the focused attention that each pupil gave their own work, one could observe groups of twos or threes swapping headphones and listening to each others' work, occasionally commenting on parts they liked. Albeit that this was one of the suggestions made on the assessment criteria document, it occurred without formal prompting. Moreover, from the responses of the pupils in the interview, this is one of the methods that students like to use in order to gain new ideas.

While listening to others' work is a technique often used in regular classroom lessons, I have noticed that some students are reluctant to share their work in front of the class in this way. In music technology, students can choose the recipients of their work and this is beneficial to those who fear criticism from their peers. In addition, the fact that the exchange is voluntary increases the significance of the experience: the extent to which one chooses to become the recipient of new ideas is up to the individual. A situation is thus established whereby the learner takes ownership of his/her learning in a safe environment:

G: I was really bad at music tech at first but once you've heard other people's ideas you can develop your own and stuff and you can keep on listening to your old pieces and you can keep on going back to them and trying to improve them.

There may be an issue here about the effectiveness of recording techniques in regular music lessons. One of the reasons that this girl finds Dance eJay so helpful is because it enables you to continually evaluate, refine and adapt your work aurally. This is not always possible in classroom situations where composition is geared towards performance and in which different demands are placed upon the student.

From the interview, it became evident that there is a real divide between pupils who enjoy working by themselves and pupils who enjoy group work. Interestingly, boys appear to dislike group work in composition: the results of the composition questionnaire revealed that 36 per cent of boys did not like group work compared to

13 per cent of girls. This may shed some light on the popularity of music technology among boys since it allows for a degree of flexibility.

Wright singles flexibility out as a factor leading to the relative success of boys in Key Stage 3 music, because choosing how to work enables boys to achieve their potential (Wright 2001, p. 288). Moreover, by allowing the individual to choose, Wright claims that teachers avoid much of the conflict that has been shown to adversely affect boys' performance in other subjects. In music technology, each student is encouraged to develop their independence by working at their own computer. At the same time, students themselves organize opportunities to share ideas. One pupil sums it up:

> B: I think it's better to work – well not all round one computer using Dance eJay – in a club, with the different computers cos that way you can have people listening but then they'll be on their own bits rather than bothering people and having to compromise or whatever and they've still got their ideas as well.

It is interesting that this particular boy talks about his ideal Dance eJay experience in terms of a club (possibly referring to the lunchtime Dance eJay club which this boy attends), rather than in the context of a lesson, although his description could fit either context. This would suggest that even in music technology lessons, which students seem to enjoy very much, there remains a feeling that students prefer to experience music learning outside of the classroom. This would be an interesting field of enquiry to develop albeit that it goes beyond the boundaries of this particular investigation. It remains to be said that this student's reflection was not echoed by any of the other students and therefore may not be representative of a general opinion.

> G: I think it's easier than to play normal instruments cos you have to be quite co-ordinated to play some instruments and with Dance eJay you don't have to have much co-ordination. You can just put your ideas down.

The above statement reflects an opinion frequently given in the interview: namely, that the motivation of students in regular music lessons is adversely affected if they do not play an instrument. Students who do not study an instrument often feel insecure about their musical ability in regular classroom lessons. When using Dance eJay, however, this problem does not exist:

> B: I just want to say that I'm not very good at playing normal instruments but I can do that [Dance eJay] really well cos I'm the Best!

In music technology lessons, these students can feel confident about participating on a par with those who learn an instrument. Music technology can provide a level playing field in which everyone's work is equally valid. Since no-one is discredited from playing, it is possible to learn something from everyone and for a true 'community of learners' to exist.

Boys' and Girls' Approaches to Composition

Comparison of 'Leaf' by Sophie and Hannah: Both compositions were inspired by an image of a leaf floating in a pool of water

It is noticeable in these two compositions that both girls have concentrated on timbre to conjure up the image of the leaf. Sophie takes quite a minimalist approach, producing a sophisticated composition by the subtle use of the track 'heaven drop' and its variations. Hannah's composition is not as well balanced in terms of form as Sophie's: her composition is over-crowded with many different sounds being played at the same time. It is clear, however, that she paid special attention to the timbre of the tracks chosen, most of which exhibit a dry quality. This leads me to think that Hannah was focusing on the leaf. In contrast, and as a result of the 'drop-like' qualities of Sophie's work, I think it is clear that Sophie was focusing on the water in which the leaf lay. It is apparent in this particular comparison that both girls avoided a linear approach – rather than build their work in layers, they constructed their compositions around the timbral qualities of the tracks used.

Comparison of 'Blue Fronds' by Ziaf and Lottie: Both compositions were inspired by an image of a luminous, blue sea anemone against a black background

Both Lottie and Ziaf chose to have one foundation track that sounded throughout their composition. In this sense they both used linear composition techniques. Lottie's composition, however, relied heavily on timbral effects: the sounds she chose were highly suggestive of the watery underworld of the sea anemone. By contrast, Ziaf's tracks were less representative, evident in his use of the same tracks for representing the image of molten lava in the second part of his composition.

Once established, Lottie's composition is entirely repetitive. In one sense, it is as though she has developed a snapshot of sound, and through the time qualities of music, has extended this image for 'x' many seconds. In this way, Lottie might be said to have been composing vertically. In contrast, Ziaf's composition, despite being based around a foundation track, is malleable with time and is constantly shifting shape and form. More dependent on the time axis and clearly constructed in layers of sounds (looking at his work on Dance eJay makes this more obvious), Ziaf may have been composing in a more linear style.

While not wishing to make any strong assertions about the general compositional styles of boys and girls, it is my tentative suggestion that boys seem to build up their composition in layers, adopting a linear approach to composition, while girls are more dependent on the timbral qualities of sound and thus approach composition with a more vertical mindset. Previous research has shown that pupils employ distinct horizontal and vertical compositional strategies without making any explicit reference to gender as a factor. Rather, it was suggested that compositional approaches varied between individuals and between different styles of music (Folkestad *et al.*, cited in Hodges 2001). Work done by Colley *et al.*, however, delves into the gender issue and claims that there is 'some evidence to suggest that girls and boys adopt different compositional strategies when composing with computers' (Colley *et al.* cited in

Hodges, 2001). Furthermore, according to Colley *et al.*, 'Some [teachers] described an important difference in the way in which boys and girls use music technology: once using it, girls treat it as a tool which helps them to produce music to the best of their ability, while boys are inclined to use the technology as an end to itself or to play around' (Green 1997, p. 125). It would be interesting to develop the field of enquiry further as to whether or not girls and boys adopt different approaches to structuring composition.

How Effective is Music Technology in Teaching Composition to Boys and Girls?

As previously discussed, there is a tendency for boys to be more enthusiastic about using technology than girls. With regard to the preferred learning methods, 60 per cent of girls compared to 36 per cent of boys prefer to compose in groups. In addition, there is an indisputable preference for boys and girls to work in single-sex groups. Interestingly, this preference is more evident amongst the boys than the girls.

Yet, despite the obvious attraction of the program for boys, the analysis of the seven compositions do not show any difference in the quality of work done by the boys and girls. This makes it hard to argue that, despite the fact that technology in general is more popular amongst boys, one is placing girls at a disadvantage by using music technology in music lessons. I would argue rather that the effectiveness of using music technology to teach composition in music lessons is not compromised by the gender factor. The question therefore remains: how effective is music technology as a tool for teaching composition?

By using Dance eJay, it is possible for students to develop many relevant and useful composition skills:

- sensitivity towards timbre
- an ability to be selective about sounds from a limited pool of resources
- an understanding of how a composition is affected by combining different sounds (texture)
- an ability to structure a composition through repetition of individual sounds or chunks of sounds
- the necessity of contrast
- the use of variation
- the development of self-evaluation skills, the ability to compose through trial and error.

Most importantly, Dance eJay helps the student focus their skills on the *process* of composition, while simultaneously allowing the teacher some insight into the *process* of composition. Kratus makes an important distinction between composition as a process and composition as a product, highlighting the point that, as teachers, 'it is much easier for us to compare and evaluate musical performances' (Kratus 1994, p. 131). However, is it right, or useful to students for our attention to be focused on product? As Kratus points out, 'Unless we find ways to describe, compare and conceptualize these fluid processes [*of composition*], we cannot hope to teach compositional processes' (*ibid.* p. 131).

Kratus developed a three-tiered analysis of the compositional process comprising exploration, development and repetition. Through using Dance eJay, with its highly graphic representation, the elements of composition are laid bare and it becomes easeir to monitor a student's progression over time. It is important to realize, however, that Dance eJay limits the type of exploration available to students since each of the tracks are pre-recorded. Exploration does take place but in a different form: a student must explore the tracks available in order to select the right sound. This has significant repercussions for the way in which it is possible to teach composition and is a point that needs further attention.

According to the National Curriculum, or indeed models of learning to compose, Dance eJay would not be sufficient for the learning of all the necessary composing skills. A significant intention of the National Curriculum is that pupils should be taught to improvize musical ideas when performing, as part of their composing syllabus. For this reason, Dance eJay and similar programs need to be used in conjunction with other approaches to composition in order to fulfil National Curriculum requirements. Besides which, as already mentioned by a boy in the interview, Dance eJay limits pupils' access to other styles of music. Looking at the National Curriculum requirements as a whole, Dance eJay is particularly useful in aiding the development of appraisal skills and in facilitating the use of ICT, as well as developing some composing skills. One of the most significant drawbacks of using the technology, however, is that it negates the development of performing skills. This is certainly one of the reasons for the program's popularity and in effect it acts as a leveller among students who do not have the same technical fluency on an instrument.

A more significant point is that by losing the performing element of music lessons, the kinaesthetic element is also lost. Dance eJay is highly audio and highly visual, but barely kinaesthetic. This raises further questions about the extent to which the music can be internalized. Music, the cousin of dance, is fundamentally about movement and it is therefore unnatural, and perhaps misleading, to divorce the two.

I would argue that Dance eJay represents music in a very superficial way, but this is not to say that Dance eJay does not have its place within a musical education. In fact, it may be a necessary starting block to give students confidence to compose. As one boy in the interview astutely suggested, Dance eJay could be used as a starting point from which ideas could be developed for use with classroom instruments.

Propositions to be Tested

1. The relationship between music technology and gender:
   (i) Boys are more interested than girls in using music technology, both in lessons and in extra-curricular clubs.
   (ii) Boys are more likely to use ICT at home than girls.
   (iii) Ability to use Dance eJay – perceived and actual – is not dependent on gender.
   (iv) Boys are more openly confident about their ability to use Dance eJay than girls.
2. Dance eJay is a popular program:
   (i) It allows pupils to work independently and at the same time to share their work with others.
   (ii) It is easy to evaluate and improve your own work.
   (iii) It is accessible to students who do not play an instrument.
   (iv) It is easy to use.
3. Issues that need to be considered if music technology continues to be a part of the music curriculum:

(i) Use of appropriate musical language needs to be integrated into the lessons and should become a part of ongoing teacher-pupil dialogue.

(ii) Students need opportunities to learn about composition through improvisation and the development of their own motifs.

(iii) Students need to learn composition through a variety of styles of music.

(iv) Students need the opportunity to develop fluency on instruments and the voice.

In conclusion, there are many benefits to using music technology (in the case of this study, Dance eJay) in music lessons as a tool for teaching composition. It clearly motivates the students and enables them to achieve musical results. In this study, boys were more interested in the technology, but this did not inhibit the girls from achieving equally effective work. Dance eJay can be used to supply several strands of the National Curriculum, although alone its use is inadequate to fulfil the requirements for composition. Finally, it is necessary to supplement the use of music technology such as Dance eJay with more physical responses to music if music is not to become divorced from its roots in movement.

References

Coomber, C., Hargreaves, D. and Colley, A. (1993), 'Girls, boys and technology in music education'. *British Journal of Music Education*, 10, 123-34.

Dibben, N. (2002), 'Gender identities in music', in R. MacDonald, D.J. Hargreaves and D. Miell (eds), *Musical Identities*. Oxford: Oxford University Press, 117-13.

Green, L. (1997), *Music, Gender, Education*. Cambridge: Cambridge University Press.

Hodges, R. (1996), 'The new technology', in C. Plummeridge (ed), *Music Education: Trends and Issues*. London: Institute of Education, University of London.

Hodges, R. (2001), 'Using ICT in music technology', in C. Philpott and C. Plummeridge (eds), *Issues in Music Teaching*. London: Routledge Falmer.

Kratus, J. (1994), 'The Ways Children Compose'. Proceedings of the 40th Conference. International Society of Music Education. Tampa, USA.

MacDonald, R., Hargreaves, D., and Miell, D. (eds) (2002), *Musical Identities*. Oxford: Oxford University Press.

Noble, C. and Bradford, W. (2000), *Getting it Right for Boys and Girls*. London: Routledge.

Wright, R. (2001), 'Gender and achievement in music education: the view from the classroom'. *British Journal of Music Education*, 18(3), 275-91.

Chapter 4

Finding Flow Through Music Technology

Serena Croft

Introduction

Prior to my first teaching post, at a co-educational comprehensive school for 11 to 19 year olds in rural Suffolk, I had little experience of using the computer as a means of musical expression. I had not attended the voluntary music technology lessons offered as part of my music degree, choosing instead to devote my energies to piano practice and performance. Only once I started teaching did I realize the potential of ICT in music. I began to investigate ICT's effectiveness, using my ongoing evaluations of classroom practice informed by the students I was teaching. This fitted well with the school's development plan which, in line with government policy, placed a high priority on the integration of ICT into all teaching and learning.

The chapter that follows is a reflection on a particular phase of action research during which it became clear that there was a strong relationship between students' musical engagement with ICT and Csikszentmihayli's theory of flow – a theory concerned with human motivation and the pursuit of happiness. As the chapter progresses, I elaborate further on flow theory as a way of explaining both my students' increased levels of commitment to composing and my own developing commitment to music teaching with music technology.

Flow Theory and Motivation

Csikszentmihalyi describes flow as an optimal experience where actions become spontaneous, self-consciousness disappears, time ceases to exist and skills are maximized (1992): you become completely involved in what you are doing for its own sake and have a self-driving interest. Although many writers discuss the advantages of music technology, making claims about its motivating qualities (see Hodges 1996, Webster 1998, Airy and Parr 2001 and Pitts and Kwami 2002, for example), it is remarkably difficult to find explicit references to a link between music technology and particular theories of learning and motivation. The work of Csikszentmihalyi differs in that it provides a useful way forward, linking motivation, engagement and learning.

A common way to understand motivation involves the simple yet valuable distinction between the intrinsic and the extrinsic. Csikszentmihalyi follows this approach and describes intrinsic motivation in terms of 'wanting to do it [the task]' and extrinsic motivation as 'wanting to do it to get the reward' (1996). The nature of the task, as seen by the student, is critical to intrinsic motivation; if the task is interesting, curiosity will be aroused automatically. Csikszentmihalyi describes this as the task becoming 'autotelic' or worth doing for its own sake (1996).

Intrinsic motivation is present when flow occurs. Csikzsentmihalyi proposes nine dimensions of flow, which I use to form the basis for understanding my students' responses. According to Csikszentmihalyi, at least some of these dimensions need to be present in order for flow to occur while being engaged in a task:

1. There are clear goals each step of the way.
2. There is immediate feedback to one's actions.
3. There is a balance between challenges and skills.
4. Action and awareness are merged.
5. Distractions are excluded from consciousness.
6. There is no fear of failure.
7. Self-consciousness disappears.
8. The sense of time elapsed becomes distorted.
9. The activity becomes autotelic.

(Adapted from Csikszentmihalyi 1996, pp. 111-13)

Context

Key Stage 3

Between the ages of 11 and 14, music lessons are compulsory and music technology has been incorporated across the music curriculum in the Suffolk secondary school. In Year 7, students are introduced to notation software, such as Finale Notepad or Sibelius, through a project focusing on 'Renaissance Dance Music'. One activity involves developing technical and musical skills alongside each other using the computer to voice their creative ideas. By copying and pasting improvised repeating patterns, such as the rhythmic and melodic ostinato and the drone, students create the accompaniment of a Pavane. Later this can be performed from notation on acoustic instruments and an improvised melody line can be added. Students learn the basic workings of the computer program, selecting instruments and inserting notes while being able to hear their ideas. The aim is to support and extend musical learning in composition, performance, improvisation and responsive listening.

Beyond Key Stage 3

After the age of 14, students who opt for examination study use the computer primarily for composition. They are free to develop their compositional ideas in class or at home. The study and analysis of students' solo performance pieces often provides a starting point for composing; recognisable rhythmic and melodic devices can be developed and transformed into original musical ideas. Students study the use of all the musical characteristics in their performance pieces, including dynamics, structure, texture, melodic line, phrasing, modulation and accompaniment, and take musical examples from these, such as sequenced triplets or an imitative accompaniment. Once identified, ideas are easily adapted and extended in composition exercises.

Alternatively, students first acquire an understanding of a particular genre of music through performing and analytical listening, and then compose using similar stylistic techniques. They can start 'from scratch' at the computer or prepare ideas on paper at home or in school.

A computer projector is used to introduce lessons, to demonstrate the workings of music programs and for sharing students' achievements. Like a traditional blackboard, the projected screen shows the aims and the intended structure of the lesson. Students are invited to the front of the class to help demonstrate the step-by-step processes of the task set before attempting it on an individual or group level. The lesson often ends with the projector displaying the individual or group work achieved.

The Study

The Sample and Data Gathering

This study is based on an investigation of 51 students, aged 14–16, preparing for their GCSE in music. The students were both male and female, with varied musical backgrounds and experience. Initial perceptions were gathered from student diaries and written statements, which also formed the basis for individual and group interviews. This data was combined with additional data collected from observations in the daily classroom routine and through discussions with students during activities involving music technology. I have interleaved the results obtained from my research with Csikszentmihalyi's nine dimensions of flow (1996) in an attempt to better understand the commitment and motivation of my students.

Dimension 1: There are clear goals each step of the way

Csikszentmihalyi states that 'in flow we always know what needs to be done. The [performing] musician knows what notes to play next' (1996, p. 111). When using music technology to compose, the ultimate goal is the completion of a good quality, well-refined composition. To achieve this, a well-defined task and clear expectations are important. Carefully planned musical activities aid concentration and can gradually introduce students to the workings of the computer, hopefully inducing flow with 'clear goals each step of the way'.

When using computers, the process of composition can differ from traditional methods. The computer lends itself to a logical approach, building up a texture by sections. As Michael described it:

> *I learnt by composing on this [the computer], you have to do it in lots of small parts, bit by bit.*

The task given to the students was to compose music for a western, with a written storyboard as a starting point. The arrange window visually highlights the structure or form of a student's composition.

The composition starts with percussion, repeating a short phrase. The music is built up gradually as the brass section enters. Later, the texture becomes thicker with most instruments playing and with the percussion repeating the initial ideas.

The student's approach to music composition using technology is often governed by musical background (Webster 1990, Green 1990, Folkestad 1998, Younker 2000). A student who lacks knowledge of traditional notation will typically use the arrange window to structure their ideas. The process of building up ideas helps establish the next goal of arranging the ideas, which eventually results in a product where ideas can be further manipulated if desired.

Hickey (1997) uses a computer program that guides students through a process of selecting sounds and experimenting with different musical elements such as melody, rhythm, texture, dynamics and timbre. The computer presents the student with choices that lead to the student setting clear and well-defined goals, such as the structural arrangement of instruments or timbre and changes in dynamics. Hickey suggests that the students need to be given time to experiment without interruption or checking progress – in other words, the teacher must be careful not to interrupt the students' flow.

In order to induce flow, it is important that goals are realistic. Below, Michael highlights the use of the MIDI (musical instrument digital interface) keyboard that is connected to the computer:

> *I love the easiness of playing straight to manuscript, much easier than pencil and paper.*

According to this quote, the composition goal was made 'easier' by introducing a computer in the place of pencil and paper. Students could listen to their achievements each step of the way, receiving immediate feedback, which helped establish the next goal.

Dimension 2: There is immediate feedback to one's actions

Csikszentmihalyi states that to experience enjoyment and to induce flow there is a need for immediate feedback to actions. Knowing how well you are doing is crucial to the experience of flow since 'the musician hears right away whether the note played is the right one' (Csikszentmihalyi 1996, p. 111).

The computer presents results while the notes are played on the keyboard, in either conventional staff notation or an arrange window. The student can immediately see what has been produced and listen to the composition through the playback facility:

> *If you haven't got the people and the instruments then you don't know what it sounds like. On the computer you've got the exact rhythm, time and beat.* (Sarah)

> *If you play it and don't like it you can always change something or add an extra bit.* (Amy)

> *You can go over [hear and see] what you have done to help you realize what would be another good part.* (Laura)

Laura was 'going over' and evaluating her own work by listening to her composition. This led to the setting of clear future goals; she knew what needed to follow, for example whether to add 'another good part' or instrument. The computer gave immediate feedback to her actions and aided the process of self-assessment.

Black and William (1998) argue that a student who has learnt the skill of self-assessment will be committed to learning and more motivated. The student assesses the work that has been completed and continues to make further decisive improvements. The suggestion is that because of these processes, motivation is increased and the concept of flow is supported. Feedback helps the student to self-regulate the learning process, retaining control of the composition and deciding on the next objective – the student has ownership of his/her creativity. Encouragement to self-evaluate and assess their own work ensures that the student's creativity is not lost through following a step-by-step process (Reese 1996, Webster 1998). In my classroom, students are also encouraged to evaluate each other's composition, whether performed by the computer or by an instrumental ensemble.

Dimension 3: There is a balance between challenges and skills

According to Csikszentmihalyi, 'In flow, we feel that our abilities are well matched to the opportunities for action' (1996, p. 111). Figures 4.1 and 4.2 illustrate Csikszentmihalyi's graphical representations of how the equilibrium between challenges and skills is required in order to experience flow.

Figure 4.1 shows that if you are faced with a major challenge and you feel you do not possess the required skills to meet the challenge, then you are likely to experience anxiety. Alternatively, if the task is not challenging and you have greater skills, then you are likely to experience boredom. In Figure 4.2 Csikszentmihalyi defines emotional states as directly relating to challenge and skill.

From observation, I have noticed that a few students consider music technology to be difficult at first. Csikszentmihalyi recognizes that an initial period of time is

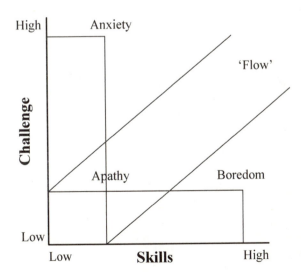

Figure 4.1 A graph showing the required equilibrium between skills and challenges to achieve flow (Csikszentmihalyi 1991, p. 74)

necessary to achieve focus for an activity. He gives the example of practising an instrument:

> It takes at least half an hour of often dull practice each time one sits down at the piano before it begins to be fun. In other words, each of the flow-producing activities requires an initial investment of attention before it begins to be enjoyable. (Csikszentmihalyi, 1997 p. 68)

During introductory lessons in music technology, students require technical support in order to 'get to grips' with the technology. Most of the comments relating to technical difficulties appeared in the first entries of the student diaries. As students became more familiar with the workings of the computer program, these initial worries disappeared.

Some of the students in my study regarded the computer program as 'easy', and immediately more straightforward to work with than traditional methods of composition. For these students, the challenges presented to them in the traditional way with manuscript and pencil did not match their level of personal skill in notation and composition, whereas new computer skills were easily mastered:

> *I was dreading the painstaking ordeal of writing my composition out by hand, slowly and with extreme difficulty.* (Louise)

Dimension 4: Action and awareness are merged

> In flow our concentration is focused on what we do – you're doing it [achieving the goal] without realizing it. (Csikszentmihalyi 1996, p. 112).

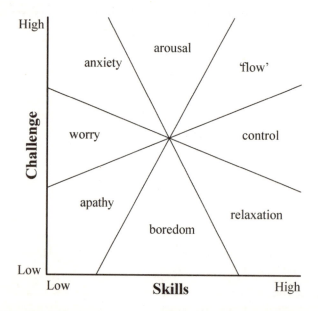

Figure 4.2 Emotional states represented through the relationship between challenges and skills (Farmer 1999)

When students become familiar with the computer program, the technical actions and workings become automatic and secondary to the primary goal of creating a musical composition. The student becomes part of the compositional action and takes ownership of this action through reflection and further interaction with the computer. Evidently this relates to the merging of awareness and action. Folkestad formulates an equation: 'composition equals improvisation plus reflection' (1998). This is the technique commonly used by jazz musicians and is now employed even more when composing with computers.

Csikszentmihalyi (1996) discusses how creativity is possible through shifting from ideas and action to the evaluation of the outcomes of action, leading back to ideas, thereby establishing a cycle that repeats itself as illustrated in Figure 4.3. The student reacts and makes decisions related to the self-evaluation of the playback that the computer provides. The 'cause and effect' relationship of flow is established. The student knows what needs to be done next to improve the final result. These steps are based on an evaluation of the musical elements within the arrangement. The merging of action and awareness follows as the cycle repeats itself without interruption; evaluation and setting goals become spontaneous. When this occurs it is likely that time passes without the student being aware of it and flow has been achieved.

Dimension 5: Distractions are excluded from consciousness

> we are aware only of what is relevant here and now. If [during performance] the musician thinks of his health or tax problems when playing he is likely to hit a wrong note. (Csikszentmihalyi 1996, p. 112)

Concentration has to be focused. As long as clear goals have been established and the activity is understood, the student can achieve focused concentration. If, for example, the task is to compose a waltz highlighting the strong characteristics of the style, the development of this task could involve adding a contrasting middle section to the waltz with a change of key. The interactive nature of the computer helps to sustain the focused attention required to complete the task. The use of headphones allows the student to enter into a personal creative space. On occasion, my students have been so engrossed in the task that they have not noticed my observing presence, nor when the lesson has ended.

Dimensions 6 and 7: There is no fear of failure, and self-consciousness disappears

> We are too involved to be concerned with failure ... or to care about protecting the ego ... The musician feels at one with the harmony of the cosmos ... (Csikszentmihalyi 1996, p. 112)

The computer allows students to lose their self-consciousness and be less concerned about failure in performance. Jessica, one of my GCSE students, commented:

You can just play [the composition on] the computer and it will sound perfect.

Jessica had been totally involved in the composition process, with the computer relaying her creative ideas. She stated that she would perform the composition from the computer because if a live performance were attempted there would almost definitely be mistakes.

Using the computer also enables students to feel less self-conscious about the presentation of their work, whether in aural or written format. While a handwritten score could be said to have more 'character', a computer-generated score aids a more effective rehearsal and live performance. This was observed during a student's composition of a string quartet. The computer indicated notes that were not within the range of certain instruments and the student was then able to edit these notes before printing out the parts for rehearsal. The players in the string quartet were presented with clear, concise notation and this resulted in a short rehearsal followed by a successful performance. For these reasons, students are much happier to share their creative ideas with an audience when the computer is used as the means of expression. As Dominic puts it:

> *The computer eliminates getting things wrong or making errors.*

Maslow (1954), a humanistic psychologist, considers self-esteem to be a basic human need which, if satisfied, will produce what he describes as the 'self-actualized person'. Taking on this paradigm, it follows that the interactive nature of the computer satisfies the social needs of the student, in particular the need to achieve self-esteem and self-concept. I have observed a Year 9 boy (13 years old) gaining a greater acceptance from his peer group by his creative application of music technology. He later created a website where his compositions could be heard.

Dimension 8: The sense of time elapsed becomes distorted

> 'Is it lunch time already?' asks Tom, as the surprise of the bell signals the end of the lesson.

Experience at my school shows that the students have sometimes been so absorbed in the task that the sound of the bell is an interruption to flow. In addition, they allocate their own free time to using music technology. 'Generally in flow we forget time, and hours may pass by in what seem like a few minutes,' explains Csikszentmihalyi (1996, p. 113). The students appear to be self-regulated and self-motivated in the learning process.

> 'Time flies when you're enjoying yourself,' I tell them as we bring the lesson to a close.

Dimension 9: The activity becomes autotelic

Autotelic is the term used to describe something that is worth doing for its own sake, for being intrinsically motivating. Csikszentmihalyi emphasizes that in flow the goals are provided by the activity becoming autotelic. Students feel that they have achieved a worthy composition, for example, and are quite satisfied to have produced rather sophisticated sounds. Evidence of their intrinsic motivation is apparent in the extra time spent using the computer program. Students with behavioural difficulties become completely absorbed when composing with music technology. They achieve worthwhile musical results and disruptive behaviour is considerably reduced.

Conclusion

I have found flow theory and its nine dimensions helpful in explaining the increased motivation of students. It has also been beneficial in redefining my understanding of what is required for my students to feel intrinsically motivated. Although I have relied on student self-reporting and my own observations, I am aware that the random contact strategy devised by Csikszentmihalyi, and other strategies yet to be devised, would yield useful data with which to isolate more specific learning situations that lead to optimal experience.

The students' perspectives, as gleaned from diaries, interviews and written statements, provided strong indicators of the achievement of flow states. Furthermore, as an action researcher and a music teacher seeking to understand how my students learn, I found that the study refreshed my own practice. In Figure 4.3, I present a personal way of thinking about the nine dimensions of flow.

This model was derived from the many explanations and definitions of flow found during my research. It takes the form of a continuous cycle, beginning with an achievable task that is either given or identified. Moving clockwise in the inner circle, the skills and challenges must be balanced before absorption, concentration and involvement take place. With this established, timelessness is accepted. Having completed this inner cycle of the initial process, reflection may lead to choosing the next step of the process and hence it is possible to move into the outer dimension, which is on a more personal level. Choosing the task aids ownership and promotes motivation to triumph over any limitations. Once this part of the process has been achieved, work becomes a joy and the pace at which the individual continues through the outer dimension of the circle is spontaneous.

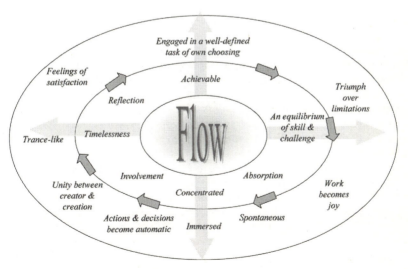

Figure 4.3 A diagrammatic representation of flow

The cycle repeats itself and continues until interruption from an outside force. The arrows stretching outwards from the centre demonstrate the ability to enter the second dimension of the cycle at any time of progression in the inner circle. The time of initial concentration needed before entering flow varies between individuals and tasks. It is likely to take place in the beginning stages of the inner circle, whether on the first cycle or one thereafter.

When I moved schools to take up a position of Director of Music, I was faced with a myriad of challenges that put the flow model to the test. There were no computers in the main music room, few classroom instruments apart from keyboards, the pressure of GCSE composition, a shortage of staff, concerts to be organized before the end of the first term and a flood. Although I was soon travelling round my cycle of flow as though it were a whirlpool, being able to relate to these experiences through the model was extremely useful.

Over the years that I have taught, appreciating the value of flow has undoubtedly contributed to my well-being and happiness as a music teacher. As such, I recommend it to the reader.

References

Airy, S. and Parr, J. (2001), 'MIDI, music and ME: student's perspectives on composing and MIDI'. *Music Education Research*, 3(1), 42–9.

Black, P. and Wiliam, D. (1998), *Inside the Black Box*. London: King's College London.

Csikszentmihalyi, M. (1991), *Flow: The Psychology of Optimal Experience*. New York: HarperPerennial.

Csikszentmihalyi, M. (1992), *Flow: The Psychology of Happiness*. London: Rider.

Csikszentmihalyi, M. (1996), *Creativity: Flow and the Psychology of Discovery and Invention*. New York: HarperCollins.

Csikszentmihalyi, M. (1997), *Finding Flow*. New York: Basic Books.

Dunnigan, P. (1993), 'The computer in instrumental music'. *Music Educators Journal*, 80(1), 32–7, 61.

Farmer, D. (1999), *'Flow' and Mihalyi Csikszentmihalyi*. Narraweena: Austega. Available at www.austega.com/education/articles/flow.htm. Accessed in November 2006.

Folkestad, G. (1998), 'Music learning as cultural practice: as exemplified in computer-based creative music-making', in B. Sundin, G. McPherson and G. Folkestad (eds.), *Children Composing*. Malmö: Lunds University, pp. 134–46.

Geirland, J. (1996), *Go with the Flow*. San Francisco: Wired Digital. Available at www.wired.com/wired/archive/4.09/czik.html. Accessed in November 2006.

Green, L. (1990), 'Assessment of composition'. *British Journal of Music Education*, 7(3), 191–6.

Hickey, M. (1997), 'The computer as a tool in creative music making'. *Research Studies in Music Education*, 8(3), 56–70.

Hodges, R. (1996), 'The new technology', in C. Plummeridge (ed.), *Music Education: Trends and Issues*. London: Institute of Education University of London.

Maslow, A. (1954), *Motivation and Personality*. New York: Harper and Row.

Pitts, A. and Kwami, R. (2002), 'Raising students' performance in music composition through the use of information and communications technology (ICT): a survey of secondary schools in England'. *British Journal of Music Education*, 19(1), 61–71.

Reese, S. (1996), 'MIDI-assisted composing in your classroom', in G. Spruce (ed.), *Teaching Music*. London: Routledge.

Rettie, R. (2001), 'An exploration of flow during internet use'. *Internet Research: Electronic Networking Applications and Policy*, 11(2), 103-13.

Webster, P. (1990), 'Creative thinking, technology and music education'. *Design for Arts in Education*, 91(5), 35-41.

Webster, P. (1998), 'The new music educator'. *Arts Education Policy Review*, 100(2), 2-6.

Wilce, H. (2000), 'Technology Tempo'. *Curriculum Specials - Times Education Supplement*, dated 25 February 2000, pp. 10-11.

Younker, B. (2000), 'Thought processes and strategies of students engaged in music composition'. *Research Studies in Music Education*, 14(2), 24-39.

Chapter 5

The Mobile Phone and Class Music: A Teacher's Perspective

Alex Baxter

Introduction

This chapter is based on data collected from two sources:

1. questionnaires completed by 540 students from all classes at Key Stage 3 in a Hertfordshire secondary school
2. observations and informal conversations with students involved in a Year 9 project offering the opportunity of sending classroom musical transactions to mobile phones.

The Year 9 project spanned the summer term and was devised to run concurrently with a second project, which involved students using Apple iMac computers to compose in a style that interested them. A local university had recently donated the Apple computers.

These projects were conceived as an attempt to inspire a cohort of students who showed a lack of enthusiasm for their music lessons. It was the first time the students had been given access to ICT in their music lessons. I was interested in finding out whether drawing on an object of personal significance, in this case the mobile phone, might lead to positive musical outcomes.

Cultural Dissonance and Music Education

By Year 9, many students have given up hope of gaining the identity of a musician as defined by success in school music (QCA 2005). At the same time, they are experimenting with who they are musically by exercising their musical preferences out of school as they become attached to particular forms of musical expression. In view of the central role that pop music plays in young peoples' lives, this 'identity', so argue Hargreaves *et al.* (2003) and Lamont *et al.* (2003), is constituted by pop music.

During my first years of teaching music in secondary schools, I have observed the strength of musical identities in my daily encounters with my students. I have noted the enthusiasm with which students have 'lent me an earpiece' of their MP3 player and I have been intrigued by the extent of their knowledge as they told me about their music. In the process, I have learnt to discern subtle differences within a whole range of musical styles previously unknown to me - I now know about 'grime', and what constitutes a 'grimy bass', for example. I am also aware of Swanwick's point that if students place such an importance on their own musical identity, music that falls outside of that identity is likely to be rejected and with this comes a rejection of school music:

> The accessibility of music from the ends of the earth and high levels of music-specific information technology compete with conventional school activities. One consequence is that students can have very little time for 'school music' and may probably see it as a quaint musical sub-culture. (Swanwick 1999, pp. 36–7)

Research carried out into students' perceptions of music at home and at school tends to view music teachers as being at the 'heart of the problem', for they are seen as being products of the Western Classical tradition and the conservatoires that maintain that tradition (Sloboda 2001, Hargreaves *et al.* 2003). Using pop music in the classroom may appear to be one obvious solution. Yet if, as Elliott points out, 'Music (including one's conception of what music is) divides people as much as it unites them' (Elliott 1989, p. 12), then any style selected is likely to create a good degree of discord. A scheme of work focusing on popular music or some aspect of popular music needs to be expertly planned in order to cater for all students, be of relevance and overcome sectarian responses.

While Hargreaves *et al.* argue that it is teachers that affect the authenticity of school music, it is the authenticity of the resources available to music teachers that has caused me to question the viability of music in school. Green makes a compelling statement:

> When school resources do not match the cultural expectations students have of the subject the result is cultural dissonance. Metallophones and tambourines are no substitute for electric guitars and drum kits; try to make them so and the results are seen as a bit of a joke. (Green 1988, pp. 142–3)

Cultural Dissonance and my School Experience

After working in two schools in Hertfordshire, the first as part of my initial teacher training (ITT) and the second as a newly qualified teacher (NQT), I realized that there was a significant 'mismatch' between students' views of school music and their views of out-of-school music. It is a problem that I am sure is not confined to Hertfordshire.

In my first school, keyboard activities featured in almost every lesson and emphasis was placed on the performance of basic notated passages found in a commercially available scheme of work. Students would generally work in pairs, although broken keyboards resulted in some students working in threes to ensure involvement with a keyboard. Students worked without headphones, and the music emanating from the room would often be filled with pre-set rhythmic backings, demos or the phrase 'DJ' which students would claim they had 'caught by mistake'. During class performances of work there was a notable kafuffle of keyboard-centred fidgeting where the kinaesthetic charm of the keyboard took precedence over the auditory sound of peer performance. The keyboards had the facility to record two musical ideas but there was no disk drive and so musical ideas could not be saved. Hence the composition would be recorded over, often by the next user of the keyboard.

It did not help matters that prior to my appointment at the second school (where I was an NQT), the students had been taught by a number of non-specialist music teachers. On arrival I found that the students' expectations were low and they were not easy to motivate. The equipment with which to 'make music' consisted of old keyboards with a very small sound palette of around ten sounds and a few broken percussion instruments. This was hardly the most inspiring canvas and yet there was no budget with which to make the canvas more stimulating. While the Year 7 students were excited about using the keyboards at first, the Year 8s and 9s were considerably less so, with a number of students happily voicing complaints about an excessive diet of keyboard use.

The school purchased a junior samba set of 12 instruments and I sourced 18 empty water-cooler bottles. I hoped to generate a more varied curriculum and offer an alternative to the constant use of keyboards, even teaching ensemble rhythm skills through the bouncing of basketballs. I was still aware, however, that due to a lack of space for small group compositional work, and the need to address all rhythm activities as a whole class, the majority of Year 9 students continued to find music uninspiring and of little relevance.

A Change in Fortunes

The music department's luck turned when the local university donated seven old-style Apple iMacs running OS 9 and Propellerheads Reason v2.5. Reason, I consider to be an outstanding piece of software since it provides, in essence, a studio in a box. Although complex, especially for Key Stage 3, it offered our students the opportunity, for the first time, to create music which interested them and which they found relevant.

As a user of Reason, I felt comfortable with demonstrating compositional techniques. The positive response of the students was of great encouragement to me as I set about trying to change our situation. Having read music technology to degree level and developed expertise as a composer using various software and hardware, I could set up, monitor and maintain each workstation. In both my training school and my current school, I had noted just how significant music was in the students' lives and so I decided to design a project that would attempt to 'tap into' the resource that was my students, in particular their own knowledge of specific musical genres.

Making use of what we know about how popular musicians learn, watching, imitating and talking would be central to the learning process (Green 2001). The project would be 'student-led' and my role would be no more than a facilitator of learning. Students needed to feel a sense of autonomy by working with the music that motivated them and using it as a stimulus to create their own similarly-styled compositions. I hoped that listening would become integral to their composing and that it would be the kind of listening that students were well practised in outside of school. Boal-Palheiros points out that:

> Enjoyment and emotion are neglected in school music listening, yet they are among the most important functions of music for children … The cultural dissonance between school and home music listening deserves greater attention from music educators. (Boal-Palheiros and Hargreaves 2001, p. 116)

Among the Year 9 classes that took part in this project, there was a strong allegiance to both R&B and hip hop. The students worked in groups of two to four and, while interacting with the software, I repeatedly heard them discussing how to improve their compositions so that they might become more authentic. 'Just where should the beat drop?' and 'How should this instrument sound?' were typical questions. Some students produced lyrics, written to 'spit over' their tunes, and it was notably the boys who wanted to MC or rap over their musical creations. I knew that I had struck gold when the students started asking to come in at lunchtime to continue with their work.

The following statement is part of the National Curriculum's justification for music education:

> As an integral part of culture, past and present, it helps students understand themselves and relate to others, forging important links between the home, school and the wider world. (DfEE 2000, p. 14)

I felt confident that this project was enabling students to understand and relate to others. They were working together, generating their own success criteria, and were happy to revise their work in order to meet their musical criterion. Forging links between the home, school and the wider world, however, was still problematic. I had failed to see any musical link between home and school other than extra-curricular activities and school concerts in both of the schools where I had worked. Music that was created within the classroom lived and died within the classroom. Concerned that it was in danger of being Swanwick's 'quaint musical sub-culture', I wondered if there was a possibility that the products of school music could have a life outside of school.

The Mobile Phone and School

I first became aware of the potential of the mobile phone as a musical instrument when I was called to cover a Year 9 geography lesson. As I entered the classroom, I was surprised to find the vast majority of students listening to music on their mobile phones. Furthermore, it interested me that so many students had mobile phones on the school premises despite the school's policy that mobile phones should not be heard or seen in school.

This situation led to me asking Key Stage 3 students about the ways in which they viewed their mobile phones. The results of an anonymous questionnaire surveying 180 students in each year group revealed that 81 per cent of Year 7s, 88 per cent of Year 8s and 92 per cent of Year 9s brought their mobile phone to school on a daily basis. These results concurred with the results reported by *The Times Educational Supplement* (*TES*) claiming that around 90 per cent of secondary school students own a mobile phone and bring it to school (Roberts 2005). The results of an open question probing students' perceptions of their mobile phones further proved to be remarkable: the term 'very important' was used in the responses of 68 per cent of Year 7s, 77 per cent of Year 8s and 78 per cent of Year 9s. Many students stated that their mobile phone allowed them to keep in touch with friends and parents, assuring them that they would be able to contact people if they found themselves in danger or had, for example, missed the bus.

The results generated from the question of what mobile phones were used for revealed that the most frequent use after calling and texting was indeed listening to music. While 85 per cent of Year 7s, 88 per cent of Year 8s and 82 per cent of Year 9s used their mobile phone for regular calling; and 57 per cent of Year 7s, 73 per cent of Year 8s and 76 per cent of Year 9s used their mobile phone for regular texting; mobile phones were regularly used for listening to music by 44 per cent of Year 7s, 62 per cent of Year 8s and 69 per cent of Year 9s.

Although research into the benefits of the mobile phone as part of an 'educational toolkit' is still limited, the *TES* has reported various attempts to put this potential resource to good use. The *BBC Bitesize* revision website offers a downloadable game with questions covering the core subjects of English, mathematics and science. *GCSETxt Bites* allows students to receive revision questions and answers by text message. Both of these services can be accessed by mobile phone. The company ICUE offers a service that combines mobile phone technology with research into reading techniques and allows a user to download written material, from books to newspapers, for reading on a mobile phone. In its 10th March 2006 *Friday* issue (Horn 2006), the *TES* reports that the learning2Go initiative in Wolverhampton found that boys' and girls' reading improved when they used handheld devices to read ebooks. At the least, this research provides a positive argument for a device which, in an educational environment, has seen much in the way of negative reporting (being implicated with issues such as 'cyber bullying', health risks, exam cheating and interruption to lessons).

In order to further my research, I posed four investigative questions:

1. Would it be possible to enable students to send their finished compositions to their mobile phone so they could listen to them at any time?
2. Would students be interested in doing such a task and would this have a direct impact on motivation for music in Year 9?
3. Would the quality of compositional work be enhanced? [Students would surely not want music that they were not proud of on their phone.]
4. Would there be any effects on students' self-perception in music? [Students would be able to show others the results of their musical transactions in class.]

1. Is it possible for students to send their finished compositions to their mobile phone?

For some time, mobile phones have been able to connect wirelessly to other electronic devices such as computers and other mobile phones, originally through infrared technology and later through a technology known as Bluetooth. In their constant efforts to design products that utilize technological advances, mobile phone manufactures continually redesign or add to their products. A significant majority of modern mobile phones have either Bluetooth or infrared connectivity technology built in and many have both technologies available.

The Procedure

This section outlines the procedure and equipment that I used for sending students' compositions to their mobile phones. No departmental budget was available for this project so it was important to keep costs as low as possible. The equipment used consisted of an old Pentium II PC laptop, a USB Bluetooth dongle complete with software costing a total of £7, the free audio editor/recording software 'Audacity' and a free 'Lame.dll' encoding MP3 library file recommended by Audacity since they are not allowed to distribute MP3-encoding software themselves. The USB Bluetooth dongle,

'IVT BlueSoleil 1.6', was manufactured by IVT and had a range of 30 metres. A visual demonstration of the procedure can be found at www.freewebs.com/cellularcompositions.

Since the students in Year 9 had been composing with Reason on computers running OS 9, their final compositions were exported by Reason as .wav files, which were then transferred to the laptop where they were imported into Audacity. The .wav files were stereo (the file fed information to left and right speakers), but it was necessary to make the files mono since mobile phones usually only have one speaker. None of the students had explored panning in their compositions, and so splitting the stereo track to create a separate left and a separate right track followed by deleting one of the tracks sufficed. The file was then ready to be exported as an MP3 file.

Table 5.1 How to transfer MP3 files

Step 1	Attach the Bluetooth dongle to a spare USB port and load up the software supplied with the dongle.
Step 2	Turn Bluetooth 'On' on the mobile phone, or set it to 'Bluetooth Enabled'.
Step 3	On the computer, select 'Bluetooth Discovery Service' to find all the Bluetooth compatible devices in range. Icons for each of these will then be displayed on the screen.
Step 4	Select the displayed icon that represents the mobile phone that the MP3 file is to be transferred to. This will enable a range of options.
Step 5	Select 'Bluetooth File Transfer Service'.
Step 6	A passkey prompt is generated and sent to the device that the computer is attempting to communicate with (i.e. the mobile phone). Enter a pass key - any numbers (normally up to four are allowed).
Step 7	A passkey prompt is generated and sent to the computer. Enter the same number that was entered on the mobile phone. Transferring a file this way requires no knowledge of a mobile phone number, it requires both parties to be present, and ensures that no third party can hack into the transfer.
Step 8	Providing the two passkeys are identical, a window is generated that shows the various folders already present on the mobile phone.
Step 9	Drag the MP3 file into the window for the file to be uploaded and the transfer to be completed.
Step 10	The file is now on the mobile phone and can be assigned as a ring tone or stored with the other sounds.

It is worth noting that it is the MP3 player on many mobile phones that allows a user to listen to music, hence the requirement to convert the compositions from the stereo .wav format to MP3 format. However, while mobile phones are increasingly available with large memories (the students interviewed for this investigation reported having memory cards ranging from 3 megabytes to 100 megabytes to allow them to keep music on their mobiles), the other reason for converting the file from .wav to MP3 is that a default mono MP3 file created in Audacity is approximately only 10 per cent of the size of a stereo .wav file. This enables whole pieces of music to fit in the memory of a mobile, and allows a user to keep a large selection of songs, although the amount directly depends on the size of the mobile phone's memory. A smaller file like an MP3 is also transferred from a Bluetooth device to another Bluetooth device much more quickly.

Table 5.1 outlines the procedure that was used for transferring the student's MP3 file to their mobile phone.

Although this procedure used a composition that had been created with ICT, it is also possible to use the process to send an acoustic recording. Options include recording the composition/performance directly into a computer through the soundcard, either into a sequencer or into a program such as Audacity; or else recording the performance onto a CD and then importing the chosen track into Audacity or similar program.

2. Would students be interested in sending their compositions to their mobile phones and what impact would this have on motivation?

As outlined above, it is possible for students to create or perform music and then begin a process to enable the finished results to be sent to a mobile phone. For this facility to be of use in the music classroom, however, students need to be motivated by the possibility. Do students actually want their own musical transactions to be published, and can these transactions measure up to the professional music they already download and listen to on their mobile phones? While many theories of motivation can be drawn upon to explain students' behaviour, I found Pintrich and Schunk's broad definition of motivation as 'the process whereby goal-directed activity is instigated and sustained' (2002, p. 5) simple and helpful. Would students see the creation of a ring tone as the 'goal' instead of the musical experience involved?

The mobile phone is certainly a technology relevant to many students, and its use supports Smith *et al.*'s exploration of the variable 'value' within the context of motivation, suggesting students are more stimulated and therefore motivated if a lesson, or an aspect of a lesson, 'explores personal relevance' (Smith *et al.* 1999, cited in Nash 2001). In order to provide preliminary data for comparison against the actual results, the Year 9 cohort of 180 students responded to a short questionnaire. This revealed that 91 per cent thought the idea of sending their own music to their mobile phone was a good idea, whilst 78 per cent felt they would want to actually send their music to their phones. Interestingly, 74 per cent felt it would offer an incentive to produce better quality work.

3. Did the fact that students could now send their compositions to their mobile phone lead to better quality compositional work?

This project coincided with the students' first use of ICT to create music of their own choice. It is therefore difficult to claim whether it was the possibility of transferring a composition to a mobile phone, the use of ICT, or both that generated the findings. From a Year 9 cohort of 180 students, it became normal for 20 students to make use of the music department at break time and lunchtime each day in order to continue work on their compositions, although the vast majority of these were boys.

From a teacher's viewpoint, it was interesting to observe large numbers of students listening to each others' compositions in progress, giving comments and relating the musical similarities to tunes made by professional artists. A significant number of students brought in CDs or played MP3 files over and over again in an attempt to internalize phrases in order to create similar beats or patterns. The complexity of some of the hip hop style rhythms proved difficult to master, yet a number of students showed not only perseverance but also that they could easily attain some of the higher assessment sub-levels set out in the National Curriculum. The students or artists (as I now considered them) knew exactly how they wanted their compositions to sound. At times it seemed that they were challenging themselves in the extreme as they tried to perform rhythmic and melodic patterns to meet the approval of the others in their compositional groups, but with hindsight perhaps this represents a 'real' and natural peer success criterion.

Students were careful to select their sounds with consideration and used high level techniques such as filtering and effects to ensure that their work sounded authentic. A positive outcome of the project was the marked effect it had on the motivation of students who had previously found music, especially keyboard work, frustrating. They were developing greater ownership of and interest in their musical transactions. At the end of the project, the compositions ranged from short, looped patterns to complete $3\frac{1}{2}$ minute 'grime' style compositions. All students sent their finished products to their mobile phone.

The following is a transcript of a taped interview with two Year 9 boys. They worked on their composition every day for a period of two weeks and the questions were not pre-planned.

Interviewer	*Have many people heard the tune that you made?*
Joe	*Yeh quite a lot, although we haven't sent it out to too many people, just close friends.*
Interviewer	*What were their views?*
Moses	*They thought it was quite good.*
Interviewer	*Can I ask how that made you feel?*
Moses	*[laughs] – Yeh I felt alright.*
Interviewer	*Did any of your friends ask you to send it to them?*
Joe	*Yeh, so we did, but we asked them not to send it out.*
Interviewer	*Any reason for that?*
Joe	*Yeh cos people could say that they'd done it.*
Interviewer	*Would you say you were proud of your work?*
Moses	*Yeh – we put in a lot of effort.*
Joe	*Yeh – trying to make it sound convincing.*
Interviewer	*How have you found this topic compared with other topics?*
Joe	*Better.*
Moses	*Yeh we're actually doing proper stuff rather than just keyboards.*

It is encouraging that these students were taking pride in the music they had produced and didn't want others to take the credit for it. The fact that others outside of the music class had heard their music also lends itself to the generation of a musical identity amongst peers. Indeed, each student who composed a piece of music, either on their own or within a group, reported emotions of feeling 'proud' or 'happy' if other students listened to their compositions on their mobile phone and gave a positive response.

4. Would there be any effects on self-perception in music? A positive story.

One student (Craig) was interested in the melody that runs through the song 'Ghetto Kyote', released by Kamikaze. He learnt the melody from sheet music, played it into Reason and then created three separate drum patterns and a bass pattern to accompany the melody. It was interesting watching Craig show his peers his arrangement and it was encouraging hearing their positive responses – many wanted Craig to teach them the melody to 'Ghetto Kyote' too.

The following is a transcript of a taped interview with Craig. Again the questions were not pre-planned before the interview.

Interviewer	*So Craig, what made you choose a tune that already exists?*
Craig	*I liked the tune and just wanted to learn it.*
Interviewer	*Was it your original plan to make your own drum and bass line?*
Craig	*No, I just wanted to learn the song but the sounds were much better on the computers so it made the tune sound better. I then thought I would add drums and a bass.*
Interviewer	*A lot of people thought your version was good didn't they; can I ask how that made you feel?*
Craig	*I felt proud that other people wanted to hear my work, especially when they told others that they thought I'd made a good tune.*
Interviewer	*Did any of your friends ask you to send it to them, and if so did you?*
Craig	*Yeh some people have asked me to send it to them so I did. Some people have made it so that if I call them it's my ring tone.*
Interviewer	*Is it your ring tone?*
Craig	*No.*
Interviewer	*How have you found this topic compared with other topics?*
Craig	*Yeh good. I think I'm better at music now.*

Craig's work was a real success story: it demonstrates not only a motivation to perform a piece of music well but also a desire to experiment to create a personal version. When Craig used his mobile phone to call someone who had assigned Craig's tune to Craig's number in their address book, they knew instantly that Craig was calling. Craig had previously found the keyboard frustrating, but by learning the melody to a song that he liked, he became highly motivated. The fact that Craig now thinks that he is better at music is also significant; his perception of his musical self has improved, and I feel that he places more trust in his musical competences.

Conclusions

When it comes to music, young people at secondary school undoubtedly know what it is they like and are capable of making informed musical judgements about the music they consume. As educators it is important that we harness this enthusiasm, while developing their discrimination skills further to allow them to interact with music beyond their experience and make sound judgements on a whole range of musics. Using music that students have ownership of in class can present a risk, but perhaps the key is to allow the students some freedom to explore their own musical styles in a way that allows their goals to be reached.

In this case, the role of the teacher may be largely to offer technical advice. Students are more than competent judges and are more than capable of setting themselves high standards. When it comes to their school music departments, it is important then that they have opportunities to interact with music that they find relevant and spend considerable time immersed in, especially in the domain of composition. Our students are the next generation of music makers and we should offer them opportunities to speak many musical languages and to discover through this speaking a personalized musical voice.

That students were able to use ICT for the first time in a school environment to compose music was a major aspect of this investigation. In addition, it was the first time that students were not required to perform live, removing significant anxieties that occur when having to perform to others in a class. It was also the first time that they were able to create musical layers without relying on others. It is possible that in a music department where students have access to computers regularly as compositional or performance tools, this investigation might yield very different results. While this project saw increased motivational levels, particularly from boys who in previous units of work had become easily distracted, there is the chance that it was simply the novelty of experience that captured students' imaginations – and that enabled some students to challenge perceptions of themselves as potential musicians and artists.

It was encouraging to observe students engaging in 'music for music's sake', making sound judgements, working together to compose and, more importantly, wanting to compose enough to gladly give up their free, out-of-class social time. It was heartening to see students focusing on the process of composition and forgetting the end game of sending their finished work to an electronic device. Students were clearly proud of their work and happy to have their musical transactions on show on the same device as the music they consume. They had the opportunity to take their musical transactions away with them, along with the freedom to share these with whoever they chose. Since they could also send and receive compositions, many students assigned compositions to people in their address book.

I am left wondering how these students will use their mobile phones in the future. Further research needs to be conducted in other schools, perhaps schools that regularly have access to ICT for composition. It would also be valuable to discover whether students would be interested in recording their acoustic music for transfer to their mobile phone, and indeed whether it offered any incentive for improved quality of work or motivation.

For me, the next cycle of this action research is to investigate the uptake rate of students choosing to send their musical products to their mobile phone if generated from a new scheme of work that does not overtly fall under the umbrella of popular music. I am interested to know whether students might choose to listen to their 'non-popular' music transactions at their leisure following the music's new mobility, and whether this leads to an increased recollection of musical discussion, thought and empathy.

In the same way that having a mobile phone is now the 'norm' for many students of school age, other technological advancements with which students will want to engage will follow. The challenge for the music teacher is to keep abreast of such developments and to find ways of utilizing them for positive means, thus continuing to build the bridge between out of school and in school. Facing such future challenges will prove enlightening, especially if what is found yields evidence of students building stronger perceptions of self as artist and musician – or simply providing an outlet for creative self-expression.

References

Boal-Palheiros, G. and Hargreaves, D. (2001), 'Listening to music at home and at school'. *British Journal of Music Education*, 18(2), 103–18.

DfEE (2000), *The National Curriculum for Music. Qualification and Curriculum Authority*. London: DfEE & QCA.

Elliot, D. (1989), 'Key concepts in multicultural education'. *International Journal of Music Education*, 13, 11–18.

Green, L. (1988), *Music on Deaf Ears*. Manchester: Manchester University Press.

Green, L. (2001), *How Popular Musicians Learn: A Way Ahead for Music Education*. Aldershot: Ashgate.

Hargreaves, D., Marshall, N. and North, A. (2003), 'Music education in the twenty-first century: a psychological perspective'. *British Journal of Music Education*, 20(2), 147–63.

Horn, C. (2006), 'Mobile Library'. *The Times Educational Supplement*, Friday Supplement, dated 10 March 2006, pp. 6–7.

Lamont, A., Hargreaves, D., Marshall, N. and Tarrant, M. (2003), 'Young people's music in and out of school'. *British Journal of Music Education*, 20(3), 229–41.

Nash, R. (2001), *Motivating your Students*. http://cvc3.coastline.edu/Telelearning2001Web/Motivation.htm. Accessed on 5 July 2006.

Pintrich, P. and Schunk, D. (2002), *Motivation in Education: Theory, Research and Applications*. Ohio: Merrill Prentice Hall Press.

Qualification and Curriculum Authority (2005), *Music 2004/5 Annual Report on Curriculum and Assessment*. London: QCA.

Roberts, C. (2005), 'Making Sense of Mobile Phones'. *The Times Educational Supplement*, Friday Supplement, dated 9 September 2005, pp. 13–16.

Sloboda, J. (2001), 'Emotion, functionality, and the everyday experience of music: where does music education fit?' *Music Education Research*, 3(2), 243–54.

Smith, P. and Ragan, T. (1999), *Instructional Design* (2nd edn.). Columbus, OH: Merrill.

Swanwick, K. (1999), *Teaching Music Musically*. London: Routledge.

Part II: Researching Digital Classrooms

Chapter 6

The DJ Factor: Teaching Performance and Composition from Back to Front

Mike Challis

Introduction

This chapter sets out an alternative approach to composition, one that acknowledges the strong identity felt by many young people, especially boys, to DJ culture. The musical genres of this culture – whether garage, drum and bass, house or R&B – have a motivating power to engage even the most difficult of students in creative music making, while providing fringe benefits, such as improving self-confidence and learning to work as a team.

In the pages that follow, I will describe a process I have used with students to develop their compositional skills. Starting with other people's music on vinyl and learning to manipulate it using turntables, students learn performance skills. They listen carefully to the basic structures of music they identify with and would like to make themselves. Using state of the art, but affordable, software they can be shown how to make tracks in a virtual studio. With the addition of drum machines, synthesizers, samplers and loop players to create their rhythm, bass line and thematic elements, they compose an entire track of their own. In a final move that incorporates the computer into a live session, using loops or original material, a complete performance is created.

This chapter will outline the project, discuss identity and motivation and describe the process in detail. Two case studies will be provided, as well as discussion relating to the technical and practical problems in scaling up the process for larger classes.

Project Background

This chapter is informed by a case study looking at the way in which teenagers in a Pupil Referral Unit (PRU) have engaged in music making. They began by DJing commercial material (deconstructing and re-organizing it), then created their own material to mix in with the commercial material, and eventually produced an original track or piece.

For one reason or another, the students at the PRU do not fit into the mainstream education system and have usually been excluded from at least two schools. They exhibit various behavioural problems and as such have a tailored curriculum in the unit, consisting of core subjects, vocational training and activities. Because of the nature of the PRU and the current trends in youth culture, the majority of students at Key Stage 4 (14 to 16 year olds) like either garage, drum and bass or, to a lesser extent,

R&B or hip hop. Although this trend has been relatively constant over the last three years of this project, other genres could be accommodated using the same approach.

The process used in this project builds on the DJ practice of mixing different musical sources by allowing the students to create and mix their own sounds with commercial ones. A DJ will take two tracks and mix elements of one with another. This could be a simple layering of the two tracks, getting the beats in time, or it could be a more dynamic, repeated rhythmic cross-fade. It could be a mix of the bass elements of one track with the treble elements of another. Whatever techniques are used, the DJ is creating a new mix from parts of the original track, deconstructing and reconstructing elements of the original. Students can begin by learning the art of mixing, and then learn to create their own material on computer, which they can mix in with the commercial material.

A key point is that this approach works with so called non-musicians, usually defined as students who don't play an instrument. Musicality is so inbred in our society that to say someone isn't musical by this definition seems somewhat limited.

> The concept of musical enculturation refers to the acquisition of musical skills and knowledge by immersion in the everyday music and musical practices of one's social context. Almost everyone in any social context is musically encultured. It cannot be avoided because we cannot shut our ears, and we therefore come into contact with the music that is around us, not only by choice but by default. (Green 2001, p. 22)

None of the students at the PRU would be described as musicians by the traditional school system and yet, given guidance, they can compose their own material and often have very clear ideas of what they want to achieve. In addition, the students in this process are disillusioned and outside the traditional school environment. An opportunity to create original material with a professional sound in a genre with which they identify does wonders for their self-esteem.

This music project has been developed as an activity and so does not have the constraints of following an exam track. The outcomes are student centred and student directed. Though formal music qualifications are not obtained, several of the students have continued their music activities after leaving the unit, either semi-professionally or as a hobby.

The process of the project has been developed in an experimental way, aided by the small numbers involved at any one time. The author believes that the process is scalable and could be adapted to other situations. Expanding the process and the technical requirements for these adaptations will be discussed at the end of the chapter.

Identity and Motivation

> The notion of 'musical identities' may help us to understand the origins of the 'problem of secondary school music', which seems to be particularly acute in the English secondary school. Students' musical identities are strongly bound up with the importance of pop music outside school, and the distinction between 'music in school' and 'music outside school' may be very significant for them. (Hargreaves and Marshall 2003, p. 263)

Hargreaves and Marshall (2003, p. 264) report that music plays a major role in the lives of young people, who often spend two to three hours a day listening to music. They define 'music in identities' as 'the ways in which music may form a part of other aspects of the individual's self-image, such as those relating to gender, age, national identity, and disability and identity.'

The young people at the PRU identify with music that is, to a large extent, 'underground', that is not mainstream. To find it you have to look for it – although the internet has made it easier for young people to find this underground music. The author has watched them share internet website addresses in the same way that in the past they may have shared football cards.

> When affirmative experience of music's inherent meanings is accompanied by positive attitudes towards its delineated meanings; when . . . two such meanings seem experientially transparent and unproblematic, music then becomes a complete reflection and celebration of the self . . . when music is like this it draws together our world: it *celebrates* us. (Green 1988, p. 137)

When youth feel alienated from authority and the perceived adult system that surrounds them, they feel the need to rebel. Often a part of that rebellion involves aligning themselves with a particular style of music that is underground, alternative and not understood by the status quo. While in the past this may have been progressive rock or heavy metal, nowadays it tends to be garage, drum and bass, hip hop, jungle, house or any other underground musical style. Regardless of the style, young people find something to identify with or which gives some kind of meaning to their existence, a kind of tribe to which they wish to belong. For the youth of the Westbridge PRU, from ages 14 to 16, that music is overwhelmingly garage, drum and bass or hip hop.

Hip hop is a good example of a music that was born out of an underground society:

> Hip hop culture emerged as a source for youth of alternative identity formation and social status in a community whose older local support institutions had been all but demolished along with large sectors of its built environment. Alternative local identities were forged in fashions and language, street names and most important, in establishing neighbourhood crews or posses . . . Identity in hip hop is deeply rooted in the specific, the local experience, and one's attachment to and status in a local group or alternative family. (Rose 1994, p. 34)

Hip hop culture, which includes graffiti and breakdancing as well as rap music, grew out of the specific cultural and economic situation that existed in the Bronx, New York in the mid 1970s. The rap music itself was developed within this hip hop culture as a result of the coming together of three basic strands: the African-American oral tradition, the emergence of sampling technology and the socioeconomic situation of post-industrial New York City.

Garage has a convoluted history, too complex to describe here. Suffice to say that UK garage has become an underground music force. UK garage works well as deconstruction material since much of it comes in quite a raw state, asking for more material to be mixed into it. This might be in the form of another vinyl, or 'chat', or skilful dynamic mixing using the mixer to blend different parts of the mix, sometimes making changes every bar.

One of the main features of garage is that it allows for 'MCing' or chatting over the music. Like rapping in hip hop, MCing allows for free expression of thoughts and ideas over the music. For those that chat, this is an integral method for expressing their identity. Identity, and therefore the writing of these chats, can be a key motivator and can also be supported as creative writing by the English department.

If these factors are taken into consideration when planning compositional work, if the students identify with the music and the challenge set for them, if their music can be put up alongside the music of their idols and worked with, if they can be proud of their achievements and the work boosts their self-esteem – then identity can be used as a strong motivator and its effects may be felt far beyond the music department.

The Process and the Technology

The approach adopted in this project varies from individual to individual and is tailored according to individual needs. While the following approach is the one that I most commonly adopt, there are other approaches, particularly if a student wants to use live instruments or vocals at an early stage.

Stage 1 – DJing

This involves finding out where the students are musically, giving them the chance to talk about what they want to achieve and letting them know what is possible. It assumes that the students are listeners to music but have not developed a high level of DJing skill or composed before.

We start by mixing commercially available music on vinyl using a standard DJ set-up of two turntables and a mixer. A collection of UK garage or drum and bass and hip hop vinyl is made available. (In buying music for the project I am guided by the students themselves and helpful record shops. Material can also be auditioned and purchased from internet sites.)

The students learn to listen to the beat and the structure of the piece. They try to match the beats by adjusting the speeds of the turntables and mixing the two tracks together so that they both play at the same time, in time, with the rhythmic elements of each track combining to create a whole. This can be quite difficult for some and requires practice. The aim is to learn about tempo, count beats and bars, and listen to the structure of the music.

The tracks are generally constructed out of eight-bar phrases and the students learn to listen to these and count the bars. By starting the second vinyl you want to mix in with the first, at the same point in the phrase of eight bars, it becomes much easier to mix. As the students progress, they can use the mixer as a tool. One example of this would be to cut from one vinyl to another, not just at the end of the track but also during the track or even at the same point in every bar. If the music is in time, then part of the rhythmic elements of one track can be 'punched' into the other to make a rhythm that is a combination of the two.

The approach to teaching this stage is important. For many students, access to DJ turntables or decks is difficult to obtain and this may be the first time that they have had access to a high quality set-up (even if often they will know someone who has a set-up). I find that the majority of them want to use decks. Culturally they identify with this method of music production, although there is a gender imbalance: while boys tend to be keen to use decks, girls are usually more reluctant, often not even trying when boys are present. I have found, however, that the girls in the project are ready to move on to composition, as well as being more likely to want to sing over their completed track.

Stage 2 - Making a Beat

Once DJing with decks has been explored, students are given the opportunity to make their own beat (drum pattern loop) on a computer. For this project, I use Reason software made by Propellerheads. Reason is a virtual studio that allows you to use drum machines, synthesizers, samplers and loop players in a virtual rack inside the computer. (See 'Technical information' at the end of the chapter.) Other software with virtual instruments, or even hardware drum machines, could also be used for this stage.

The technology is introduced as a tool to make the beat the students want. It is not taught by a detailed introduction of the software and all its functions, but rather by instruction and intervention at the point at which a particular function is needed. Using the drum machine, the students load up a set of sounds to use and programme a beat onto these sounds. The software emulates a hardware drum machine and gives visual feedback. Working in 4/4, the students hear what works and what doesn't by immediate audio feedback. They trial and improve sounds until they get a basic beat. The tempo can be adjusted to any value required. For garage this is usually around 135 bpm. Drum and bass will run at around 165 bpm, with hip hop and R&B running at around 80–90 bpm.

Once a beat has been set up in the computer, it is possible to feed the output signal from the computer to the mixer and to mix it in with a commercial vinyl. The students get immediate feedback: they can hear their beat mixed in with the commercial material and begin to see the possibilities. This motivates them to create more variations on their beat. Several patterns can be stored, enabling the student to switch the beat and make changes at various points in playback. These can be automated and the basic layout of a track can be structured.

Stage 3 - Adding a Bass line and Thematic Elements

Using a virtual synthesizer or sampler, the students add a bass line. This can be achieved by either writing it into the edit grid using the mouse in non real-time, or by playing a MIDI keyboard into the computer to trigger the virtual instrument. Thematic elements can be added using the other instruments as they begin to build a track.

The quality of the sounds the students hear is very good. In fact, much of the commercially made music that they are listening to uses the same sort of software that they are using. Hearing their own material being played next to music they admire gives a great sense of achievement.

Stage 4 - Developing a Structure

The students listen to the commercial tracks and study their structure. They look at how the pieces are put together and then structure their own track into phrases. (In Reason this is particularly easy to see as the phrases can be grouped and colour coded.) Their music is then put on CD. This is very important since the students value the ability to take a product away with them from the project.

Stage 5 - DJing with Their Own Material

Although putting their material on vinyl would be possible using a dub plate cutter (in much the same way that Edison made his original recordings), this is prohibitively expensive. Instead, we use computers to play work in progress and a CD deck for students to mix their finished material with other tracks created during the project or with commercial vinyl. This is less tactile than vinyl but expedient. If they are so inclined, they can chat or sing over the tracks, making recordings of their performances.

Case Studies

Beckie

Most participants in this project were male, since most females lean towards wanting to sing to backing tracks rather than compose their own material. Beckie (not her real name) was different. In the unit she is a 'live wire' and can be very difficult to pin down and get working, although she is motivated about music. She came to the music sessions and played hip hop vinyl on the decks. Many of these vinyls come with instrumental and a cappella versions, so she could easily mix the rap lyrics of one with the instrumental track of another. The various parts of the track - the beat, the bass line, the addition of thematic elements such as a piano chord or a loop of jazz music - were pointed out as she played with the decks.

Once confident that Beckie knew what she was listening to, we sat down and made a basic beat on the drum machine in Reason. She quickly became quite good and finished off her first lesson with three variations of her beat that could be switched between and played.

At the following session, Beckie played some more vinyl and mixed different tracks. She played with reverse, got used to stopping the vinyl and even did some elementary scratch movements. Then we worked on her track. We added a piano loop to go with her beat, and a bass line. The piece was 5 bars long but because Reason can play this as a loop it seemed continuous. We put it together with an a cappella track. By now, it was break time and some other students dropped in to the room to listen. They assumed the track was being played from the decks and were surprised to learn that Beckie had made the beat herself. This gave her a great sense of achievement and improved her self-confidence.

Most of the students at the PRU suffer from acute lack of self-esteem, and this cannot be underestimated as one of the key factors in their lack of achievement. Being able to improve on their esteem is therefore one of the primary objectives of the music programme at the unit.

Nathan and Pedro

Nathan and Pedro, again not their real names, had a love of chatting. They already had some DJing skills and came to the sessions to DJ and chat. Recording the outcomes of these sessions was important to them. They wanted a product and liked to go away and listen to what they had done and, no doubt, play the mixes to their friends. They were challenged to write some original music to mix in with vinyl for a concert performance. They began by making beats with the drum machine in Reason. They quickly got the hang of the machine and produced a variety of beats. These were played back from the computer and mixed in with commercial vinyl straight away. The effect was good: they liked their beats.

The next step was to structure a song. Pedro worked on this and made a song that had a bass line to go with his beat. He structured the song to have different beats and bass lines in different sections. He then added some thematic elements using the sampler and the Graintable synthesizer in Reason. This track was exported to CD.

Nathan worked on his own material and made several tracks over a period of two months. The resulting compilation of tracks was burnt to CD and then mixed with commercial vinyl. Nathan and Pedro wrote their own chat words or lyrics to MC over the music and several mixes were recorded. Finally a video was shot of the two lads performing their material. It was shown during a concert performance.

The process described works for these students in this particular environment, as well as for small-sized groups. It is for the reader to reflect on how relevant these case studies are with regard to their own students. All schools have a fair share of difficult students. Could these techniques be useful in motivating them to be creative and productive, rather than negative and a drain on the system?

Conclusions and Outcomes

Students with no prior knowledge of composition can be motivated to compose their own material by being encouraged to DJ commercially available material with which they identify. This identity can then be harnessed to motivate them to make their own material using computers. By beginning with basic beats and mixing these with commercial tracks, they can increase their confidence. They can then extend their composition to include a bass line and thematic elements, creating their first section. By working on form and structure they can produce a track that can be mixed and maybe even MCed or chatted over. This project shows that the process can work with Key Stage 4 students who have had little or no experience of composition.

Outcomes

- Students get to be creative in an idiom with which they identify.
- They create an object that they may be very proud of and that may be comparable to commercial material.
- Their self-esteem is improved and, with this, their motivation and behaviour.
- They learn basic skills doing something they enjoy.
- Working as a group can develop their ability to cooperate and share.
- Often the more able students will help the others.
- They direct the composition themselves.

Opportunities may exist for students to show their work to others. These could range from informal showings at school to CD recordings played to friends, shows recorded for community radio stations or even live performances on stage (such as concerts or club-style parties).

Making music can have life-changing consequences. Take the example of Dizzee Rascal:

> The experience of Dizzee Rascal, the acclaimed rap star, is a wonderful example of this child-centred practice. Dizzee was just 19 years old when he won the 2003 Mercury Music Prize. On receiving the prestigious award he said that he couldn't have made it without his secondary school teacher Tim Smith – not the acceptance speech most of us had anticipated!
>
> For many years Dizzee had had serious problems with behaviour and faced constant exclusions: whether he could remain in school had been in doubt. This situation transformed when Tim Smith started working with him. Tim said of him, 'I remember noticing how talented he was … I was gobsmacked by the quality of his work. Each time he came he seemed to have new ideas and he wanted more and more knowledge from me. Eventually he did get excluded from virtually all his classes and spent most of his time working with me in the music room – in a little store cupboard.'

There is an important message in Dizzee's story – indeed in recognition of this Dizzee gave all the £20,000 prize money to youth clubs in East London to buy musical equipment for young people. What did Tim Smith do that enabled Dizzee to stay in the school system, change his behaviour and achieve his potential, and what does it mean for whole school practice? (Kehoe 2004, p. 2)

Dizzee Rascal's success is obviously quite unique. At the same time, the child-centred approach employed by his teacher can be applied to help many whose behaviour is jeopardizing their own and other's education, and maybe even the future direction of their lives.

> According to Dizzee, if he hadn't got into music he would have been drawn into crime – we can thank his music teacher, Mr Smith, formerly of Langden Park school, for encouraging Dizzee to develop his musical talent. (dotmusic 2003)

Strategies for Scaling up for Schools

Since we were working on a small scale, vinyl decks and laptops were used to facilitate these projects. When working with larger groups, other set-ups may be necessary. It is important to note that you do not need excellent DJing skills: the ability to mix one sound with another is enough to get started. Facilitation and encouragement on the part of the teacher is more important than flashy DJing techniques. Bringing in a DJ to demonstrate various techniques could develop advanced DJing skills and possibly motivate the students even more.

Although vinyl is the most tactile medium, other ways of mixing are available. A CD-mixing set-up could be used along with computers. The finished material created by the students can be burnt onto CD and used just like any other CD.

One approach for large groups might be to use software-based mixing packages. An entire class could mix tracks in a computer room. They could make their own material, using appropriate software, and import it into the mixing package. This would remove the need to learn the art of beat matching (the software would do it) and therefore students could progress faster to the stage of mixing in their own material.

Technical Information

Vinyl Mixing

To get started all you need is a pair of vinyl decks and a DJ mixer, a pair of headphones and something with which to amplify the music (most schools would already have this). Oh, and of course, some vinyl to play. Vinyl is the most tactile way of mixing. Cheap set-ups can be had for £200 – but these will have poor performance and may not last the rigours of school use. You should, however, be able to acquire decent decks with a mixer for around £500 at 2005 UK prices. A useful reference book on the art of DJing is *How to DJ (properly)* published by the Bantam Press (Broughton and Brewster 2002).

CD Mixing

Although CD mixing is less tactile, it has the advantage of the students being able to mix music they own themselves on CD, as well as being able to burn and mix material they have made. A basic CD set-up would cost from £200 upwards.

Computer Mixing

Computer-based mixing packages enable students to work in the school computer room, mixing tracks that are saved as files on computer. This makes it possible for schools to provide multiple stations. There are lots of different packages out there – check on www.hitsquad.com. Hardware interfaces can be used to control your files on the computer. Two such devices are the Behringer B-CONTROL DEEJAY BCD2000 (www.behringer.com/BCD2000/) and Hercules DJ Console (www.hercules.com/), which can be bought for around £100 and include mixing software in the package.

Final Scratch (www.stantondj.com) and Serato Scratch Live (www.serato.com)

These are systems whereby vinyl decks are used to control files held on the computer. They are excellent for skilled DJs since they allow them to use all their advanced techniques to control any sound file on the computer as if it were actually on the vinyl. The vinyl itself only plays back time-code information, which the computer then uses to play back the required sound file. They are quite expensive and complex systems, however, and may not be the right thing for schools just starting out.

Reason (www.propellerhead.se)

Although there are other programs that try to emulate it, Reason is the king of the virtual studio instrument world. It gives you an almost bombproof virtual studio environment in which to play samplers and synthesizers and drum machines and loop players, applying effects with full libraries of sounds and excellent support for importing your own sounds into the instruments. It can work as a stand-alone program, or it can connect to programs such as Cubase Logic or Digital Performer using Rewire technology. For the price of a good synthesizer you can buy a licence for five or ten stations and have large numbers of students using it. It is a complex program but a template can have individuals writing beats in the Redrum Drum Computer within minutes. The program can be set to open this template by default. It is the program widely used to make commercial vinyl beats.

Cubase/Logic

Most schools already have Cubase or Logic. If you have virtual instruments in these programs, they can be used to make a beat. While the learning curve for this might be higher than for Reason, using Cubase or Logic means that live recordings can be incorporated (such as vocal or instrumental performances).

Live

Ableton Live is an incredible piece of software. The full version is not cheap but you can do a lot with the demo, which is downloadable from www.ableton.com. The X-session controller is an excellent device that allows you to control Live and comes with a cut-down version of the program for around £80. (See www.evolution.co.uk/products/evo_xsession.htm)

Other Software

If budgets are tight then freeware or shareware software, such as drum machine editors, might be useful, as might any creative software that students have access to outside school. AudioMulch (www.audiomulch.com) is a very powerful package that runs as a time-limited demo and has a shareware pricetag. There are many other packages available – check out websites such as www.hitsquad.com.

Drum Machines

Hardware drum machines can be simple to use. Transportable drum machines can be used with mixing desks. Since most schools would only have one or two of these, they are more appropriate for individuals than groups.

More Useful Websites

Equipment:

www.mveducation.com
www.studiospares.com

Vinyl:

www.baserecords.co.uk
Good source of UK garage and house music
www.redeyerecords.co.uk
Good source of drum and bass

Info:

www.bbc.co.uk/1xtra/

Final Word

I hope that this chapter has whetted your appetite for exploring the possibilities of working on composition in this way. I firmly believe that these techniques can make a difference.

In my sessions, I use different styles in different forums. I don't always use DJ mixing as a starting point and often work solely with computers. There are some wonderful pieces of software out there that can be adapted and used to motivate students. New equipment is being released all the time, at lower and lower prices. Music production has been opened up to all, not just those who have access to an expensive computer. Virtual studios give today's students access to stuff that I would never have dreamed possible, even ten years ago.

Immense power is available – what matters is what we do with it. I hope that you have been inspired to experiment and explore this amazing area.

Sample music made on this project can be auditioned on the author's website at www.mikechallis.com

References

dotmusic. (2003), http://uk.launch.yahoo.com/l_reviews_a/30229.html.

Broughton, B. and Brewster, B. (2002), *How to DJ (Properly)*. London: Bantam Press.

Green, L. (1988), *Music on Deaf Ears: Musical Meaning, Ideology and Education*. Manchester: Manchester University Press.

Green, L. (2001), *How Popular Musicians Learn: A Way Ahead for Music Education*. Aldershot, Hants: Ashgate.

Hargreaves, D.J. and Marshall, N.A. (2003), 'Developing identities in music education'. *Music Education Research*, 5(3), 263-74.

Kehoe, I. (2004), *Including 'Dizzee Rascal': Transforming Behaviour, Attendance and Learning Through Child-centred Practice*. London: The Grubb Institute of Behavioural Studies.

Rose, T. (1994), *Black Noise: Rap Music and Black Culture in Contemporary America*. Hanover, NH: Wesleyan University Press.

Chapter 7

Composing with Graphical Technologies: Representations, Manipulations and Affordances

Kevin Jennings

Musical composition is by definition a practical art. For the composer who is just starting out, this can create a tricky bind. In Donald Schon's words:

> The paradox of a really new competence is this: that a student cannot at first understand what he needs to learn, can learn it only by educating himself, and can educate himself only by beginning to do what he does not yet understand. (Schon 1987, p. 93)

In a musical context the problem becomes, 'I cannot learn to compose without composing, but I cannot compose without learning how'. Beginning composers need to plunge into composing in order to learn how to compose. They need to try to do what they do not know how to do in order to gain the experience that will help them learn how to do it. They may encounter obstacles in their attempt, such as the need for instrumental competence (so as to be able to realize musical ideas) and for some form of notation reading and writing skills. A basic competence in musical rudiments may also be perceived as a requirement for formal studies in composition, making it exceedingly difficult for students without these prior skills to get a foot on the composing ladder.

For the many students entering secondary school music classrooms already in possession of these skills, there are likely to be other obstacles to composition. The ability to play an instrument, for example, can be a double-edged sword. While it enables students to realize their musical ideas, it often constrains these ideas to those that they can physically play, so that music arises from 'the automatism of our fingers' (Smith Brindle 1986, p. 6) rather than from considered compositional thought. Those with the ability to read standard music notation will find that it serves a different purpose in a composing context to that served in performance. Students who are skilled in using notation as performers will not necessarily be similarly skilled in using notation in the manner of a composer. Finally, for those with some background in music theory, it is often difficult to transfer rudimentary musical concepts, which have been learned formally and discreetly, into a holistic composing context. Knowledge 'about' music may not necessarily translate into knowing 'how to' compose.

It has often been suggested that these difficulties might be overcome by adopting approaches that make use of computers and associated technologies. The problem is that much of the music software in common usage is either based on notation (using a computer representation of traditional score) or on the sequencer model (designed primarily to facilitate note input via a musical instrument, usually a keyboard). In the first case, standard music notation is just as opaque to the novice user when presented on the computer screen as it is on paper, while in the latter, the young composer's creative imagination may still be limited by what he or she can accomplish technically at the instrument. In order for a computer-based approach to have real value, it must attempt to overcome one or both of these problems.

This chapter will briefly describe two graphical music software applications that employ alternative forms of representation of musical information. These novel applications, Hyperscore and DrumSteps, attempt to enable beginning composers (particularly those in the early years of secondary schooling) to engage in music composition independently of any physical instrument. They seek to provide students with a vehicle for compositional thought, while at the same time making the results of their ongoing work immediately available to the teacher for discussion and analysis. Based on a series of closely observed case studies, the pages that follow will:

1   describe a variety of behaviours and interactions observed in learners and teachers working with these software applications
2   show how these behaviours are to an extent a function of the interfaces themselves
3   suggest that using computer music software may lend itself to an 'improvisational' pedagogic approach that is quite different from the teaching approaches employed in more traditional, non computer-based settings.

Notation

'Notation is the servant of expression, but equally a medium of independent thought' (Maconie 1990, p.113)

While the experience of music is time dependent, a notation system may hold the music steady in a way that enables a variety of interactions. Bamberger describes music notation systems as:

systematic frameworks within which the noticeably invisible relations of pitch and time that are necessarily experienced as continuously going on, come to be represented as spatial, static and invariant properties. (Bamberger 2004, p. 171)

It is evident that notation acts as a vehicle for recording, communicating and disseminating the results of composers work. Less evident but crucially important for composing is the manner in which notation acts as an 'object to think with' (Papert 1993, p. 11). Notation systems provide a vehicle for compositional thought, which enable the composer to hold in mind a multiplicity of musical ideas, shift attention seamlessly from one musical entity to another, find connections between things, and observe patterns and attributes of musical ideas that, in turn, may themselves suggest further ideas, manipulations or connections.

In this regard, notation systems are not neutral. Any representational system (including standard staff notation, tonic sol-fa and computer-based piano-roll) will act as a filter, serving to surface some aspects of the material and conceal others. As Bamberger describes it:

> When events are 'turned into objects' the representations of those events are necessarily partial and they are so in two senses: they are *incomplete*, and they favor, or are *partial* to certain aspects of the phenomena while ignoring others. (Bamberger 2004, p. 171)

The process of composition involves selecting, from a range of possibilities, musical objects for consideration, reflection and manipulation. The success of this process depends on both the transparency of the notation system used and the ability of the user to parse it. For the beginning composer, the value of using a computer-based notation system lies in the degree to which it can *reflect back* aspects of the musical materials in a manner that may be intuitively understood, while simultaneously making these materials available for *manipulation*.

Affordance

The concept of *manipulation* of musical materials is vital to understanding the true nature of computer-based composing. Since computer interfaces are not neutral, their design will not only conceal some things and surface others – in the manner of any other notation system – but will also subliminally direct the actions of users, in both musical and non-musical ways. The characteristic of objects to themselves suggest how they should be acted upon is commonly referred to as *affordance* (Gibson 1977, 1979; Norman 1988):

> Affordances provide strong clues to the operation of things. Plates are for pushing. Knobs are for turning. Slots are for inserting things into. Balls are for throwing or bouncing. (Norman 1988, p. 9)

Computer-based systems afford direct action on, and manipulation of, graphical objects that represent musical entities. This makes them fundamentally different from paper-based notation, where the only action that can be carried out on an object is to erase it and replace it with another. Furthermore, computer software commonly enables operations on groups or aggregations of notes simultaneously. A simple example of this is copy-and-paste. Most computer music software *affords* this action, making it possible to replicate musical material much more easily and immediately than with pen and paper. The suggestion inherent in the idea of affordance is that if a functionality is provided, it will be used. This influences both the composing process and the musical outcome. As we will see later, the *affordances* of music software have a fundamental influence on the work of both students and teachers.

Alternative Software Designs

> Ideally what we want is a notation that could be mastered in ten minutes, after which music could be returned to its original state – as sound. (Schafer 1976, p. 247)

The challenge for software designers is to create software that represents musical information in a manner that is easy for the novice composer to understand and manipulate. This chapter is concerned with two novel software applications that attempt to do just that. Each application provides an alternative to more common notation and sequencer-based approaches, both in the manner in which the music is represented, and the opportunities provided for manipulation of this material. The first of these is Hyperscore.

Composition activities in the Hyperscore environment proceed on the premise that the piece of music will be based on a number of short musical ideas or motives. Motives are made by placing notes in the motive window (see Figure 7.1). Users may create as many short ideas or motives as required. Motives, which are colour coded, may then be placed in the main sketch window by using the mouse to 'draw' them in with the appropriate coloured pen. In playback, the play head scrolls from left to right across the sketch window. As it passes over a line or stroke, it plays the associated motive, repeating it for the entire length of the stroke.

If a stroke is contoured, the software will interpret the stroke according to a 'best-fit' between the content of the particular motive window and the overarching shape of the stroke. The resulting melody will embody both the internal melodic and rhythmic shape of the motif and the overarching melodic contour. Hyperscore also provides various levels of automated help, which act to fit the contents of strokes to an underlying pitch set, based either on a scale or a triad. The exact nature of this pitch set may be controlled to a degree by shaping the harmony line, which runs horizontally through the middle of the sketch window.

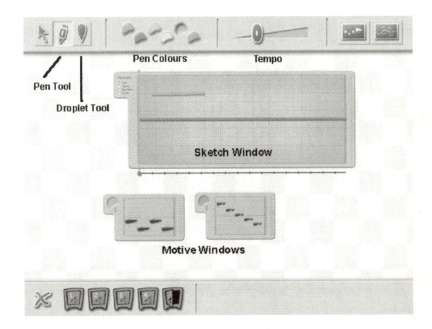

Figure 7.1 The Hyperscore Workspace

The second software application referred to in this chapter is called DrumSteps (Figure 7.2).

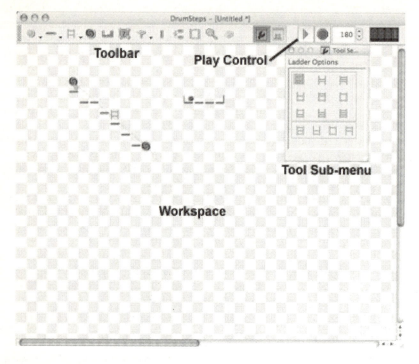

Figure 7.2 The DrumSteps Workspace

DrumSteps operates as a 'percussion construction-kit'. Users construct sets of steps and various other static elements. Sounds are produced by causing balls to fall through the construction and collide with its static elements. The basic time unit is the step, while timbre is embodied in the ball. Steps may be arranged so as to produce a wide variety of rhythmic patterns. The basic step pulse may be subdivided by using ladder elements, while sets of steps may be grouped between 'wormholes', causing the ball

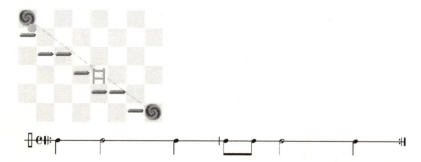

Figure 7.3 Rhythmic patterns in DrumSteps

to repeat the contained pattern (see Figure 7.3). Step sets may be linked so that an action in one set may be used to cue an action in another.

The application supports multiple voices and the grouping of elements at various levels of aggregation, as well as multi-user collaboration via the internet. While a full description of each software application is not practicable here, the reader is encouraged to explore these applications, both of which are freely available for download.

Case Studies: Representations, Manipulations, Affordances and Teaching

Clearly Hyperscore and DrumSteps differ in many respects from both traditional notation systems and other computer-based representations. This chapter seeks to explore the nature of these differences with respect to the manner in which non-standard interfaces:

a) represent and filter the available musical information
b) afford opportunities for, and place limitations on, possible manipulation of this musical information
c) afford opportunities for non-musically motivated interactions
d) influence the manner in which teachers engage in the business of teaching composition.

In order to examine how these interfaces might affect the work of students and teachers in practice, a series of workshops were conducted. Participating students, who were between 11 and 12 years old, used each piece of software over a number of weeks.

Context for the Case Studies

Setting Workshops took place during the school day but outside the normal classroom. In each study, two students at a time worked on separate computers at opposite ends of a large room, with the teacher/researcher dividing his time between them as deemed appropriate.

Task time Each student spent between 5 and 8 one-hour sessions working with each software application to make a single extended piece of music.

Prior experience Students had little prior formal music training; they did not play a musical instrument or read standard music notation.

Teacher/researcher The author, an experienced musician who has worked for many years in secondary school music teaching, acted as teacher and facilitator for each of the workshops.

Data capture All student and teacher actions were captured on digital video, yielding a complete record of each student's composing pathway. The student's work was also saved on the computer regularly throughout each session.

Students were chosen at random from the general school population. They were broadly representative of those students entering secondary school without much exposure to formal music tuition. The teacher/researcher adopted a reactive role, initially offering minimal guidance to students beyond what was necessary to begin the compositional process and thereafter making spontaneous interventions as deemed necessary. It was hoped that this strategy would be broad enough to allow a variety of unscripted interactions, thereby providing a window into not only the student's processes but also those of the teacher.

Case Example (A) – Kevin Discovers Nothing (How representations can affect learning)

The representation of rests marks an interesting difference between the note level representation in Hyperscore (and in both DrumSteps and piano-roll) and staff notation. In staff notation, a rest is represented by the presence of something – a 'rest' symbol – whereas in Hyperscore (and DrumSteps), a rest is simply the absence of a note-icon. The excerpt from the following case study illustrates how one student accessed the fundamental concepts of rest, pulse and rhythm as a direct result of the manner in which the interface filtered and represented this musical information.

Kevin has made two motives (Figure 7.4a and Figure 7.4b).

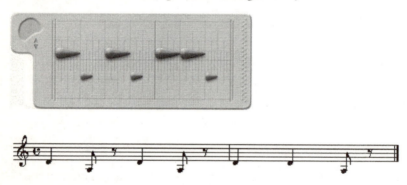

Figure 7.4 (a) Purple Motive

Figure 7.4 (b) Blue Motive

The teacher asks Kevin to 'draw' the two motives together in the Sketch window (Figure 7.5 a).

As the motives play back together, they get progressively out of sync with each other (Figure 7.5b), due to the fact that one is seven beats long (Figure 7.4a – Purple) while the other is eight (Figure 7.4b – Blue).

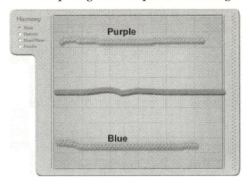

Figure 7.5 (a) Motives in the Sketch window

Figure 7.5 (b) Motives in Score

Kevin looks quizzical, as if the result was not quite what he expected, but doesn't say anything. The teacher tries to focus his attention on the problem. His initial strategy is to have Kevin count the number of beats in each motif. For the purple motive, Kevin counts seven beats accurately. In the blue motive, however, Kevin counts the rhythm of the notes themselves rather than beats (Figure 7.6).

He fails to count anything in the gaps (rests), placing a count on each note rather than on each beat. He has confused pulse and rhythm and does not have the concept of a rest as a beat unit.

The teacher points to the 'gap' in the motive window representing the first crochet rest in the blue motive:

T: *See that ... count it or don't count it?*
K: *Ehhh ... don't count it ...*
T: *Why not?*
K: *Because there's no ... there's no notes there ...*

Kevin's answer is tentative, as if he recognizes that there may be an unresolved issue. The teacher then suggests that he think of this gap (rest) as an 'imaginary' or 'invisible' note and count again. After two attempts, Kevin laughs and says:

K: *It was eight ...*

Kevin has begun to internalize the concept of rest and has established the relative lengths of each motive. The teacher then returns to the problem of synchronization between the two motives:

ONE   TWO   Three - Four - Five - Six   SEVEN   EIGHT

Figure 7.6 Kevin counts notes

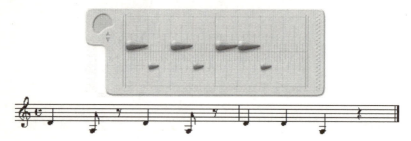

Figure 7.7 Purple motive final version

> T: *But, we said that that's a silent note [pointing to the rest in the blue motive (Figure 7.4b)]. Why couldn't there be just a silent note at the end [pointing to the end of the purple motive (Figure 7.4a)]?*
>
> K: *Yeahhh?*
>
> T: *But it would still count?*
>
> K: *Yeah.*

The purple motive window is extended so as to have a quarter note rest at the end and then played back (Figure 7.7).

> K: *[spontaneously counts along evenly] … one, two, three, four, five, six, seven, eight.*

Kevin has understood the concept of 'rest' and has decoupled pulse from rhythm. His learning has emerged from the real musical task of making two musical ideas 'go together'.

The key factors in Kevin's learning relate to the simplicity of the drawing metaphor (which enables functional comparison of the relationship between the two motives) and the clarity and directness of the representation (enabling the teacher to quickly identify Kevin's misconception). The nature of both the teacher's intervention and Kevin's understanding are predicated on the notion of a rest as the absence of something, clearly reflecting the manner in which the information is filtered and represented in the interface.

Although this is a short example drawn from a single case study, conversations about similar issues - pulse, rhythm, rhythmic alignment, relative lengths of motives, melodic contour, texture and form - arose in almost all of the Hyperscore cases examined. Albeit that the issues emerged spontaneously and were not a reflection of any overt agenda on the part of the teacher, they are clearly relevant to the everyday work of secondary school music teachers.

While the influence of the teacher was a factor in Kevin's learning, so was the nature and structure of the interface. The issues discussed seemed to be those made most immediately accessible by the interface. More specific, pitch-related issues, including intervals, triads and harmony did not seem to arise as often, despite the teacher's efforts to introduce them. This could be explained by the fact that individual pitches are not explicitly labelled in the interface, making some pitch-related issues difficult to tackle. Clearly the interface lent itself to discussion of certain topics but not others.

Case Examples (B) – Stacy Makes a Motive (How manipulations embody concepts)

One of the functions of a graphical music interface is to enable students to engage in manipulation of musical material. Fundamental musical concepts will often emerge from the seemingly more superficial exploration of interface affordances. In the following example, Stacy discovers a variety of musical relationships through simple note-level manipulations and the use of copy-and-paste functionality to 'group' and manipulate note events.

Stacy spends about 15 minutes randomly dotting in notes of various lengths and pitches, without making any discernable progress. She fills and clears a short motive window several times with random arrangements of notes (Figure 7.8).

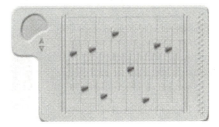

Figure 7.8 Stacy's random exploration

Suddenly she seems to hit on an idea. She clears the screen and makes a three-note descending figure (Figure 7.9).

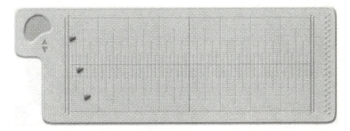

Figure 7.9 Stacy's initial idea

She follows it with its inversion (Figure 7.10).

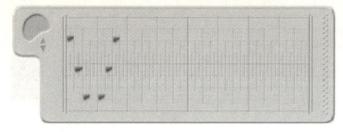

Figure 7.10 Stacy discovers inversion

Having made the six-note figure, she copies-and-pastes it so as to make a repeat, then shifts the lower two notes of the second figure up a semi-tone (Figure 7.11).

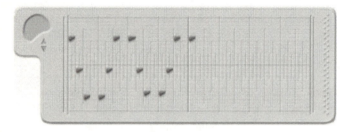

Figure 7.11 Stacy discovers repetition and variation

She sings the melody to herself, tracing the melody on the screen as she does so, but continues to sing, completing the melody with three more notes. She then finds these notes and adds them to the end of her motive (Figure 7.12).

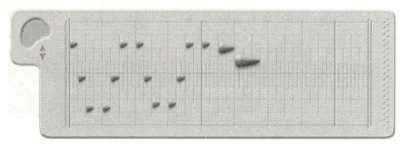

Figure 7.12 Stacy's final motive

In building this motive, Stacy makes use of inversion, repetition and variation. Although these are standard techniques for developing and altering musical material, none of them has been suggested to her previously. They seem to have simply emerged during her exploration of the representation and manipulations afforded by the interface. Three notes descending are followed by three notes rising, copy-and-paste creates a repeat, and the variation is created by simply highlighting and moving a two note group.

While the motive itself was created relatively quickly once the initial idea had become manifest, its creation was preceded by a long period of exploration and experiment, both with the interface and with the musical materials represented. This was characteristic of all students' work throughout the workshops. Periods of seemingly more productive work were interspersed with these periods of seemingly random exploration or *bricolage* (Papert 1993, p. 143), which Kevin referred to at one point as 'just messing around'. These exploratory behaviours were necessary simply to become familiar with the interface, but were also seen to constitute a valuable form of quasi-musical exploration, out of which more concrete ideas frequently emerged. Although teachers may often feel constrained to intervene so as to keep students 'on task', it is important to recognize these explorations as part of the process of composing with graphical technologies. They should be regarded as a kind of graphical process of 'improvisation' that may ultimately lead to productive musical outcomes.

Case Examples (C) - Becky Plays Chasing (How musical interfaces can engender extra-musical actions)

While most students used the interfaces to musical ends, it was interesting to note the wide range of other non-musical motivations that seemed to inhabit students' work.

See one of Emer's Motives in Figure 7.13. It has a sense of pitch contour, but beyond that, very little in the way of an organizing principle. Examination of the Hyperscore motive window, however, quickly surfaces its underlying structure (Figure 7.14). The motive is clearly the result of a graphical/visual rather than a musical process. In this case, Emer is not using the note icons to access musical information, but rather manipulating the visual entities themselves. Her work here is most likely not a reflection of musical intent.

Figure 7.13 Emer's motive (score)

Figure 7.14 Emer's motive (Hyperscore)

Emer's work in the Sketch window showed similar characteristics (Figure 7.15).

Figure 7.15 Emer's work in the Sketch window

Her long, crossing strokes (top and bottom) are symmetrical. The blue (middle) stroke is a zigzag pattern, with the surrounding dots placed so as to partly mimic the shape. The four short strokes at the end are symmetrical around the central axis (the outer ones are purple, the inner ones are blue), while the final lines of dots are initially also symmetrical, although the lower is later extended.

Stacy, on the other hand, seemed to work in the sketch window in a more kinaesthetic manner (Figure 7.16). Many of her strokes were neither attempts to create a musical outcome, nor organized as visual patterns. Rather, they represented an intuitive physical gesture or scribble.

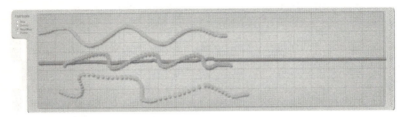

Figure 7.16 Stacy's kinaesthetic drawing

Becky's work in DrumSteps was an extreme case of this extra-musically motivated work. Despite repeated teacher interventions, Becky seemed to make almost no progress, and spent the first two sessions aimlessly placing and erasing step and ladder elements and auditioning timbres for the balls. However, towards the end of the second session, she seemed to suddenly become energized, creating the step set shown in Figure 7.17.

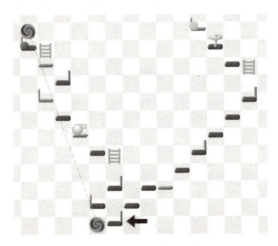

Figure 7.17 Becky's initial idea

The key to understanding this construction lies in the number of steps in each ball-path. Up to the point at which the two paths converge, the left-hand path has 13 elements while the right-hand path has 14 (including spaces, which count as a rest). The effect is that both balls arrive (at the step indicated by the arrow) one after the other. The wormhole at the bottom routes the balls back to top left, and they then appear to 'chase' each other down the steps. Becky's work is clearly motivated by aspects of animation rather than musical concerns.

> T: *Ok, so ... what you've done is that you've made a plan for the way you want the ball to go on the screen.*
> B: *Yeah.*

Becky describes how the two balls will follow each other.

> B: *Yeah ... it's a game of chasing ...*

She adds several more voices, counting the path length of each so as to ensure they all pass the merge point sequentially, creating a 'caterpillar' effect (Figure 7.18).

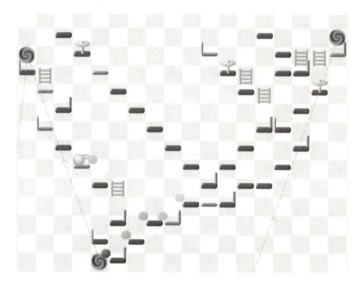

Figure 7.18 Becky's 'Game of Chasing'

Becky describes her motivation for the second part of her piece.

> T: *You have an idea for something to do? What's your idea ...*
> B: *I'm gonna shape it kind of like a diamond ...*

She then proceeds to do just that (Figure 7.19).

Becky's piece displays little evidence of any musical organization beyond that imposed by the software. In fact, she doesn't seem to use the software as a means of engaging with music at all. The first section of her piece is motivated by notions of animation and procedure, while the latter part is graphical. She attends primarily to

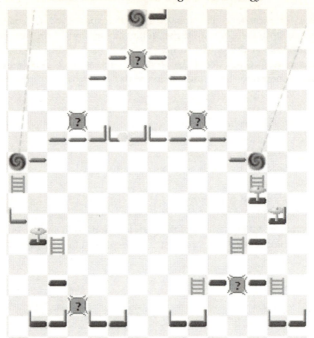

Figure 7.19 Becky's diamond shape

the affordances of the interface and engages with construction, animation and process, viewing the sound output as a secondary by-product of her work.

The examples above illustrate what might be considered one of the drawbacks of working with graphical music interfaces. In attempting to provide a vehicle for musical interaction, other modes of activity are inevitably facilitated. While this rarely causes any difficulty for students, it may create a degree of discomfort for music teachers who, naturally, wish their students to be engaged in musically motivated work.

Case Examples (D) – Variations on Teaching (How interfaces can afford teaching approaches)

Not only were the specific musical areas that arose a function of the interfaces, but also in many cases the teaching methodology itself seemed in some way to arise out of the possibilities offered by the software. During the workshops, for example, the teacher frequently reacted spontaneously to things that the students had done and improvised methodological approaches using the affordances of the interface. Often this included attempts to use functionality provided by the interface to *model* a variety of compositional techniques. The degree to which the interface itself provided a mutually well-understood medium for student–teacher dialogue was observed to be a key factor. Students could observe the teacher's actions, understand their musical meaning, and then use the interface to explore these techniques in their own work

In the following example, the teacher engages in a spontaneous demonstration in order to try to engage a student with standard compositional techniques in the area of pattern and variation.

Emer's initial motive-making seemed to be limited in scope, with the result that her motives seemed repetitive. The teacher suggests that in making her new motives, she think about the idea of pattern.

> T: *What would you mean ... what would you understand by patterns?*
> E: *Kinda like ... the same thing ...*
> T: *Something that you'd recognise ... ?*

Without formally defining the idea of pattern in music, there is agreement that there is some element of repetition involved. The teacher uses the interface to illustrate how this notion might be applied in composing. He makes a semi-random motive and then asks Emer to listen to it and see if she can pick out any sections of the motive that sound interesting and might form the basis for a repeating pattern (Figure 7.20).

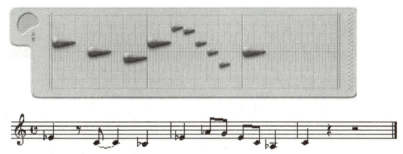

Figure 7.20 Pattern example

The teacher is trying to get Emer to listen to the motif in a different way – to 'zoom in' to the motive, break it into sub-units and consider each unit in isolation. Emer doesn't understand the task so the teacher demonstrates using the interface. First, he loops the opening syncopated three-note descending figure. Emer immediately 'gets it'. The teacher uses the copy-and-paste function to make a new motive consisting of three repeats of this figure. He then makes small variations to the figure, by raising the first note of each three note group (Figure 7.21).

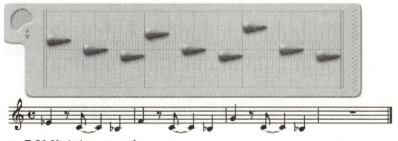

Figure 7.21 Variation example

He then repeats this illustration twice more, taking different sub-units of the original, 'copy-and-pasting' to make a new repeating motif and making variations.

In this instance, the teacher perceived a need for intervention, seized on the aspect of the tool at hand which seems to best fit his requirements, and attempted an unscripted demonstration. The subject of the intervention arose spontaneously out of Emer's perceived need, while the manner of its execution was to a large extent a function of the software. The working material was created on the spot and the idea of creating simple variations was entirely unscripted – it simply arose from what was possible. Emer proceeded to make extensive use of this technique in her later work. Having observed Emer's response to this demonstration, the teacher proceeded to use this technique successfully with each of the other participating students. The teacher's methodological approach has been guided and expanded by the affordances of the software.

Summary

> The tool should have many possible uses, both imagined and unimagined (Upitis 1989, p. 244)

Graphical Interfaces Afford Musical Interactions

Throughout each set of workshops there was clear musical engagement and learning on a variety of levels. Musical interaction and learning were, to an extent, a function of the interface – each interface made musical descriptors and parameters explicitly available for consideration and provided a set of manipulations through which a variety of musical ideas might be actively explored. Musical ideas and concepts sometimes arose as a result of deliberate teacher intervention, but also emerged naturally and spontaneously out of student's exploration of these affordances of the interface.

Graphical Interfaces Afford Non-musical Interactions

While both interfaces supported a range of musical actions and manipulations, they equally afforded the user a range of actions that were not primarily musical in nature. In fact, the likelihood is that all computer graphical music interfaces (even those based on staff or piano-roll notation) will afford at least two modes of interaction: musical and graphical. Other modes of interaction may also be afforded depending on the particular design of the interface. In Hyperscore, these 'third' affordances were kinaesthetically motivated 'drawing' actions; while in DrumSteps they were an emphasis on procedure and causation.

Graphical Interfaces Break Down Barriers Between Domains

The interfaces described here made musical structures and concepts available to students through intuitive graphical descriptors. In so doing, they also facilitated other forms of interaction such as Emer's graphical constructions, Stacy's 'physical' gestures or Becky's animations. Students' responses to the interfaces varied from the clearly musically motivated to interactions with more 'superficial' aspects of the interface. In fact, most students were seen to move fluidly and comfortably along this continuum – the question as to whether they were making a piece of music, a picture with music attached or an animation with sound did not seem to trouble them. It appears that these interfaces break down barriers and make connections between differing modes of engagement and the different domains they represent. While this may be disconcerting for teachers, it is evidently not a problem for students.

Teaching with Graphical Interfaces

The main focus of this chapter has not been to examine in-depth, specific aspects of teaching methodology when working with and through graphical computer interfaces, yet it is worth noting that these interfaces will affect the manner in which teachers go about their work. Teachers may need to adapt their methodological approaches in order to make the most effective use of these tools. In this regard, it may be useful to consider the following points.

1 **Teaching 'with' the Interface**
   Most interfaces lend themselves to surfacing some issues and not others. Teachers should try to be aware of particular affordances of the interface and work *with* – rather than against – these.

2 **Interfaces as Windows on Cognition**
   Graphical interfaces can provide a valuable 'externalization' of student's composing processes. Close observation of student's work in these interfaces may enable the alert teacher to focus on issues that could otherwise be difficult to uncover.

3 **Interfaces Facilitate Improvising and Modelling**
   Much of the value of graphical interfaces lies in the manner in which they provide a mutually well-understood medium for joint musical exploration. Characteristic of this exploration is its improvisatory nature. Teaching approaches based on unscripted responses to students' work and improvised interactive demonstrations may be especially appropriate in this context.

4 **Interfaces as Vehicles for Conversation**
   Perhaps the most important attribute of graphical interfaces is their ability to act as a vehicle for teacher–student interaction. The interface enables the student to explore, and the teacher to both observe and demonstrate. It is in this fluid combination of ongoing musical conversation between student and teacher that real teaching and learning is most likely to occur.

For the teacher working with a graphical music interface, there is a clear trade-off between facilitating access to musical materials and manipulations, and enabling other modes of behaviour. Any interface design which attempted to prevent all non-musical interactions, however, would need to be so restrictive that it would exclude most, if not all, of the user group observed here. These students simply do not have the necessary prior musical experience and note-reading skills to benefit from more rigidly designed systems. For such students, these interfaces represent an accessible path into the musical domain.

Finally, any well-designed interface will stimulate students' imaginations in many different ways. This will afford a multitude of possible modes of engagement and interaction, *'both imagined and unimagined'*. Awareness of these *affordances*, musical and non-musical, can only enhance a teacher's ability to maximize the teaching and learning opportunities offered by graphical music technologies.

References

Bamberger, J. (2004), 'How the conventions of music notation shape musical perception and performance', in D.E. Miell, D. Hargreaves and R. MacDonald (eds), *Musical Communications*. Oxford: Oxford University Press, pp. 171–92.

Gibson, J.J. (1977), 'The theory of affordances', in R.E. Shaw and J. Bransford (eds), *Perceiving, Acting and Knowing*. Hillsdale, NJ: Lawrence Erlbaum Associates, pp. 67–82.

Gibson, J.J. (1979), *The Ecological Approach to Visual Perception*. Boston: Houghton Mifflin.

Maconie, R. (1990), *The Concept of Music*. Oxford: OUP.

Norman, D.A. (1988), *The Design of Everyday Things*. London: MIT Press.

Papert, S. (1993), *Mindstorms: Children, Computers and Powerful Ideas*. Cambridge, MA: MIT Press.

Schafer, R.M. (1976), *Creative Music Education*. New York: Schirmer.

Schon, D. (1987), *Educating the Reflective Practitioner*. San Francisco: Jossey-Bass.

Smith Brindle, R. (1986), *Musical Composition*. Oxford: Oxford University Press.

Upitis, R. (1989), 'The craft of composition: helping children create music with computer tools'. *Psychomusicology*, 8(2), 151–62.

Chapter 8

Networked Improvisational Musical Environments: Learning Through Online Collaborative Music Making

Andrew R. Brown and Steven Dillon

Introduction

This chapter explores the potential for using computers, linked via a network, as vehicles for collaborative musical improvisation. The term 'networked improvisation' suggests a 'contemporary musicianship', which embraces the computer as instrument, the network as ensemble and cyberspace as venue. Networked improvisation provides a multitude of learning opportunities, which the authors will discuss. Drawing on a selection of school- and community-based case studies, they will focus on issues, approaches and strategies for educators using networked musical environments. The chapter will also illustrate the potential of such environments to provide collaborative and supportive learning spaces, where both action and reflection can take place.

The Computer as Instrument

A computer can respond, in the same way as a piano, to gestures resulting in real-time expressive changes in sound. While DJs and contemporary bands frequently utilize the computer as an instrument for playing recombined chunks of music rather than individual notes (as in sound samples and loops of sonic materials), it still has a significant role as an expressive instrument for contemporary musicians. Networked improvisation with generative music algorithms involves using the computer as both an instrument and a partner, providing musical experiences through meta-level control.

Networked improvisation can be broadly described as collaborative music making over a computer network. It may be useful to differentiate two further classifications: a) those systems that directly send musical gestures over the network as MIDI, audio or OSC data, and b) those that send parameter data for controlling generative algorithms. Programs such as 'Band-in-a-box' have been using this kind of algorithmic representation of contemporary music styles for many years, but have been neither interactive nor networked.

The authors of this chapter pay particular attention to networked improvisation using algorithmic functions because we believe such systems provide unique educational opportunities and an elegant solution to the technical limitations of network latency (Chafe and Leistikow 2001). For many decades computer musicians, such as David Cope (1992) and Iannis Xenakis (1991), have used generative algorithms in the production of complex music compositions constructed over many hours, days or weeks. The recent advances in computer technology have made it possible to design music algorithms based upon specific pitch, timbre and rhythmic qualities. They can be manipulated in real time with a simple interface that a child can control. Furthermore, this operation can be a collaborative one that utilizes a network to facilitate virtual ensembles.

Is It the Same as a Real Instrument?

The personal satisfaction and meaning gained by users of computer instruments have been documented as being similar to those described by musicians using acoustic instruments (Brown 2000, 2003; Dillon 2001). Computer instruments with specifically designed algorithms, based on the theoretical rules of known musical styles, can provide a focused curriculum experience. The student is able to directly manipulate style, actively influencing the sound and reflecting on the changes in musical elements. The computer can also be used as an instrument within a mixed ensemble, as in many contemporary performances where electronic and acoustic instruments are combined.

The Network as Ensemble

Prior to the internet, real-time interaction was only possible for musicians who were physically collocated. Now it is possible to interact in real time over a network. This allows ensemble activity to occur at separate sites for musicians sharing a network and software. They are able to play together in collaboration, each seeing and hearing the result of their gestures, as real musical communication is facilitated between them. Cyberspace becomes a new meeting place, not unlike a musical chat room, with music taking the place of speech as the primary mode of communication between users.

Cyberspace as Venue

Networked musical environments allow cyberspace to become a 'venue' where improvisers can participate in a musical dialogue, perform solo, or listen to the performances of others. With algorithmic musical instruments that are not dependent on continuous gestural input, the user can be both listener and performer, both producer and consumer. In the same way that chat rooms facilitate online communities, networked musical environments create a cyber venue for participatory cultural experiences.

What is Networked Improvisation?

Networked improvisation involves two or more musicians operating software that connects over the internet or a local area network. Musical information generated by the musicians is sent over the network, linking them via their computers in real time, that is, so quickly as to be perceived as immediate. The musical information sent over the network can be raw audio data, parametric data (controlling key and density levels, for instance) or symbolic form, such as Musical Instrument Digital Interface (MIDI) note data. Communication between musicians during the session is asynchronous: information can simultaneously flow in any direction, like speech in a telephone system. A networked music environment is therefore an interactive distributed computer system with which multiple users can make music in real time.

Elements of an Environment for Networked Improvisation

Networked improvisation activities reinforce existing musical skills that focus on sonic expression and communication. They also involve new skills and understandings that take into account the new digital context. This section explores the skills, knowledge and resources used in a networked improvisation.

A Contemporary Musicianship

Musicianship in a networked environment acknowledges the computer as an instrument, a networked group as a form of ensemble, and cyberspace as the venue for their music making. Since the instruments utilize digital technologies to store, represent and communicate musical knowledge and experience, it is necessary for the musician to have a reasonable understanding of how these technologies operate. For this reason, contemporary musicianship includes skills in using computer hardware and software to record, review, generate, produce and publish music. It acknowledges the unique techniques and knowledge demonstrated by DJs, sound designers, electronic composers and music producers. Furthermore, in place of common practice notation, the contemporary musician uses digital representations of music – such as waveforms, graphs, event lists and computer code – to analyse, compose and perform.

Modes of Creative Engagement

Networked environments using algorithmic processes allow a variety of modes of creative engagement. The facility to participate in the changing of parameters, as well as to sit back and analyse the current state of the music, provides an increased range of relationships with the music-making process. An improviser can choose to play, direct, explore, select or listen. In turn, the technology used by the musician can serve as an instrument, tool, model, generator and container of musical knowledge (Brown 2000, 2003). This means that students can engage in different ways within the same performance experience, enhancing the opportunities for learning music.

Using generative networked improvisation systems, we have observed improvisers collaboratively switching from being listener (judging the quality of the rhythmic groove) to being explorer (experimenting with the pitch range of instrumental parts) and then director (making adjustments to the tempo so that the groove 'felt' danceable). While the generative nature of the software provides the ability to oscillate between acting and reflecting during performances, the real-time nature of the algorithmic music generation provides instant feedback to the student on the musical choices they make. These provide opportunities for increased development across a broad spectrum of musical intelligence.

Resources for Networked Improvisation

Networked improvisation systems fall into two main categories:

1. Systems where the musician's gestures are directly controlling the note level detail of the music in the way of traditional co-present acoustic improvisation.
2. Systems where musicians (such as DJs or live algorithmic music performers) control meta-level parameters and the details of the sound material are based on prepared or generated material.

Systems are available that support one or both of these methods of operation but the most established networked improvisation resources come from the academic computer music community. A number of these require significant computing expertise and may be beyond the reach of many school students or teachers. Since they illuminate the history and future of this field, however, a brief overview follows.

A Brief Overview of Networked Improvisation Resources

In the same way that MIDI was a revolution in connecting synthesizers together in the 1980s, the Open Sound Control (OSC) specification (Wright and Freed 1997) has been the catalyst for a number of real-time music systems to embrace network-jamming capabilities. Programs that implement the OSC standard can communicate with each other sending text, symbolic or audio data between computers over a network. Some of the programs that support networked musical performance using MIDI or OSC are SuperCollider, Max/MSP, Pure-data, Algorithmic Composer and AudioMulch. With these systems, the user builds a musical patch (instrument) from components and programs the way in which instructions and data are sent and responded to when received. Another format that is emerging to do a similar job as OSC via MIDI is the RTP payload format for MIDI (Lazzaro and Wawrzynek 2005). It is worth keeping an eye on the development of this format since it specifically intends to foster networked music performance applications.

Code Jamming

An even more flexible, and challenging, trend in the academic computer music community is live programming. This involves lines of computer code that are written and sent out over a network during live performances. The lines of code describe the music and sounds to be played. Examples include ChucK (Wang and Cook 2003), Co-Audicle (Cook *et al.* 2005), SuperCollider (McCartney 1996) and Impromptu (Sorensen 2005). Code fragments describe synthesis processes, generative music algorithms or commands to currently running operations and functions.

Although the flexibility of such systems is vast, immense coding skill and knowledge of digital music systems is required to manage the task under the time pressures of live performance. As a result, these systems are rarely used in schools, although they are increasingly common in university music programmes and electronic music festivals. The TopLap website provides further detail about systems for live programming.

Networked improvisation software suitable for classroom usage includes the jam2jam program (Brown *et al.* 2002), described later in this chapter; the PitchWeb application that is part of William Duckworth's Cathedral online music project; John

Klima's GlasBead application for sharing musical fragments in a virtual space; and the Cyberjazz system, a performance network where instrument gestures are sent as note-by-note MIDI messages directly over the network. A reasonably simple live programming system based on a conversational narrative model is Quoth (Latta 2005), which may be suitable for use in school music programmes. The Continuator (Pachet 2002) is a generative improvisation instrument that works as a call-and-response system. It reflects the student's performance through imitative variations, but does not support multiple users over a network.

A Networked Improvisation Example

jam2jam is a networked improvisation system designed specifically for music education. It aims to enhance engagements with music at personal, social and cultural levels. The vignette described in this section – in which students used jam2jam in a music and dance activity – will illustrate how networked improvisation can be conducted. Observations across a variety of age groups, contexts and cultural groups using jam2jam suggest that the meaningful experiences achieved through networked improvisation share the same qualities as a 'real' ensemble experience.

The jam2jam Software

jam2jam is a networked improvisation system that allows users to modify the musical parameters of an algorithmically generated musical style. Since parameters are altered by adjusting sliders, it provides users with next-to-immediate audio feedback. Any number of jam2jam systems can be connected into an 'ensemble' over a network, which can be a local network or the internet. Users are connected by the shared music and the mirroring of moving sliders across each connected computer. A built-in instant message chat-box provides text communication between performers, but the more important communication occurs as students listen to the collaborative sounds that they share. Music can be 'played' by one or more of the connected computers. It is sensible to only have one machine playing at each physical location, with the others at that location acting as remote controllers.

A Networked Improvisation Session

A series of music lessons using networked improvisation was set up with four Apple iMac computers. Two were located in a city school and two were in a country school. Each school had a classroom ensemble comprising about ten Year 8 students. Each classroom had several Orff percussion instruments; acoustic guitars; a Theremin or synthesizer; and a turntable plugged into a mixing desk. Four students at each location had been selected to play the computer, while the remaining students played other instruments or sang/rapped. The musical results were coordinated similarly at each school, with jam2jam linking the classrooms over the internet. The performance was loosely synchronized but instruments were heard only locally at each site.

The teachers had prepared printed charts with the rhythmic and note possibilities of the 'Vox pop' algorithm for students. Based on these, each group composed a short ostinato for acoustic instrument use in the performance. They practised separately in their classrooms using jam2jam as a backing track and prepared graphic scores that indicated when each instrument was to play. Several students had composed short vocal choruses and raps for the event.

The learning objectives focused on the core content of musical knowledge found in contemporary hip hop style. The key objectives were to demonstrate an understanding of the elements of hip hop through composing/improvising, listening/analysis and performance. More specifically, students were expected to demonstrate an understanding of form/structure, syncopated rhythm, timbre and texture.

The teachers made audio recordings of each iteration of the improvisation. In reflective sessions the students listened critically to these recordings, adjusting their performances and scores. The musical descriptors on the jam2jam interface – such as volume, solo, density, range, length, progression and sound (timbre) – were used to frame the reflective sessions and guide the discussion. The students using the computers on the network had to attend to the acoustic performances and the generative possibilities of the computer. The acoustic performers focused on the structure of the piece, and keeping in time and in tune with the computer-generated music.

The learning was apparent in the evolution of the piece from chaotic early performances to more considered and tasteful later rehearsals. It was also evident in the development of scores and the demonstration of individual control over musical elements. Most important for the students was the idea that the music they created sounded like an authentic contemporary piece. This was made possible through the use of computer-based sounds and generated drum and bass parts.

After the initial rehearsals as class groups, the two classes did a series of networked performances at an agreed time. In the same way that the individual class performances had taken shape as rehearsals progressed, the networked performances developed as the computer players learnt to cooperate and synchronise their combined ensembles.

The text chat-boxes in jam2jam enabled students to coordinate activities between sites during the performance. Initially they used the boxes simply to chat across the network. Then gradually they began using musical terms in the chat to communicate what they had planned on their scores or to respond to what they heard. Some of the more 'musical' chat comments included:

'Let's solo the bass guitar the next time round.'
'Put more hi hats in the chorus.'
'The guitar is too loud in the mix.'
'The last chorus is next.'

The students learnt to use appropriate musical terms for each instrument and its activity. Concepts such as 'shuffle', range, density and length (the names on jam2jam sliders and dials) became associated with a musical change that could be identified aurally. The repeated association between the experience, the sound and the naming reinforced the use of musical terms to direct the music; as a result of the software design, the students were guided to use the musical terms with understanding.

The factor specific to online music making in this vignette was that the same piece of music simultaneously had two different interpretations in two locations. Furthermore, the networked performance enabled an authentic basis for a style with musical phrases and rhythms, which acoustic players could either play in unison with or in counterpoint against. The learner could be immersed in an environment where several modes of engagement were available. They could listen, play and improvise with materials or select effective passages and replicate them.

Networked improvisation provides a new form of educational experience through which students are able to share a networked aural environment and develop an extended form of musicianship. Musical knowledge is encountered through real-time experience, constructed and focused by the generative musical algorithm. The algorithm directs the style and focuses the learning experience on specific musical knowledge.

For educators using networked improvisation, there are questions about how software and lesson design can inform and enhance each other. In the situation described above, the teachers used the characteristics of the generative algorithm (the inherent harmonic and rhythmic ideas) as the core musical knowledge for their unit plan. Clearly, many musical ideas are rule-based and it is relatively simple to turn rules into an algorithm, or conversely derive musical lesson from an analysis of the algorithmic rules and constraints. There is an opportunity to focus on gaining core musical knowledge, while involving aesthetic decisions affecting the intensity, density and texture of the piece. In addition, students are able to encounter analytical and intuitive (Swanwick 1994) musical knowledge, as well as encountering composing/improvising, performing and focused listening/audition (Swanwick 1981) experiences.

In such a constructivist context, educators become the designers of improvisational environments that enable experience and engage students with collaborative music-making. The software design needs to include, as jam2jam does, the capacity for this kind of engagement by embodying conceptual frameworks and philosophies that promote meaningful interaction.

Operating a Networked Improvisation

Although understanding computer networks may not be a traditional part of a music teacher's skill base, a small amount of this understanding is required in order to operate a networked musical environment. Organizing students to maximize the benefits of these interactions has a significant impact on their learning.

Maximizing the Learning Benefits

A networked improvisation environment using a generative algorithm can encourage shifts in modes of engagement during performance by maintaining a musical phrase while the user listens to it and discusses future changes via text chat. This 'freeze frame' capacity has great potential for ensemble learning and for developing students' aural perception. It enables a change of focus from local to global musical detail without fear of the music's surface level failing. It affords the exploration of style, with a range of quickly and easily accessible genres, while providing an accessible and inclusive virtual learning environment. In addition, there are opportunities for distance education and, with a suitable interface, for physically and mentally impaired musicians to access complex musical experiences.

A networked improvisation environment can be used as the heartbeat of a mixed electric/acoustic ensemble, focusing and facilitating both real and virtual experiences. Students are able to see the computer as an instrument or 'just another' vehicle for expressive music. The system can help them connect with digital music making, demystifying the process and its abstract presentation in commercial video and audio forms.

Interactive experiences with networked improvisation systems encourage the development of musical intuition and enable meaningful learning. Each type of networked improvisation system accentuates particular skills and learning outcomes. The systems that transmit real-time MIDI or audio data focus primarily on traditional performance techniques such as timing, phrasing and pitch selection. These will be of particular benefit to students who are isolated and have limited access to ensembles. Systems that use generative engines, on the other hand, focus on higher order structure including arrangement, texture, instrumentation and form. These will be most effective as an adjunct to other improvisational and ensemble experiences, allowing for meta-cognitive development and the breaking down of geographic music-making boundaries. Students can, for example, focus their understanding upon the structure of a song over time, while the algorithm takes care of surface-level compositional detail. Or, alternately, they can focus on parameter changes to the drum densities in order to achieve just the right amount of drive for a dance track.

Secondary students working in pairs at one school made the following comments:

> *'It's pretty snazzy I like the way u can talk to them as well as compose!'*
> *'Jam 2 Jam was heaps good and it's good that you can be connected with heaps of people at the same time and also how u can chat at the same time.'*
> *'We both found the program very fascinating. It is effective as an alternative to MSN.'*
> *'It looks cool when one of us moves the buttons and the other sees the results.'*

These students made the association between gesture and sound. They valued the opportunity to be able to talk to each other about music while creating sounds in real time. The teacher commented on how the chat-boxes encouraged musical conversations that focused student attention on making a 'good groove' together.

Teaching Strategies for Networked Improvisation

In the same way that a good lesson plan contains core content knowledge, so an algorithm contains the rules that circumscribe a musical style. Interaction with the software provides interaction with that content. This makes it an effective curriculum resource.

Critical reflection on the relationship between the gesture of moving the slider and the sound is important for learning. In a classroom, this can be done with headphones and a set of reflective questions as a basis for discussion. On a network, students can respond in writing using chat-boxes. Aural exercises, such as listening to and replicating a groove sequence, focus on developing aural perception skills that deal with larger chunks of musical information than individual pitch and duration. Improvising in networked pairs or groups increases the range of possible changes and makes the aural perception activity more complex.

Working with student pairs – one playing whilst the other describes the activity – is a good reflective strategy. The listening student's task is to use musical language to describe what is happening and to recognize the intensity of the instrument activity. Students can listen to and identify timbres or instruments, go through each instrument solo and listen to the changes that each slider makes to the sound, or create a groove using different style presets and describe the differences in groove using musical terms.

A creative activity for individuals or small groups could involve writing song lyrics or a rap to a generative groove. The jam could be recorded using an audio capture program, tape or video recorder; published as an MP3 file or podcast of the music; and pressed as a CD with labels and promotional material. Alternatively, a MIDI file saved from a generative groove could be used as a starting point for composition within a sequencing program.

More teaching ideas for the use of networked improvisation systems are described in the subsections that follow.

Dance Party in the Lab

A metaphor for motivating students to participate in a networked improvisation session is to present the experience as part of a dance party. Since DJs and laptop performers use this kind of interaction in nightclub dance venues, the activity replicates a common performance activity in electronica. The jam can involve extra students using live percussion, acoustic instruments or vocals. Others may dance, sing or VJ (perform as Video Jockeys who process live and prepared images which are projected) to accompany the jam.

Mixed Ensemble

The networked improvisation environment can be one part of an electronic/acoustic performance that uses algorithmic material as a basis for live performer improvisation. It can be passive, as 'music minus one' with a printed chart, or it can involve the interaction of computer performer(s) and acoustic musician(s). More exciting performances tend to combine the interaction of several networked performers with live performers, such as in the jam2jam vignette described earlier in this chapter.

Style Analysis

Networked improvisation software that uses generated styles can be used to better understand those styles and the nature of style differentiation. As an aural perception activity, students can describe and identify musical features of generated music and compare it to recordings of music in a similar style. The repetition allows for deep focus on short fragments of music, while the use of mute and solo buttons allows for specific and isolated focus on a single part. The varying of parameters can be used to test the boundary of style definitions: students can experiment with how much different parameters can vary while still maintaining the integrity of the style.

Multimedia Producers

The idea of VJs who use video mixers to interact with both live and recorded image material is common in dance clubs and electronic music venues. VJing can involve a live performance or a video production. For live video mixing, programs such as Union by Livid Software can be used, whereas programs such as Apple's iMovie are useful for editing video footage and cutting in the recording of the jam. Students can prepare, produce and present a digital video of their improvised song, using voice and live instruments. They can videotape it; or pre-record it using an audio program, then edit the recording to separate video footage.

Curriculum Integration

The potential of cross-curricular outcomes are strong with ICT and computational music algorithms. They can include the writing of lyrics for language studies; the discussion of digital network communication potentials in media studies; the science of sound in physics classes; the mathematical concepts of beats and time; performance considerations in drama; backing music for dance; and issues of culture and style in studies of society and the environment.

Conclusion

A networked improvisation environment is an immersive, interactive, virtual sonic stage where music making can be experienced by groups of participants having a dialogue, shaped by their own gestures, over a network. The environment is delimited by the musical rules that govern compositional structures, as imbued in the system's design. The educational benefits of networked improvisation are that it is accessible and engaging, embodying musical knowledge in an aural environment that allows simultaneous reflective discussion or demonstration of musical understanding.

Networked improvisation environments provide the opportunity to develop a contemporary musicianship that takes into account ICT and interpersonal skills. They are similar to other musical activities in terms of the need for skills of control over media and gesture in order to be expressive and sonically communicative. They are unlike instrumental improvisations in their ability to provide meta-control of musical parameters and to break down the barriers of geography.

In the development of curriculum materials for networked improvisation environments, teachers should encourage intuitive and creative activity by focusing on the expressive qualities of music. Reflective structures should be encouraged to draw out the knowledge and to turn experience into understanding. Constructivist and transformative teaching methodologies are required rather than mimetic teacher-centred approaches.

The potential for networked improvisation environments is to provide access to complex musical systems and to engage participants in musical understandings that link gesture and sound with concepts of musical knowledge and interaction. The dynamic development of these systems relies on designs which encourage and sustain meaningful interaction, while being sufficiently complex to allow the revisiting of musical knowledge at progressively deeper levels, both within the moment and over time.

References

Brown, A.R. (2000), 'Modes of compositional engagement'. *Mikropolyphony*, vol.6. Available at http://eprints.qut.edu.au/archive/00000168/. Accessed 24 November 2006.

Brown, A.R., (2003), 'Music composition and the computer: an examination of the work practices of five experienced composers'. University of Queensland, Brisbane: Unpublished PhD.

Brown, A.R., Sorensen, A., and Dillon, S. (2002), *jam2jam* (Version 1) [Interactive generative music-making software]. Brisbane: Exploding Art Music Productions.

Chafe, C. and Leistikow, R. (2001), 'Levels of temporal resolution in sonification of network performance'. Paper presented to the International Conference on Auditory Display. Espoo, Finland.

Cook, P.R., Davidson, P., Ananya, M. and Wang, G. (2005), 'Co-audicle: A Collaborative Audio Programming Space'. Paper presented to The International Computer Music Conference. Barcelona, Spain: ICMA.

Cope, D. (1992), 'Computer Modelling of Musical Intelligence in EMI.' *Computer Music Journal*, 16(2), 69–83.

Dillon, S.C. (2001), 'Making Computer Music Meaningful in Schools'. *Mikropolyphonie-online journal.* Available at http://pandora.nla.gov.au/pan/10054/20011007/farben.latrobe.edu.au/mikropol/volume6/dillon_s/dillon_s.html. Accessed 24 November 2006.

Latta, C. (2005), *Quoth Description and Demonstration.* Available at http://netjam.org/. Accessed 24 November 2006.

Lazzaro, J. and Wawrzynek, J. (2005), *RTP Payload Format for MIDI*. Available at http://www.cs.berkeley.edu/~lazzaro/sa/pubs/txt/current-mwpp.txt. Accessed 24 November 2006.

McCarthy, C., Bligh, J., Jennings, K. and Tangney, B. (2005), 'Virtual Collaborative Learning Environments for Music: Networked DrumSteps'. *Computers and Education,* 44(2), 173–95.

McCartney, J. (1996), 'SuperCollider: A New Real-time Sound Synthesis Language'. Paper presented to the The International Computer Music Conference. San Francisco: ICMA, pp. 257–8.

Pachet, F. (2002), 'The Continuator: Musical Interaction with Style'. Paper presented to The International Computer Music Conference. Göteborg, Sweden: ICMA, pp. 211–18.

Sorensen, A. (2005), 'Impromptu: A Live Programming System using AiME'. Paper presented to the Australasian Computer Music Conference. Brisbane: ACMA.

Swanwick, K. (1981), *A Basis for Music Education*. London: NFER, Nelson Publishing.

Swanwick, K. (1994), *Musical Knowledge: Intuition, Analysis and Music Education*. London: Routledge.

Wang, G. and Cook, P.R. (2003), 'ChucK: A Concurrent, On-the-fly, Audio Programming Language'. Paper presented to the International Computer Music Conference. Singapore ICMA.

Wright, M. and Freed, A. (1997), 'Open Sound Control: A New Protocol for Communicating with Sound Synthesizers'. Paper presented to The International Computer Music Conference. Thessaloniki, Greece: ICMA.

Xenakis, I. (1991), *Formalized Music*. New York: Pendragon Press.

Web Links

Algorithmic Composer users: http://www.users.bigpond.com/angelo_f/AlgorithmicComposer/algorithmicComposer.html

AudioMulch: http://www.audiomulch.com/

Band in a Box: http://www.pgmusic.com/

ChucK: http://chuck.cs.princeton.edu/

Continuator I: http://www.csl.sony.fr/~pachet/Continuator/

CyberJazz: http://www.ccd.net/projects/search.html?projectID=1076574545
GlasBead: http://www.cityarts.com/glasbeadweb/
Impromptu: http://impromptu.moso.com.au
jam2jam: http://www.explodingart.com/
Max/MSP: http://www.cycling74.com/products/maxmsp.html
MICNet!: http://collaboratory.nunet.net/micnet/index.html
Open Sound Control: http://www.cnmat.berkeley.edu/OpenSoundControl/
PitchWeb: http://www.pitchweb.net/PWMU.htm
Pure-data: http://sourceforge.net/projects/pure-data/
Quoth: http://netjam.org/
Supercollider: http://www.audiosynth.com/
TopLap: http://www.toplap.org
Union: http://www.lividinstruments.com/software_union.php

Chapter 9

Music e-Learning Environments: Young People, Composing and the Internet

Frederick A. Seddon

Introduction

Future e-learning environments will create exciting opportunities for computer-based collaborative composition. Students will interact within and between schools in the UK, as well as across a global community. In order to provide effective learning, new teaching and learning strategies – adopted and adapted specifically for future music e-learning environments – will be required.

This chapter seeks to inform readers of the technological opportunities currently available. It encourages them to adapt their teaching practices so as to maximize the opportunity for young people to compose in e-learning environments. The teaching and learning strategies proposed, based on collaborative learning and peer-evaluation, resonate with the practices employed by popular musicians as discussed in *How Popular Musicians Learn* by Lucy Green (2001).

In order to illustrate some of the advantages of e-learning environments, an overview of a small pilot research study is presented (Seddon 2006). The study took place in a collaborative music e-learning environment. It reveals some of the potential benefits of this environment for future music education practices.

e-Learning Environments

Information Communication Technology (ICT) is driving change in teaching and research in education (Cain 2004). ICT is frequently employed to facilitate more student-centred learning. Music sequencing computer programs (such as Cubase, Finale, Cool Edit Pro and Musicator Delta), for example, make it possible for students to engage in creative music making without first having to learn to play a traditional musical instrument. Students can learn at their own pace and engage with styles and genres of music of particular interest to them.

ICT, when combined with email and the internet, allows for teachers, students and researchers from anywhere in the world to form collaborative groups, transmit information and share expertise. Composition files can be saved and exchanged over the internet. It is the linking of music-sequencing programs and the communication possibilities provided by the internet that enable the creation of e-learning environments.

Music e-learning environments are really just ways of exchanging and being able to discuss, evaluate and develop the contents of music files without necessarily having to be in the same physical space or time. Music files are created with music-sequencing software (e.g. Cubase), and then exchanged and discussed either via email (see below) or an online conferencing tool (e.g. First Class).

Music files can be created as MIDI files, using inexpensive musical keyboards that provide a wide variety of sounds generated either in the keyboards themselves or through 'software synthesizers' (e.g. Roland Sound Canvas). Software synthesizers can be installed in the computer and accessed through the music-sequencing software. Music files can also be created as audio files: a microphone is inserted into the computer and records the voice or a 'natural' musical instrument (e.g. flute) into the music-sequencing software (see the pilot study reported below for details).

ICT is continually becoming more affordable and user friendly. While this means that specific technologies are likely to be superseded by new emerging technologies, the fundamental educational issues governing the exchange of composition remain constant. These include:

- teaching and learning strategies
- collaborative learning
- constructive criticism
- self-and peer-critique/evaluation.

In this chapter, discussion of the above issues is informed by a pilot study investigating the responses of students when working with Musit Interactive. Musit Interactive is a Norwegian music-sequencing software program from which previously saved music and text files can be emailed between students thus creating a specific music e-learning environment.

An Experimental Music e-Learning Environment

A secondary school in the UK was linked with a secondary school in Norway to enable students to engage in computer-mediated collaborative composition via email without teacher mentoring. The main aims of the study were:

- to test the logistics of collaborative computer-mediated composition via email
- to elicit participant responses
- to investigate the relationship between prior experience of formal instrumental music training (FIMT) and both the communication processes and composition strategies adopted.

The Students and Equipment

There were eight participants (four Norwegian, four English), aged 13–14 years, who formed four composition pairs as follows.

1   Pair 1: both non-FIMT (one from UK, one from Norway)
2   Pair 2: both FIMT (one from UK, one from Norway)
3   Pair 3: one FIMT (UK), one non-FIMT (Norway)
4   Pair 4: one FIMT (Norway), one non-FIMT (UK).

Equipment used included MIDI musical keyboards and microphones connected to computers with Musit Interactive music-sequencing software installed. This music-

New Midi is for later in the song. Not sure what to do next. Try adding some drums. I tried to make the song build up.

Figure 9.1 A screen shot of the Musit Interactive music-sequencing program

sequencing software contains an integral 'text box' (see Figure 9.1) that enables text communication from within the software.

Musit Interactive has an internal file compression system that 'packs' and 'unpacks' the music and text files automatically without requiring additional computer skills from the user. This automatic compression system considerably reduces the file size, simplifying the process of emailing music and text files between participants.

Musical 'loops' produced by professional musicians are available within Musit Interactive and participants could manipulate the position of these 'loops' in the music-sequencing program. They could add further MIDI musical material via the MIDI keyboards; and live sounds could be added by recording into the music-sequencing program via the microphone (with the recordings then saved as audio files). The 'loops' provided a stimulus for initiating the composition process. In this way the participants were not faced with the daunting task of a 'blank canvas'.

The Process

Although the participants had no prior experience of music-sequencing software, following a single ten-minute group training session Musit Interactive proved easy to use. No teaching of composition was given for the duration of the pilot study. After the technology training, each participant was invited to an individual semi-structured interview designed to reveal their expectations of engagement in the study. The composition process was initiated in the UK with the instruction: 'Using the equipment provided and working with your partner using the "text box", produce a piece you both agree sounds good'. The instruction to 'Produce a piece you both agree sounds good' was used in order to imply the importance of peer-evaluation.

Each composing pair had six composition sessions (three in each country). Each session lasted approximately 25 minutes and took place over three consecutive days. After the sessions, the evolving compositions were automatically compressed by the Musit Interactive program. They were saved in separate files that were emailed between the UK and Norway until completion of the composition process. This process produced six music files with six text files for each composing pair. When the compositions were completed, each participant was invited to participate in a second individual semi-structured interview designed to reveal reflections on their engagement in the study.

Interviews

The researchers conducted individual pre- and post-composition interviews with the participants. The questions were open-ended and the researchers asked additional questions when required to provide continuity in the interview and develop issues raised by the participants. The interview questions were as follows.

Q1. What do you think it will be [was it] like using the technology to compose a piece of music?

Q2. What do you think it will be [was it] like working with someone you have never met before?

Q3. What do you think it will be [was it] like working with someone from Norway/ the UK?

Q4. What do you think it will be [was it] like only being able to communicate using text?

Q5. How pleased do you expect to be [were you] with your piece?

Analysis

The interviews and text communications were analysed using the 'constant comparative method', a procedure for the qualitative analysis of text (Lincoln and Guba 1985). The themes that emerged indicated the participants' expectations of collaborative computer-based composition in an e-learning environment and whether or not those expectations were fulfilled.

The researchers (all trained musicians) listened to the music files and categorized them based on an adaptation of a constant comparative method validated in a previous study (Seddon and O'Neill 2003). Together with the text files, they were analysed, revealing text dialogue, musical dialogue and the different composition strategies adopted by the composing pairs. Comparisons were made between the music and text files, both within each composing pair and between composing pairs, in relation to prior FIMT.

Themes from Pre-composition Interviews

Two overall themes, common to both the UK and Norwegian participants, emerged from the pre-composition interviews.

All participants displayed high levels of confidence in their ability to use the equipment. Their confidence was evidenced through the expectation of fun and excitement during collaboration with an unknown person from another country.

Probably we'll find this fun and it ... it's more ... interactive like we get to do it with someone else. And it's not even like somebody we actually know. And it's across the world so it's going to be rather fun you can make friends as well, so it will be rather fun. (Quote from UK FIMT)

I don't know I haven't been like erm ... talking so much to guys in England but I think it will be fun. (Quote from Norway FIMT)

All participants expressed concern about collaboration during the process of composing and deciding the content of the composition. Their concern was based on the possibility of conflict arising from deleting each other's work and/or their partner's preferred styles of music.

I don't know ... I think just trying to agree on like say they take a bit of my work out of it. I'll probably get really annoyed but then if I understand their way of puttin' it then I will be alright. (Quote from UK non-FIMT)

I don't know. It depends on who they are, if they like my kind of music or they like another kind of music. (Quote from Norway FIMT)

In addition to these overall themes, various individual themes emerged. The participants in one international pair (Pair 2, both FIMT) separately expressed a view that differences in music preferences might result in a positive collaboration.

We could like different music so it could make a difference to what we have in our composition. As like I might like pop and she might like rock, or he might like rock and then ... So we would have to like try and work together and make it into a poppy-rock or something like that. (Quote from UK FIMT)

if they like my kind of music or they like another kind of music then we can maybe make a whole new kind of music. (Quote from Norway FIMT)

A UK participant (non-FIMT) felt there would be less 'social pressure' because his Norwegian partner was unknown to him and they would be working outside of the physical space of the school.

I just think erm ... it's like ... they haven't like seen you before and you haven't seen them before so it's really kind of erm ... just getting together to do like one thing there's no like pressures or you know social groups in like school where whenever you work with someone at school ... The kind of usual thing at school. (Quote from UK FIMT)

Another UK participant (FIMT) made an interesting speculation about how working with this particular technology in this situation would impact upon collaborative communication during the composition process.

If you know someone and they are like next to you, you can talk and then do it. Here we have to do it and write what we do and then they have to change it or keep it the same. And we can't really decide together, or we can but it will be a longer time to wait. And we might have to like do some things wrong and them put them back in. And, but if you have it next to you, the person next to you erm ... it would be easier because first you can talk then do it but here you have to do it and then talk, and then do it and then talk. So it's going to be a bit harder than if you are sitting next to them. (Quote from UK FIMT)

Themes from Post-composition Interviews

Overall themes emerging from the post-composition interviews confirmed the sense of 'fun and confidence' expressed in interviews prior to composition. The composition process was most often referred to as 'fun', 'interesting', 'enjoyable' and 'exciting'.

Fun because I never did it before. (Quote from Norway non-FIMT)

It was very fun erm ... If someone asked me if I would do it again then I would because it was very fun. (Quote from Norway non-FIMT)

I enjoyed it ... like doing something different like with the computer and I now know how to like use that and it was nice working with someone from a different country instead of working with someone here because it was an experience to remember. (Quote from UK non-FIMT)

Interesting 'cos I didn't know what music she liked ... he liked erm ... what he liked or anything. It was very fun erm if someone had asked me if I would do it again? ... I would ... it was very fun. (Quote from Norway non-FIMT)

The theme 'concerns about conflict while composing' from the pre-composition interviews, however, was not confirmed in reflective post-composition interviews. On the contrary, participants reported that potential conflict was not the problem that they had anticipated.

She deleted my 'heli' ... erm ... my 'gunshots' ... [Interviewer ... 'yeah ... how did that feel when she deleted your 'gunshots'?] ... I wasn't bothered really ... I just like put them in to see what they sounded like and if she didn't like them then she could change them, delete them. (Quote from UK non-FIMT)

If you couldn't have had the text it might have gone a bit conflicting at changing the wrong bits and then them putting it back and then you taking it away and them putting it back again. (Quote from UK non-FIMT)

In post-composition interviews, all of the participants reported being 'pleased' or 'very pleased' with their completed compositions, even though for some this was unexpected. They all reported positive feelings about working with someone they had never met before. The only negative reports concerned the time allowed for composition – all participants wished that they could have had more time to compose.

Collaborative Computer-based Composition in Relation to FIMT

The analysis of the music and text files revealed that the presence of an FIMT participant resulted in complex and extended musical dialogue. When both partners had prior experience of FIMT, musical dialogue replaced descriptive text dialogue, producing more exploratory composition strategies that included critical engagement with each other's ideas. When only one of the pair had prior experience of FIMT, more descriptive text was required to support the musical dialogue and if musical communication broke down, high levels of social interaction via text communication replaced it. With pairs comprising non-FIMT participants, little musical communication took place and uncritical or cumulative composition strategies were adopted. These results resonated with the three types of dialogue identified in research by Mercer and Wegerif (1999):

1 **Disputational talk** where individuals challenge each others' ideas and disagree to the extent that decision-making remains an individual process.
2 **Cumulative talk** where individuals largely agree with each other and without confrontation build positively but uncritically on what the other has said.
3 **Exploratory talk** where collaborators constructively challenge each others' ideas often resulting in modifying each others' ideas.

Mercer and Wegerif argue that exploratory talk is required before effective collaborative learning can take place.

The results of this study suggest that the most effective pairing for collaborative computer-based composition in music e-learning environments is where both participants have prior experience of FIMT. The results of this study also suggest that FIMT/non-FIMT pairings are more effective than pairs of non-FIMT participants. Although these findings need to be validated by a larger scale study, they provide a useful guide for teachers with regard to structuring of pairings for collaborative, computer-based composition in e-learning environments.

Implications for Education

Two interesting themes related to 'social pressure' and 'sequence of events' emerged from the interviews (see themes from pre- [and post-] composition interviews).

The 'social pressure' theme was indicated by a participant who felt more comfortable knowing that his composing partner neither knew nor could see him during the composition process. This will resonate with teachers who have noticed that certain personality types, such as very introverted students, find it easier to engage in collaborative computer-based composition in e-learning environments than face-to-face environments. Some adolescents, too, acquire negative identities or lack self-confidence and this can impact upon their performance during a musical task. Evidence shows, for example, that adolescents who have had no instrumental training believe that they will not be as good at computer-based composition as adolescents who play musical instruments, although there is no evidence for their belief (Seddon and O'Neill 2001, 2006). This means that collaborative computer-based composition in e-learning environments can not only make music composition possible for adolescents without instrumental training but can also help to reduce negative identity and help with self-confidence issues.

The 'sequence of events' theme was indicated by a participant's concern about the sequence of events when composing in an e-learning environment (as opposed to a face-to-face environment). It reveals how the collaborative e-learning environment can impact on the composition strategies adopted in relation to prior experience of FIMT.

Previous research indicated that when composing alone at the computer, individuals with prior experience of FIMT did not explore the possibilities made available by the computer, instead producing music that adhered to more traditional notions (Seddon and O'Neill 2001, 2003 and 2006). By contrast, in this chapter's pilot study the students with prior experience of FIMT, working with others in collaborative music e-learning environments, displayed more exploratory composition strategies than their untrained peers.

Although it was not possible to deduce whether this was a result of the collaboration process, the e-learning environment or a combination of the two, evidently levels of confidence and motivation ran high. All participants enjoyed the collaborative composition experience and were pleased with the outcomes (see themes from pre- [post] composition interviews). Since these were fairly typical young people, it seems reasonable to propose that many, if not most, adolescents would respond in similar ways when working in music e-learning environments. The challenge lies in ensuring that their motivation and confidence in the classroom is not compromised by inappropriate teaching strategies.

Teaching Strategies

When considering teaching strategies, several questions arise. Will merely engaging collaboratively with computer-based composition necessarily improve students' composition skills? Is intervention by teachers required? If so, what form should this intervention take?

A common view is that students should be taught through a curriculum grounded in recognized good composition practice, based on Western classical values (Hickey 2003). This teaching style appears to assume that, because of their training and experience, teachers know what makes a 'good' composition and that it is their responsibility to pass this knowledge on to the student by teaching composition. While this may be appropriate for some adolescents, particularly those who have chosen to study music at public examination level, others may prefer working collaboratively with their peers and creating music in genres unfamiliar to the teacher. In these cases, it is preferable for the teacher to provide a collaborative environment, enabling adolescents to share their expertise in order to improve their composition skills, rather than to try to gain new expertise in order to teach composition. Although this involves a role change from instructor to facilitator, after a period of observation the teacher will still be able to contribute musical expertise because general musical principles tend to apply across genres of music. (These teaching strategies already occur in classrooms but providing a collaborative e-learning environment connected to the internet gives the adolescents wider access to more varied musical skills and genres.)

There are several music educators who resist the 'naïve' view of student composition and support the stance of teachers adopting facilitating rather than instructional roles in the classroom. John Paynter, for example, believes that the student's natural musicality manifests itself in making up music in much the same way that music has been made up, invented and performed by untutored people across the ages (2003). Paynter also believes that composition, which he prefers to refer to as 'making up music', is a natural process that just requires opportunity and encouragement.

Lucy Green, in her book *How Popular Musicians Learn: A Way Ahead for Music*

Education, describes peer-directed and group learning music-making activities without teacher intervention. This involves learners providing their own peer-role models, teaching each other and learning by watching, listening and imitating. Collaborative computer-based composition environments provide an opportunity for teachers to recreate similar 'virtual' creative environments to those described by the popular musicians in Green's research (Green 2001).

> I've only written about two songs. Normally they're just like a riff, and then the rest of the band, we all mix together. That's what normally happens, someone gets the main riff and then we all put our bits in and it rolls into one ... Everyone likes a different sort of music so it's good. It's good because it all mixes up so you've got a bit of rock, jazz, blues, funk in there so it's all kind of – bit of grunge in there – so it's all, it's a complete mix of the lot. (Green 2001, p. 81)

There is also some evidence to show that more creative products are produced during collaborative work that is focused around self- and peer-critique grounded in constructive criticism (Crook 2000). It is more useful for teachers to focus on fostering these critical skills in adolescents when composing than to try to teach composition *per se*.

When teachers adopt facilitating roles in collaborative music e-learning environments, it usually leads to the production of more varied styles of composition. This in turn can result in problems of evaluation for the teacher. In these situations, it is useful to base evaluation on the 'subjective' criteria of whether or not the composers have achieved the effect they are attempting to create rather than 'objective' criteria inappropriate for the style or genre produced. In addition, it is important to involve the student composer and peers in self- and peer-evaluation regarding how the composer's idea was fulfilled, and encouraging them to comment purposefully and constructively. If teachers do not encourage self- and peer-evaluation, adolescents may never acquire self-confidence and competence in these very important skills.

Providing e-Learning Environments in Schools

Providing e-learning environments in schools is already technically possible. It is important to accompany this opportunity with a change in pedagogical practises (Burnard 2000, Faulkner 2003) if, as music educators, we are to bring about the changes to music education expressed in the Music Manifesto (www.musicmanifesto.co.uk). The situation is possibly best expressed in a quotation from Lucy Green:

> Many teachers would feel guilty and irresponsible if they found themselves sitting for even ten minutes outside the classroom whilst students worked at copying their favourite recordings through peer interaction and without any intervention on their teachers' parts! However, this is how young popular musicians have acquired their skills and knowledge for decades. Perhaps school teachers could bring about worthwhile results by standing back a little more than we do in many countries at present. (Green 2001, p. 204)

References

Burnard, P. (2000), 'How children ascribe meaning to improvisation and composition: rethinking pedagogy in music education'. *Music Education Research,* 2(1), 7-23.

Cain, T. (2004), 'Theory, technology and the music curriculum'. *The British Journal of Music Education,* 21(2), 215-21.

Crook, C. (2000), 'Motivation and the ecology of collaborative learning', in R. Joiner, K. Littleton, D. Faulkner and D. Miell (eds), *Rethinking Collaborative Learning.* London: Free Association Books, pp. 161-79.

Faulkner, R. (2003), 'Group composing: student interaction from a social psychological study'. *Music Education Research,* 5(2), 101-24.

Green, L. (2001), *How Popular Musicians Learn: A Way Ahead for Music Education.* Aldershot, England: Ashgate Publishing.

Hickey, M. (2003), 'Creative Thinking in the Context of Music Composition', in M. Hickey (ed.), *Why and How to Teach Music Composition: A New Horizon for Music Education.* Published in partnership with MENC by Rowman and Littlefield Education, Lanham, MD, pp. 31-53.

Lincoln, Y. and Guba, E. (1985), *Naturalistic Enquiry.* Beverly Hills, CA: Sage.

Mercer, N. and Wegerif, R. (1999), 'Is "exploratory talk" productive talk?', in K. Littleton and P. Light (eds), *Learning with Computers: Analysing Productive Interaction.* London and New York: Routledge, pp. 79-101.

Paynter, J. (2003), 'Music in the school curriculum: why bother?' *British Journal of Music Education,* 19(3), 215-26.

Seddon, F. A. (2006), 'Collaborative computer-mediated composition in cyberspace'. *British Journal of Music Education,* 23(3), 273-83.

Seddon, F. A. and O'Neill, S.A. (2001), 'An evaluation study of computer-based compositions by children with and without prior experience of formal instrumental music tuition'. *Psychology of Music,* 29(1), 4-19.

Seddon, F. A. and O'Neill, S.A. (2003), 'Creative thinking processes in adolescent computer-based composition: an analysis of strategies adopted and the influence of instrumental training'. *Music Education Research,* 5(2), 125-37.

Seddon, F. A. and O'Neill, S.A. (2006), 'How does formal instrumental music tuition (FIMT) impact on self- and teacher-evaluations of adolescents' computer-based compositions?' *Psychology of Music,* 34(1), 27-45.

Website

Music Manifesto. (2004), http://www.music manifesto.co.uk. *Accessed 3 April 2006.*

Chapter 10

Current and Future Practices: Embedding Collaborative Music Technologies in English Secondary Schools

Teresa Dillon

Introduction

Since the early 1980s the availability and application of ICT has influenced all subject areas across the curriculum. Although it was not until the 1990s that the National Curriculum referred explicitly to music technologies, today they are used prolifically and music technology has become a recognized subject area in its own right.

Despite these developments recent reports indicate that music technology practice in schools often centres on particular pieces of hardware and software. Innovative practice tends to be spearheaded by individual teachers and is inadequately disseminated. In addition, while it is common for hardware to be used in pairs and small group settings, little is known of the creative and collaborative processes engaged when working with such instruments. This dearth in understanding affects the training of teachers, the design of music technologies and the development of meaningful music activities where the technology is appropriately embedded in the learning context.

This chapter addresses these issues with reference to research into current secondary school music technology practices, which focuses specifically on young people's creative and collaborative interactions when working with sequenced keyboards and computer-based sampling software. It discusses how to improve understanding in this area and how better to embed existing technologies within the current curriculum. The conclusion presents a view toward the future and briefly describes the potential of tools such as emerging wireless and mobile technologies for collaborative music making and sharing.

Overview of Music Technology within Secondary Schools

Recent surveys carried out by the Office for Standards in Education (Ofsted) reflect a complex picture of the use and outcomes of music technologies within secondary school settings. A survey on *Music in Secondary Schools* (2001/2003), for example, reports that 'The use of music technology remains weak in Key Stage 3' (p. 7) and in some schools was considered as 'an additional - even exotic - resource' (p. 8). On the other hand, the findings of *ICT in Schools 2004: The Impact of Government Initiatives: Secondary Music* indicate that:

ICT has had a positive impact on teaching and learning in music in the majority of secondary schools. Music technology is often used successfully to enhance the development of a wide range of musical skills, as well as being an area of study in its own right. (Ofsted 2004, p. 4)

The above quotes reflect a complex situation. It is clear that although developments in music technology are encouraging, a closer examination of actual practices in secondary schools reveals the tendency to focus on the benefits or limitations of particular hardware and sequencing or notation packages (Busen-Smith 1999, Mills and Murray 2000, Pitts and Kwami 2002). While less emphasis is placed on the processes engaged in or the kinds of music created.

To investigate this, the author carried out a survey of 121 randomly selected professional music teachers from secondary schools in England and Wales (Dillon *et al.* 2001, Dillon 2006). It aimed to build on the understanding of how music technologies were applied in secondary schools. There was a particular focus on the types of music technologies and the social contexts within which they were used. Teachers' personal accounts and impressions of using music technologies were also included.

In relation to this chapter, relevant findings indicated that keyboards (93 per cent) and computers (83 per cent) were the most frequently used music technologies. Music technologies were generally used in group settings (most commonly in pairs) and, overall, teachers found them to be most applicable at Key Stages 3 and 4 (11–16 years). Teacher training varied greatly, ranging from teachers who were self-taught and those who had taken day courses to those who had diploma or degree-level experience in using music technologies.

Given these findings, it is not surprising that a recent Ofsted report noted:

Most music departments base the majority of work in music technology on one piece of software – typically either sequencing or score-writing. This can result in students gaining limited experience in the wide-ranging applications of ICT in music. A minority of departments make good use of a range of software, including audio-editing programs and CD-ROMs to develop skills such as aural perception and understanding of musical form and history. (Ofsted, 2004 p. 4)

Overemphasis on one or two pieces of software cripples innovation and creativity. Furthermore, lack of teacher training and support inhibits the realization of the full potential of these tools. Exemplary practice tends to be driven by individual teachers with passion and interest in the field (which parallels the use of ICT in art, where such practice is rare and sometimes little known outside the school or department context – see Arts Council of England, *Keys to imagination: ICT in art education*, 2003).

In order to discuss how existing and new music technologies are best embedded in collaborative secondary school settings, greater dissemination of 'best practice' within the teaching profession is required. This would involve coordination between policy-makers, the teaching profession, researchers and consultants. From a research perspective more work needs to be carried out on the kinds of musical interactions and processes, both individual and collaborative, that existing and new technology can support. This in turn could lead to more informed decision-making and the use of technological tools for meaningful musical activities.

The following sections address these issues by focusing on a keyboard study and an eJay (computer sample software) study that took place in secondary school contexts within the UK. They reflect on the use of these technologies, their advantages and disadvantages, and the collaborative creative process engaged in when using these instruments.

Collaborative Happenings – Developing Shared Musical Understandings

Although some educators have reported concern that students only experience music composition in groups (Odam 2000), others (Pitts and Kwami 2002) argue that group composition can potentially lead to better quality work. This highlights the fact that, despite group composition being commonplace within music classrooms, teachers and educators are unclear about the benefits, limitations and outcomes of such practices.

To address this gap, the author explored the group composition process of students (11–17 years) using keyboards and eJay within secondary school settings (Dillon 2003, 2004, 2006). 'Musical co-construction' – what it meant to jointly create a new piece of music with another person – was central to understanding the process (Dillon 2006). The author defines musical co-construction as the reciprocal process through which individuals co-develop a shared musical understanding of the task and their individual differences. Exploring and understanding this concept contributes to a better understanding of how students work together when making music using new technologies (Dillon 2006). In order to achieve this the author worked closely with the students' music teachers, who devised activities which were then examined in close detail.

Collaborative Keyboard and Computer Cacophonies

Making Music using Keyboards

The keyboard study took place in a comprehensive secondary school in northeast London (UK). Two tasks were given: a structured task and an unstructured task. The same 18 students, comprising 9 pairs (10 male, 8 female; mean age 14.06 years), participated in both studies. The tasks were carried out during lunchtime in the music room.

The structured task involved composing a short tune on the keyboard, using sequences labelled A, B, C and D. These sections were arranged in the order ABACADA, a pattern based on the musical form ritornello. It was up to the students to construct these sections and so this part of the task was open-ended. The average task time spent on the semi-structured task was 16 minutes.

The unstructured task instruction was 'to compose a tune as they wished' using the keyboard. This kind of instruction was familiar to the students since at the end of their normal music lessons they frequently had a period called 'free time' for 'free play' or improvisation on the keyboards. The average task time spent on the unstructured task was 18 minutes.

Facilitating Features

An aspect of qualitative analysis, which merits discussion in relation to the key themes of this chapter, is how the keyboard, as a tool in and of itself, supported the student's creative collaborative processes. Qualitative interpretation of dialogues suggested that the keyboard facilitated music and collaborative practices by creating a space in which partners could work and test ideas, explore possibilities and experiment by playing different notes and samples. The pre-recorded sample and effects bank embedded within the software was a source of inspiration in both task settings, while the save and record features allowed the students to immediately listen to and edit their work.

Repurposing Existing Music Repertoires

It was interesting to note how participants in both tasks appropriated existing pieces of music that they knew, repurposing and fitting them into the compositional structure. In some cases they remixed existing pieces by adding sound effects from the keyboard to create entirely new compositions 'on the fly'. One dyad, for example, used parts of the nursery rhyme 'Mary had a little lamb' in the ABACADA structure. Additionally, in both task settings participants created entirely new 'soundscapes', drawing on the keyboard's store of samples to create musical 'montages'. This resulted in arrangement choices and compositions that evoked particular atmospheres or images for them.

Use of the keyboard provided participants with an immediate source of sounds from which to select and compose their pieces. It acted as a mediating tool through which participants could engage in phases of critical listening and selection (i.e. the selection of specific samples, whose merits and appropriateness have been listened to and discussed in detail), arranging, editing, refining, recording and saving. One of the main advantages of the keyboard was to provide a shared space through which to physically explore and negotiate ideas: musical communications and experiments were importantly supported and augmented by verbal discussions as ideas were thrashed out and developed. Practically, it provided a means for users to save and critically listen to their work, which in turn drove further periods of exploration, editing and refining.

Making Music using eJay

The second study used eJay: a CD-ROM that contains pre-recorded vocal and instrumental samples. eJay allows users to compose, arrange, edit and record music in dance, rave and hip hop styles. Once installed, it turns a PC into a mini-editing studio.

This study took place during normal school music lessons in a comprehensive secondary school in Milton Keynes (UK). The task given by the teacher was to put into practice 'what the participants had learnt in previous lessons about riffs, hooks and repetitive motifs using Dance eJay'. Within the school a total of 4 triads and 1 dyad (14 participants; 11 males and 3 females; mean age 13.7 years) were involved. The average task session lasted 42.09 minutes.

The eJay Interface – A Rich Mediational Space

eJay provided a rich, graphic interface through which the students could discuss their ideas. In terms of collaboration, the interface was important for mediating and supporting participants' interactions. Evidence suggests that the immediacy of the software allowed the students to instinctively, and with minimal effort, jointly select and arrange samples on the colour-coded, graphic arrange page. Consequently the graphic arrange page was one of the most defining features of eJay, since it allowed participants to 'see' the compositional structure. It was believed that this encouraged richer and longer verbal discussions, particularly when compared to the types of dialogues that were observed in the previous keyboard study.

Supporting the Creative Process

Features such as the 'click, drop and drag' approach to sample selection and arranging afforded immediate modes of musical composition. The graphic playback feature allowed the participants to listen and reflect critically on what they had assembled. In addition, the range of samples stored within the software provided an instant source material, analogous to a painter's palette, from which to develop compositional ideas.

While the young people developed ideas and defined their task, eJay was found to support the continuous and cyclical creative processes of production, evaluation and redesign. As with the keyboard study, this was evident in the way that the students creatively engaged with one another, building on each other's musical suggestions and critically discussing the merits of each sample as well as their fit into the overall, evolving composition. The creative process was both convergent and divergent, with participants drawing on their previous musical experiences, the task structure and the affordances of the software to create their compositions. In summary, eJay provided a shared space though which the student could become creative, collaborative music-makers and producers.

Reflections on the Use of Keyboards and Computers

The keyboard and eJay studies contribute at first to our understanding of the creative processes, while simultaneously extending our knowledge of the advantages and disadvantages of such technologies for music education. It is clear from the findings that the design of the interface and the whole learning activity (including the task, teacher instructions and how the environment is set up) is crucial to making the most of technological tools. The following points summarize some of the key findings and recommendations for embedding music technologies within secondary school contexts, with references to current initiatives for supporting teachers.

Advantages and Disadvantages of Keyboards

1   Sequenced keyboards are hybrid musical instruments, allowing students easy access to a variety of sounds and effects. Married with the traditional keyboard playing space (e.g. the keys), students can experiment with different forms and styles.

2   Automatic functions allow students to trigger and play pre-recorded samples in real time and combine them with their work.

3   Keyboards allow students to easily save, store and retrieve previous works.

4   In the studies carried out, practical playing skills ranged from one-finger/two-finger to one-handed/two-handed playing, although the majority of students were unable to play with more than one hand at a time. For many students, playing the keyboard was considered difficult and so teachers should encourage and support students with their playing skills.

5 While keyboards currently dominate secondary school music classrooms, further research is needed as to whether such instruments are the most appropriate to support general level musical skills and knowledge.

Advantages and Disadvantages of eJay

1 The shared graphical interface allows all students within the group to 'see' how the composition is developing.
2 The interface facilitates rich verbal dialogues, especially when the students are not wearing headphones.
3 The colour-coded sample pages allow students to quickly search, find, click, drop and drag samples on to the arrange page.
4 There is a large bank of pre-recorded samples in different styles, depending on which form of eJay is being used (dance, hip hop or rave).
5 Samples tended to be predictive: the time signatures were standardized and could not be modified, which could lead to compositions sounding very similar. To overcome this pre-recorded or live samples could be added.

General Observations and Points

1 Keyboards and music software can provide a shared space around which partners can jointly make music together. The instruments' interfaces provide possibilities for small groups (minimum of two) to compose and musically co-construct ideas together.
2 When working in groups around such technologies it is necessary for the teacher to encourage turn-taking so that partners experience different roles and develop a good understanding of the software.
3 Technical breakdowns or students' lack of technical knowledge can hinder and disrupt sessions. Teachers need to ensure that all the required technical skills are taught before the music lesson begins.
4 To maximize the potential for successful musical collaboration students should be encouraged to develop critical verbal skills. Where possible they should be discouraged from using headphones in groups, since this reduces the possibility for verbally discussing ideas and critically evaluating the composition.
5 Tasks on keyboards and on computers need to be well structured. Setting clear task goals helps students to begin composing.
6 Teachers should prepare for the sessions in advance. It is important that students do not think of the time on computers as 'free time'. Students need to feel that their work on computers is taken seriously.
7 Publishing students' material, for example making a CD and playing it to the rest of the class or putting it on the school website, is a positive and motivating outcome and places a strong value on this approach to music making.

Exemplar Initiatives

1 **National Music Management Group**, funded by the British Education Communication Technology Agency (Becta) and Department for Education and Skills (DfES), has been specifically established to provide advice on embedding ICT into the music curriculum.

2 **Musical Futures** encourages and support young people to become more active in music and provides online access to specialist music technology experts and resources.

Future Directions for Music Technology in Secondary Schools

So far, this chapter has focused on current school music practices and interactions involving students who work side-by-side around the keyboard or computer. However, with the global increase of internet use, broadband and other forms of digital culture (e.g. iPod, digital radio and wireless media), music production and distribution has changed fundamentally. It is now possible to plug into, create and share music through mobile devices and networks. Such advances challenge the didactic, drill and practice teaching methods often observed within secondary school music settings, while simultaneously affording new modes of collaboration and extending creative possibilities.

Discussing the benefits of contemporary, wireless and broadband technologies, Weinberg has coined the term 'Interconnected Musical Networks' (IMNs) (Weinberg 2002, 2005). IMNs are computer systems that allow players to independently share and shape each others' music in real-time. Interestingly, the interactions in such musical networks occur *through* the technology, facilitating not only synchronous, virtual communication but also asynchronous communication and in some cases side-by-side and face-to-face interaction. According to Weinberg (2002, 2005), IMNs are flexible enough to operate both in the same physical environment and over distributed, remote networks. This allows designers to create interdependent frameworks through which players can influence, share and shape each others' music in real-time, potentially leading to rich social and musical experiences that enhance collaborative musical interaction.

The following projects are interesting in terms of showing how online, mobile and wireless networks are changing the ways in which we share, compose, distribute and manipulate music in real-world and virtual contexts. Such developments will influence future school music practices, transforming not only how they are organized but also how music is accessed, consumed and produced. This, in turn, will have an impact on how learning activities are structured and potentially lead to a more open, personalized music portfolio and curriculum.

The Beatbug Network

Beatbugs are palm-sized, hand-held, digital musical instruments that were initially designed to provide a formal introduction to mathematical concepts in music through an expressive and rhythmic group experience. Multiple Beatbug players can form an interconnected musical network (The Beatbug Network) by synchronizing with each other; users can trade sounds and control each other's music. When connected, the Beatbugs have been found to encourage collaborative creativity and composition, as well as social play (Weinberg *et al.* 2000, Weinberg 2002, Weinberg *et al.* 2002).

F@ust Music Online

Jordà and Barbosa's (2001) project, F@ust Music Online (FMOL), was part of the Catalan theatre group La Fura dels Baus' show F@ust 3.0 (1997). FMOL used the internet as a virtual synthesizer which allowed professionals, amateurs and newcomers to compose single or several electro-acoustic pieces in real time over the internet. La Fura dels Baus then chose some of these compositions to form part of their F@ust 3.0 production. In order to support online synchronous communication, FMOL's design permitted users to listen to already existing pieces and either modify them (with an inbuilt user profile and preference system) or create their own new pieces.

The user profiling system allowed users to input their preferences (e.g. preferred musical genre, favourite instruments, musical training and level of expertise). The FMOL system then provided suggestions such as potential partners for collaboration, or appropriate musical pieces they could participate in and collectively develop. After working on a suggested piece, the user could evaluate its quality. This information was stored in the system and taken into account in the user's next proposal. In this way the system was constantly being tuned towards the preferences of the users by taking into account their feedback responses. Such profile and feedback systems are useful in supporting online collaboration by providing users with knowledge about their partners. This background knowledge can play an important role in grounding online collaboration by providing a base level from which to begin developing a shared musical understanding.

Mobile Networks

Jukola, by the Mobile Bristol Centre, is a recent mobile network project (O'Hara, *et al.* 2006). Taking the form of a wireless jukebox, it allowed users to democratically select the music they listen to in public spaces. In a café or a bar, for example, instead of the staff deciding on what music to play, members of the public could view the track list and nominate which song they would like via a large touch screen display. Using a wireless hand-held computer (iPAQ) the public could collectively vote on which song to play next. As the jukebox was accessible via the internet, users could also upload MP3s or review the day's play list.

Similarly tunA allowed users in a public space (e.g. a bus) to 'tune' into each others' playlists via a wireless network and handheld computer. This mobile network was developed by members of the Human Connectedness research group at the now defunct MediaLab Europe (Bassoli *et al.* 2003, Bassoli *et al.* 2004).

Tanaka's (2004) Malleable Mobile Networks built at the Sony Computer Science Laboratory Paris allowed users to collaboratively manipulate the compositions they listened to on the fly. By attaching sensors to handheld computers, a listener's body movements (such as tapping fingers), along with their location and proximity to others within the system and length of their journey time, could change the shape and flow of the composition as they moved.

Common to Jukola, tunA and Malleable Mobile Networks is the use of such networks and hand-held computers in public spaces for social, collective musical sharing and manipulation. The emphasis in these projects is often on play and a sense of community. For readers interested in this kind of work, it is worth reading further details of these prototype research projects since they provide useful insights into how we may collectively engage with music in the future.

Final Thoughts

When developing new musical applications for education, careful consideration should be given to the end user and the context of use. It is important not to parachute technologies into schools situations without understanding how they will serve the learning and development of the end-user. In this respect, researchers and educators within the field of collaborative music technologies need to be Janus-headed.

One head should face our current situation. For this we need:

1   To carry out further research on the individual and collaborative processes that existing music technologies support.
2   Improved models of learning and teaching, so that the technology is not delivered into schools for the sake of it and teachers are capable of integrating and inventing new uses for such tools.
3   More communication and collaboration between the key stakeholders in this area – teachers, software developers, researchers and policy makers.

Our other head needs to be facing towards the future. For this we need:

1   To be aware of the advancements in mobile, locative, virtual, tangible and other such technologies, but also to be engaging and collaborating constructively with those who are working on the leading edge.
2   To learn from past mistakes; new technologies need not and should not be developed in isolation from the end-user (students and teachers) and experts in the field of music education.
3   To work within mixed disciplinary teams so as to ensure that from the beginning the instruments we develop for future musical expression and communication are usable, aesthetically pleasing and motivating.

Acknowledgements

I would like to thank all the teachers who responded to the music survey, with particular thanks to the teachers and young people at Valentines High School, London, Stantonbury Campus, Milton Keynes and Lord Grey School, Bletchley, UK, who were involved in the keyboard and eJay studies. The keyboard and eJay study discussed in this chapter was carried out as part fulfilment of a PhD thesis through The Open University, UK under the supervision of Professor Dorothy Miell, The Open University and Dr Richard Joiner, Bath University. Finally I'd like to thank Dr Pam Burnard and John Finney for the invitation to contribute to this book and Jenny Stayne of Futurelab for her original feedback on this chapter.

References

Arts Council of England. (2003), 'Keys to Imagination: ICT in Art Education'. Available at http://www.artscouncil.org.uk/publications/publication_detail.php?browse=recent&id=361.

Bassoli, A., Cullinan, C., Moore, J. and Agamanolis, S. (2003), 'tunA: A Mobile Music Experience to Foster Local Interactions'. Paper presented at the 5th International Conference on Ubiquitous Computing, Seattle, 12–13 October.

Bassoli, A., Moore, J. and Agamanolis, S. (2004), 'tunA: Synchronized music-sharing on handheld devices'. Paper presented at the 6th International Conference on Ubiquitous Computing, Nottingham, September.

Busen-Smith, M. (1999), 'Developing strategies for delivering music technology in secondary PGCE courses'. *British Journal of Music Education*, 16(2), 197–213.

Dillon, T. (2003), 'Collaborating and creating using music technologies'. *International Journal of Educational Research*, 39(8), 893–7.

Dillon, T. (2004), 'It's in the mix baby: exploring how meaning is created within music technology collaborations', in D. Miell and K. Littleton (eds), *Collaborative Creativity, Contemporary Perspectives*. London: Free Association Books, pp. 144–57.

Dillon, T. (2006), 'Exploring young people's collaborative and creative processes using keyboard and computer-based music technologies in formal and non-formal settings'. Unpublished PhD thesis, Department of Psychology, Milton Keynes: The Open University.

Dillon, T., Joiner, R. and Miell, D. (2001), 'An Investigation into Music Technology Practices'. Paper presented at the RIME, Research In Music Education, University of Exeter.

Jordà, S. and Barbosa, A. (2001), *Computer-supported cooperative music: Overview of research work and projects at the Audio Visual Institute - U.P.F.* Available at http://www.iua.upf.es/mtg/publications/mosart2001-jorda.pdf.

Mills, J. and Murray, A. (2000), 'Music technology inspected: good teaching in Key Stage 3'. *British Journal of Music Education*, 17(2), 157–81.

Murray, A. (1997), *The Music IT Support Project*. Available at http://www.becta.org.uk.

O'Hara, K., Jansen, M., Lipson, M., Unger, A., Jeffries, H. and Macer, P. (2006), 'Distributing the process of music choice in public spaces', in K. O'Hara and B. Brown (eds), *Consuming Music Together: Social and Collaborative Aspects of Music Consumption Technologies*. Dordrecht: The Netherlands Springer.

Odam, G. (2000), 'Teaching composition in secondary schools: the creative dream'. *British Journal of Music Education*, 17(2), 109–27.

Ofsted. (2001/2003), *Music in Secondary Schools*. London: Office for Standards in Education (Ofsted).

Ofsted. (2004), *ICT in Schools 2004: The Impact of Government Initiatives: Secondary Music*. London: Office for Standards in Education (Ofsted).

Pitts, A. and Kwami, R.M. (2002), 'Raising students' performance in music composition through the use of information and communications technology (ICT): a survey of secondary schools in England'. *British Journal of Music Education*, 19(1), 61–71.

Tanaka, A. (2004), 'Malleable Mobile Music'. Paper presented at the 6th International Conference on Ubiquitous Computing, Nottingham, UK, 7–10 September 2004.

Weinberg, G. (2002), 'The Aesthetics, History, and Future Challenges of Interconnected Music Networks'. Paper presented at the International Computer Music Conference, Göteborg, Sweden, pp. 349–56.

Weinberg, G. (2005). 'Interconnected musical networks: toward a theoretical framework'. *Computer Music Journal*, 29(2), 23–39.

Weinberg, G., Aimi, R. and Jennings, K. (2002), 'The Beatbug Network: A Rhythmic System for Interdependent Group Collaboration'. Paper presented at the New Instruments for Musical Expression (NIME), Dublin, Ireland, pp. 107-11.

URL

http://www.polarproduce.org

Part III: Strategies for Change

Chapter 11

Strategies for Supporting Music Learning Through Online Collaborative Technologies

S. Alex Ruthmann

Introduction

Recent advances in online technologies, coupled with increasing access to the internet in American schools and homes, have contributed toward a paradigm shift in the ways students use the internet in their daily lives (Prensky 2001). The shift towards a second generation internet, often referred to as the *Web 2.0*, is defined and encompassed by new technologies designed to enhance social collaboration, such as blogs, wikis and streaming on-demand multimedia content (O'Reilly 2005).

Along with new tools have come more efficient, flexible and easy-to-use internet interfaces for creating media-rich online content. Participation in social networking sites, such as Facebook.com and MySpace.com, has spread rapidly among students in the United States, especially those in secondary and tertiary schools. A by-product of these recent developments is a new vision of the internet – it is seen as not just a repository of information and a conduit for communication but rather a highly interactive collaborative platform that can be personalized for socializing, communicating and learning.

The chapter that follows is a description and discussion of several online collaboration technologies. It includes recent projects by music educators and researchers that take advantage of the collaborative potential of the internet. Although many of these tools were not specifically designed for music education, they can be easily adapted to use and support a broad range of music education classes in secondary schools.

The discussion concludes with a summary of strategies that music educators might use to extend both the physical and temporal bounds of their classroom by creating online music learning environments for students. These environments enable the students to engage collaboratively with music and with each other, both inside and outside of class time.

Online Collaborative Tools

Although the use of online collaborative technologies is not new in education (Jonassen *et al.* 2003) or in music (Théberge 1993), recent developments afford new possibilities in the secondary school music classroom. The defining aspect of these technologies is that in some way they enable collaboration or interactivity between the creator and the user. Regardless of whether they are used by the teacher to support in-class activities, or by students to share and discuss their work outside of class, these technologies have the potential to mediate music learning in meaningful ways.

Online collaborative technologies are often embedded in the social networking websites that students visit and participate in on a daily basis, most of which include a combination of blogs and streaming media galleries. Because students are already familiar with many of these tools from outside the formal school setting, they may be well equipped to take advantage of them in their collaborative music learning experiences. Three major online collaborative tools – blogs, podcasts and wikis – will be described and discussed in this section, as well as how these tools have been utilized in a variety of music education projects to date.

Blogs

An easy way to understand a blog is to think of it as an online journal. Just like a paper-based journal, an author makes regular entries called 'posts', usually on topics of personal interest. As authors upload and post their thoughts onto their blog, their entries appear on the blog in a serialized manner with the most recent posts often appearing at the top of the page. While a blog is an internet webpage, what differentiates it from a traditional webpage is that it consists of dynamic content that is updated frequently, and the manner of posting content does not require programming. Instead, templates that can be personalized are offered through blog-hosting sites such as Wordpress.com, Livejournal.com, Xanga.com and Blogger.com. Almost all blog sites have web-based interfaces for creating and managing blogs so that users do not need additional software or knowledge of HTML or other web-coding languages.

Most blog sites allow you to compose a post using a WYSIWYG (what you see is what you get) interface, similar to that found when writing an email. These interfaces provide the ability to easily add images, embed streaming music or video files, add hyperlinks to other websites, and have tools to customize the formatting and appearance of the text. Once a post is published on the blog, the author often has access to additional controls for managing reader comments, selecting and making adjustments to the overall appearance of the blog, and for making edits to prior posts.

Figure 11.1 shows example posts and the sidebar from my blog at AlexRuthmann.com. Readers can search my blog for posts on specific topics, view blog posts sorted by categories, peruse archived postings and access links to other sites on the internet. Sidebars make it easy to navigate large blogs with many posts.

Another difference between a blog and a regular webpage is that readers can easily add comments to blog posts. At the bottom of each post is a *Comments* link. Readers who would like to provide feedback to a particular post can simply click on that link to add their feedback, which is normally open for all to read. From this perspective, a blog becomes an interactive tool enabling readers and the author to easily engage in an online conversation through the *Comments* feature.

Podcasts

A podcast is essentially an internet-based radio station with online episodes that can be downloaded and listened to on demand. To create a podcast, one either records or uploads an audio file (e.g. a composition, a radio show or a recording of a rehearsal) to

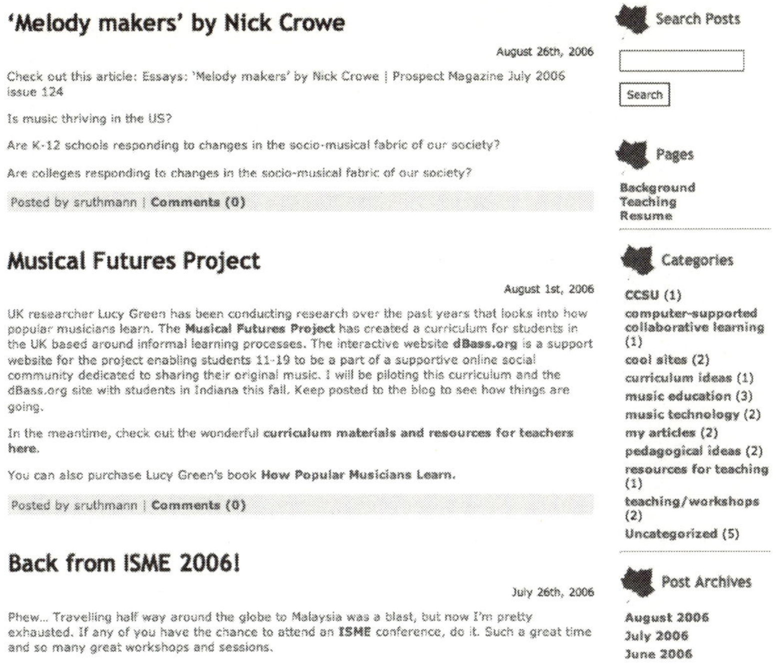

'Melody makers' by Nick Crowe

August 26th, 2006

Check out this article: Essays: 'Melody makers' by Nick Crowe | Prospect Magazine July 2006 issue 124

Is music thriving in the US?

Are K-12 schools responding to changes in the socio-musical fabric of our society?

Are colleges responding to changes in the socio-musical fabric of our society?

Posted by sruthmann | **Comments (0)**

Musical Futures Project

August 1st, 2006

UK researcher Lucy Green has been conducting research over the past years that looks into how popular musicians learn. The **Musical Futures Project** has created a curriculum for students in the UK based around informal learning processes. The interactive website **dBass.org** is a support website for the project enabling students 11-19 to be a part of a supportive online social community dedicated to sharing their original music. I will be piloting this curriculum and the dBass.org site with students in Indiana this fall. Keep posted to the blog to see how things are going.

In the meantime, check out the wonderful **curriculum materials and resources for teachers here.**

You can also purchase Lucy Green's book **How Popular Musicians Learn.**

Posted by sruthmann | **Comments (0)**

Back from ISME 2006!

July 26th, 2006

Phew... Travelling half way around the globe to Malaysia was a blast, but now I'm pretty exhausted. If any of you have the chance to attend an **ISME** conference, do it. Such a great time and so many great workshops and sessions.

Search Posts

Search

Pages

Background
Teaching
Resume

Categories

CCSU (1)
computer-supported collaborative learning (1)
cool sites (2)
curriculum ideas (1)
music education (3)
music technology (2)
my articles (2)
pedagogical ideas (2)
resources for teaching (1)
teaching/workshops (2)
Uncategorized (5)

Post Archives

August 2006
July 2006
June 2006

Figure 11.1 Example blog posting with sidebar

an internet server and attaches that file to a blog post. Using a feed aggregator, such as FeedBurner.com, the blog with attached audio files is transformed into a podcast which can be subscribed to by any podcast player (e.g. Apple's iTunes) or listened to via an embedded player within the blog.

A listener does not need an iPod, or other portable music player, to experience a podcast. All one needs is access to the Internet and the ability to play music online. One of the most popular sources for listening to podcasts is through Apple's free iTunes software[i]. In this software, listeners can browse podcasts and download 'episodes' that are of interest.

Figure 11.2 provides a sample view of the podcast window in iTunes. The podcasts shown were created by students in my secondary general music classes. Similar to a blog, the most recent episodes appear at the top of the podcast window. Listeners can read a description of the content of the show and then either download the episode to their computer or listen to the show through iTunes.

Another popular site for creating podcasts is Odeo.com. This free podcast-hosting site allows users to record or upload a podcast for free and bypasses the need to set up a separate blog for posting your audio files to. Odeo serves as the blog and file server for your podcast.

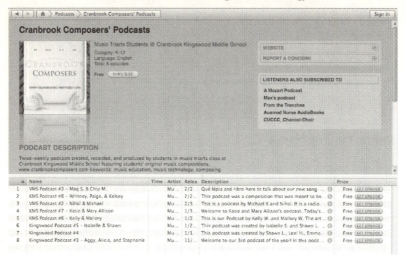

Figure 11.2 Example podcast window from Apple's iTunes software

Wikis

A wiki is a website that allows users to easily view, add and modify content on the website. It differs from blog and traditional website technology by being designed for large numbers of people to collaboratively create, edit and publish a webpage or website. The most well-known use of wiki technology is Wikipedia[ii]. Wikipedia is an online, publicly editable encyclopedia. Initially, I was intrigued by the concept of a

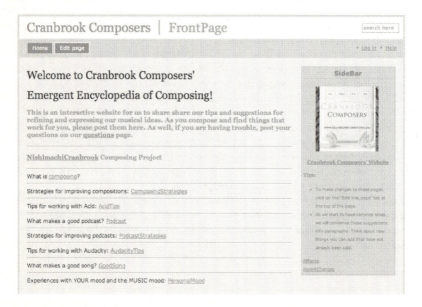

Figure 11.3 Example music education wiki

collaborate website that could be co-created by myself and my students, and would be easy to add to and modify.

There are many free wiki websites available for music educators[iii]. In my own classes, I used PBWiki because it is easy to use and has a simple design. Figure 11.3 is a snapshot of one of the wikis created in my secondary general music classes. At the top of the picture is an 'Edit Page' button. Clicking this button and signing in with the class password enables any viewer to have editing access to the content of the website. Most wikis come with a history feature that allows the wiki owner/moderator to view and approve any and all changes. As a teacher, you can choose to have all student modifications approved by you before being put up on the website, or you can cede responsibility to your students. The example wiki in Figure 11.3 is from the Emergent Encyclopedia of Composing[iv] that was created by my students to support their creative projects in class. It will be discussed in more detail later in the chapter.

Recent Projects Using the Internet for Musical Collaboration

Music educators and researchers have been using the internet to support collaborative composing experiences since the mid-1990s. Projects such as Netcomm and MICNet (Reese and Hickey 1999) and the Vermont MIDI Project (Cosenza and McLeod 1998) were pioneering in terms of using the internet to facilitate musical collaboration[v]. In each of these projects, student composers were paired with mentors, such as professional composers, teachers or collegiate music education students. Student MIDI or notation files were uploaded to a specially designed website. Mentors could view the site, read student comments, download the students' computer files and offer comments and critique. The mentors would then post their comments for students to read. These early collaborative projects required specially designed websites for their functionality. With recent developments in wiki, blog and podcasting technologies, however, any teacher or student with a basic fluency with the internet can create similar environments to support online musical collaboration.

In 2004, UNESCO launched the *Sounds of Our Water*[vi] project as part of their Young Digital Creators project. The aim of this project was to provide an online platform for students to collaboratively compose music and sound compositions using recordings of water sounds from around the world. This site was the first project to use an online sample gallery consisting of recordings of water sounds made and submitted by student musicians and sound artists in the projects. Students were directed to record water-related sounds in their local area, which they would upload to the sample gallery. Then students from around the world downloaded and integrated water sounds from the project into their own compositions. These compositions were in turn uploaded to the website for comment and feedback from members of the project.

Two recent projects (Bizub and Ruthmann 2006, Seddon, 2006) utilized online collaborative technologies to facilitate cross-cultural composing projects among students in different countries. Using email and the Norwegian-designed *Musit Interactive*[vii] internet-based composing platform, Seddon (2006) explored the relationship between formal instrument tuition and collaborative composition among students in Norway and the UK. Bizub and Ruthmann (2006) conducted an exploratory study investigating the challenges and successes throughout an internet-based collaborative composing project among students in Japan and the United States.

The collaborative tools utilized in the latter study were embedded in a central website with links to free blogging, podcast and wiki tools.[viii] Where the collaboration was primarily through email in the Seddon (2006) study, students in the Bizub and Ruthmann (2006) project used wikis along with email to collaborate with each other. While the wiki provided a space for students to collaboratively discuss and outline their compositions, students chose to communicate through a combination of wiki and email. Both the researchers and the students reported that the researcher-designed website, which consisted of an amalgamation of third-party, free collaborative tools, was at times difficult to navigate and was not as easy to use as more familiar technologies, such as email.

Collaborative music websites are not unique to music education. Musicians and music companies have recently developed collaborative websites that take advantage of similar technologies. DigitalMusician.net, AcidPlanet.com and MySpace Music (a part of MySpace.com) are among a list of many new sites where students and amateur musicians can gather online to socialize, collaborate, create and promote their music. AcidPlanet features free music sample collections from contemporary musical artists which can be downloaded by students to be remixed and uploaded to the site in monthly remix contests. MySpace Music provides an outlet for musicians to easily create free webpages with embedded streaming music players to share their music. DigitalMusician.net enables musicians to perform and record together live over the internet with embedded videoconferencing features. Nearly all of these sites allow musicians to post their compositions. Both listeners and fans can add comments to particular songs and communicate directly with the musicians.

Strategies

Online collaborative technologies afford multiple possibilities for enhancing the learning experience of our students. The research studies, collaborative projects and online music environments discussed above provide a small overview of how these technologies have been used in the past and how they might best be used by music educators. The strategies shared below are drawn from my own experience – experimenting with and researching students' experiences while using these technologies in my secondary school (Ruthmann, in press) and university music classes. My trials and experiments have been influenced by other innovative early-adopters[ix] of these technologies in music education.

Peer-feedback/Peer-teaching

In my own teaching, the greatest educational value provided by blogs was the expanded online possibilities for peer-feedback and peer-teaching. When I taught secondary school general music in a computer lab, I could not physically be everywhere to help answer students' questions and provide feedback on their compositions. Instead of viewing this negatively, I had my students create their own blogs for class where they could upload compositions[x] in progress for other students to listen to and comment on.

While many students provided peer-feedback in person to their classmates during class, they also posted their compositions and questions to their personal blog. Because blog technology is relatively simple to set up and use, students were easily able to upload their compositions (MP3 files, computer files and screenshots) and provide feedback to each other in the form of comments in class, outside of class, before and after school and at home. In addition, the blogs enabled them to document and assess their own collaborative creative process.

Blogs have a further use in supporting peer-feedback and assessment in a large ensemble performance setting. Many music educators in the United States are posting recordings of large ensemble rehearsals to course blogs. After recording the final run-through of a performance in choir, band or orchestra class, the teacher can upload that recording to a blog and ask students to listen to the recording at home. Teachers can post questions for students to reply to by adding a comment to the posted rehearsal recording and students can provide feedback to the teacher to help plan the next day's rehearsal outside of class. Blogs can also serve as a means for self-assessing individual, section or large ensemble performances. In this case, asking students to comment on rehearsal and performance recordings is one way to democratize the roles of teacher and student, providing opportunities to share responsibility for rehearsal planning and performance (Shively 2004).

Blogs as Course Websites

Teachers can use blogs as an easy way to create a website for their classes. For each class that I teach, I create a blog that includes links to the course syllabus, the course calendar and websites, documents and other files that the students will need throughout the course. As the course progresses, assignments are posted on the blog, including questions for student reflection. In class or at home, students can post their own reflections to the course blog for other students to read. Having students add their reflective comments to a class blog can be an effective and efficient way to have students read and learn from each others' comments. For the teacher, an advantage to using blogs as opposed to standard website technologies is that little knowledge of website coding is needed to create a blog. All blog-hosting sites provide a selection of professionally designed templates suitable for use in education[xi].

Online Media and Music Sample Galleries

Online collaborative technologies can provide opportunities for students to engage in a 'discourse in music' (Folkestad 1996) through the use of online media and music sample galleries. Collaborative music websites, such as dBass.org, provide an online space for students to upload music samples they create to be shared with other students on the website. This group-constructed and shared sample library allows students from different geographic locations and cultures to interact directly through the sounds and music they create. As an example, a student in the United States could upload a field recording that could, in turn, be used by a student in Japan in a composition.

These technologies are not limited to uploading and sharing short musical samples. Students' full compositions, images and even videos can be embedded in and shared through online galleries. Figure 11.4 shows the online media gallery used in my secondary general music courses. At the beginning of each term in my composing-based courses, I asked students to listen to and critique the compositions from prior courses. The student composers in my courses have often drawn on compositional ideas and techniques from music composed earlier by their peers. Throughout the

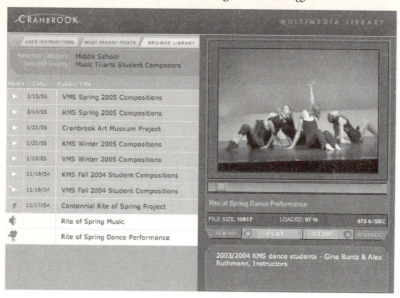

Figure 11.4 Example online media gallery

course of the term, they frequently revisit this online archive of compositions for creative ideas.

Free audio-hosting/podcasting websites such as Odeo.com provide an easy way for teachers and students to create an online audio gallery similar to that shown above. Using Odeo, students and teachers can upload multiple audio files that will be streamed on demand with the rest of the class. The website also allows students and teacher to add comments to the tracks. Though Odeo is limited to working with MP3 files, many free software programs, including iTunes and Audacity[xii], can convert between MP3 and other file formats.

New developments in Flash-based video-streaming technology enable students that have access to digital camera or internet webcam technologies to record themselves and easily share their videos online. Google Video[xiii] and YouTube[xiv] are two popular video-streaming sites where students can view videos of historical music perform-ances, lessons and virtually any other topic. These technologies enable teachers and students to upload up to ten minutes or 100Mb of digital video for free to these servers. Both Google Video and YouTube have privacy filters that enable users to limit access to the video. Once videos are uploaded to these servers, the user can embed the Flash-based video on a website, in an email or on their personal blog. The main advantage of Flash-based video streaming/storage services is that storage for the video is free and easy to manage. Since the Flash-based videos on these sites are often of low quality, however, teachers need to consider the trade-off between video quality and the ease of use coupled with free hosting.

Wikis as Spaces for Group Collaboration

The power of wikis to support music learning is rooted in the democratic and collaborative nature of the technology (Jonassen *et al.* 2003). Any user with a password can enter a wiki and add, edit or remove content. Figure 11.3 shows the main entry page for the Emergent Encyclopedia of Composing[xv], developed by my students over a period of two years. I was initially drawn to wiki technology as a way for my students to collaboratively build an emergent online database of compositional strategies. Over the course of my classes, as students found compositional techniques that were particularly effective, students posted their strategies and techniques to the class wiki. As additional areas of interest arose, new sections were created to meet the needs and interests of the student composers. Students were also encouraged to post challenges they encountered in the 'Questions' section of the wiki so that I (as teacher) or their peers could provide feedback and help in class or online. Because this wiki was used for many classes over multiple semesters, it became a valued tool by my students; the strategies and feedback on the site came from and reflected the lived compositional challenges of their peers.

As moderator of the wiki, I had the ability to review all student additions and changes before they were posted. Although most of the time I did not need to take advantage of this feature, opening the wiki to unmoderated comments may not be the best choice in all situations. In particular, teachers should take into account the maturity of their students when deciding to moderate comments.

Wikis could also serve as a useful tool to support beginning instrumental ensembles or those studying a common instrument. Teachers could set up a wiki for each instrument group in their classes and post musical exercises, warm-ups, fingering charts and tips for playing. One example could be to ask students to post on the wiki when they found successful practice strategies at home. These students could then share their successful strategies with their peers via the wiki. Alternatively, those students who faced a particular challenge could go to the class instrument wiki to find help – again from their peers. This emergent record of students' successes and challenges could serve the teacher as a useful tool for informal assessment. Wiki posts could be used to gain insight into students' habits of practice and to influence future lessons or rehearsals.

Summary

Newly emerging online music-learning communities that integrate many of the online collaborative tools discussed in this chapter (such as dBass.org, MusicDelta.com and SoundJunction.org) have the potential to address some of the difficulties faced by early users of an amalgam of free, third-party tools. Professionally designed online communities will no doubt lead to exciting possibilities for online collaborative music learning in the near future, enhancing the music learning experiences of students in secondary schools. As social networking and online collaborative technologies continue to develop and become more pervasive in students' online experiences generally, music educators should take the time to evaluate the numerous and constantly changing technologies available. They should investigate how these can enhance and extend learning, both within and outside the physical and temporal bounds of their classrooms. The challenge lies in how to connect to and adapt the online tools and social environments prevalent in our students' lives in order to best support learning and teaching in our music courses.

References

Bizub, S. and Ruthmann, A. (2006), 'The Internet and the Nature of Collaborative Experience: Cross-Cultural Composing among Students in Japan and the United States'. Paper presented at the International Society of Music Education (ISME) World Conference, Kuala Lumpur, Malaysia.

Cosenza, G. and MacLeod, S. (1998), 'Vermont MIDI Distance Learning Network: A Model for Technology in Classroom Learning'. Proceedings of the Fifth International Technological Directions in Music Learning Conference, San Antonio, Texas.

Folkestad, G. (1996), *Computer-based Creating and Music Making: Young People's Music in the Digital Age*. Göteborg, Sweden: ACTA.

Jonassen, D., Howland, J., Moore, J. and Marra, R. (2003), *Learning to Solve Problems with Technology: A Constructivist Perspective* (2nd edn). Upper Saddle River, NJ: Pearson Education.

O'Reilly, T. (2005), 'What is Web 2.0?' Available at http://www.oreillynet.com/pub/a/oreilly/tim/news/2005/09/30/what-is-web-20.html. Accessed on 4 September 2006.

Prensky, M. (2001), 'Digital natives, digital immigrants'. *On the Horizon*, 9(5), 27–39.

Reese, S. and Hickey, M. (1999), 'Internet-based music composition and music teacher education'. *Journal of Music Teacher Education*, 1(5), 15–28.

Ruthmann, A. (in press), 'The composers' workshop: An emergent approach to composing in the classroom'. *Music Educators Journal*.

Seddon, F. (2006), 'Collaborative computer-mediated music composition in cyberspace'. *British Journal of Music Education*, 23(3), 273–83.

Shively, J. (2004). 'In the face of tradition: questioning the roles of conductors and ensemble members in school bands, choirs, and orchestras', in L. Bartel (ed.). *Questioning the Music Education Paradigm*, pp. 179–90.

Théberge, P. (1993), *Any Sound You Can Imagine: Making Music/Consuming Technology*. Hanover, NH: University Press of New England.

URLs

Music Education Blogs

collective.musiced.net/
Music Education Blog Collective
www.alexruthmann.com/
Alex Ruthmann
www.jsavage.org.uk/
Jonathan Savage
etobiasblog.musiced.net/
Evan Tobias

Music Education Wikis

cranbrookcomposers.pbwiki.com/
Cranbrook Composers' Wiki
cranbrookcomposers.pbwiki.com/NishimachiCranbrook
Nishimachi/Cranbrook Wiki

Social Music Learning Websites

unesco.uiah.fi/water/
UNESCO Sounds of our Water Project
www.dbass.org
Musical Futures Project
www.acidplanet.com/
Acid Planet
www.musicdelta.com/
Music Delta
www.soundjunction.com/
Sound Junction

Notes

   i   http://www.itunes.com/
   ii   http://www.wikipedia.com/
   iii   Some popular wiki sites include PBWiki.com, JotSpot.com, and TiddlyWiki.com.
   iv   http://cranbrookcomposers.pbwiki.com/
   v   For a thorough discussion of these projects in the context of their contributions to online musical collaboration, see Seddon (2006).
   vi   http://unesco.uiah.fi/water/
   vii   This technology was recently integrated into Music Delta – http://www.musicdelta.com/
   viii   Blogger.com, PBWiki.com, iTunes.com
   ix   Special thanks to Steve Bizub and Marj Haber whose discussions, conversations, and collaborations influenced many of the ideas shared in this chapter.
   x   Students would often upload an MP3 file of the composition along with a screenshot of their composition so that students could listen to the file and see the visual representation.
   xi   A blogging service specifically designed for use by educators along with example blogs can be found at http://www.edublogs.org/.
   xii   Audacity is a free basic audio editing program available at http://audacity.sourceforge.net/
   xiii   http://video.google.com/
   xiv   http://www.youtube.com/
   xv   http://cranbrookcomposers.pbwiki.com

Chapter 12

Pedagogical Strategies for Change

Jonathan Savage

Introduction

The use of ICT in the music classroom has the potential to challenge traditional approaches to music teaching and learning. Although it can continue to reinforce existing ways of teaching music (i.e. extrinsic to the ICT itself), this chapter will argue for an intrinsic model of technological use. It will draw on recent classroom-based research that has examined the uses of technologies through this intrinsic model. It will analyse the pedagogical issues that arise when technologies are applied in this way within the classroom, drawing on the author's own experience of classroom teaching with these technologies and reflecting on their use through appropriate research methodologies. The chapter will end by considering the main implications for the teaching of music in the secondary classroom using ICT, including the importance of thorough planning, inclusion, the role of learning objectives, expanding what counts as music, efficient classroom management, assessment and integration.

> In a technology-rich world we need to review and modernise what and how we learn. Imagine how a graphic designer works today compared with 30 years ago. What should a modernised music, art or design curriculum be like? . . . They may use technology as a tool for thinking, making or doing. Technology needs to be used more effectively to help develop learners' enquiry skills, logical reasoning, analytical thinking and creativity. It should support individualised and independent learning, while encouraging wider communication and collaborative learning. (Quality and Curriculum Authority 2005)

The QCA's recent consultation on curriculum change (QCA 2005) highlights the importance of new technologies and their effective use as a key 'force for change' as educators seek to develop a school curriculum fit for the twenty-first century. This chapter will consider how music teachers should teach with ICT. But even this, in many respects, is an impossible task. There is no single, fixed solution that any given teacher should seek to implement in their teaching. Rather, this chapter will identify some principles and practical issues that any teacher will need to address in order to make effective use of ICT in their own classroom, acknowledging that these are bounded by a unique set of personal, social, curricula contexts.

Background

The background to this chapter is framed by two important documents published by the Teacher Training Agency (TTA 1999a and 1999b). One of these documents (TTA 1999a) was written to provide teachers with ideas for a range of possible uses of ICT. The second (TTA 1999b) was written to inform teacher educators of the areas they ought to be covering in training courses. The content of these publications was important since it gave clear signals about the types of knowledge and practice that music teachers and teacher trainers ought to be developing.

The TTA suggested that there were four main areas of knowledge that teachers needed to develop:

1. how to plan to use ICT to promote learning objectives
2. effective use of ICT in teaching
3. assessment and evaluation of students' progress in music with ICT
4. the development uses of ICT for personal and professional ends. (TTA 1999a, p. 4)

Specifically, the document outlined three key principles for music educators.

1. Decisions about when, when not and how to use ICT in music lessons [should be] based on whether the use of ICT supports good practice in teaching music. If it does not, then do not use it.
2. When planning, make sure that the use of ICT in a particular lesson or scheme of work directly relates to the chosen teaching and learning objectives.
3. ICT should allow the teacher and student to achieve something that could not be achieved without it; or allow them to learn something more effectively and efficiently than could be done otherwise. (TTA 1999b, p. 3)

These three principles seem well-founded and are useful starting points for our considerations. They emphasize the importance of ICT in supporting good practice in music teaching. In other words, teachers should not be seeking a new 'shiny' and modern ICT-enriched pedagogy that supplants the many excellent features of their existing music curriculum and associated good teaching practices. Effective music teaching with ICT will not appear that dissimilar to effective music teaching without it. After all, ICT is just another tool, medium or set of instruments that teachers will use to allow students to achieve the learning objectives that they have set.

This analysis, however, does not tell the whole story. The third principle is important, stating that ICT 'should allow you or your students to achieve something that could not be achieved without it'. This rightly hints that teachers and students should be encouraged to use ICT to extend and develop the music curriculum into new areas, perhaps beyond the reach of traditional methods and practices in music education.

Thinking about new technologies and how they should be incorporated into musical practice is not a new issue:

I believe that the use of noise to make music will continue and increase until we reach a music produced through the aid of electrical instruments that will make available any and all sounds that can be heard ... The present methods of writing music will be inadequate for the composer who will be faced with the entire field of sound. (Cage 1968, p. 4)

In typically provocative style, John Cage summarized what he saw as the inadequacy of traditional methods of music making in light of the changing conceptual basis on which musical materials are defined.

The revolution in musical technologies over the last sixty or so years has led to a bewildering array of electronic musical instruments and devices. Some of these offer genuinely new and exciting potential to educators, with the possibility to fulfil Cage's prophecy. The challenges that Cage and others confronted during the second half of the twentieth century have similarities to those faced by music educators today. Not least of these is the need for us to face up to increasingly pluralistic models of musical production and consumption. There is a need for educators to fundamentally reconsider what is meant by musical ability, skill and understanding as ICT becomes an integral part of our classrooms.

Extrinsic and Intrinsic Use: Two Models of Musical Practice with ICT

Within the classroom, ICT can be used in at least two ways. It can function as a tool to facilitate models of practice 'extrinsic' to the technology itself, or it can be used to generate what might be called an 'intrinsic' model of practice, one that leads to a greater exploration and engagement with sound itself.

The Extrinsic Model

The first of these models is prevalent throughout the United Kingdom's classrooms. The most common and obvious outworking is the linking of musical keyboards to computer workstations using sequencing software as a tool for tonal composition. Typical compositional tasks might include working with melodic and rhythmic ostinati, chord-based compositions, writing music for film (occasionally incorporating the use of sound effects) and many other tonal-based, piano keyboard-mediated tasks. These tasks provide valuable educational experiences for students. It is possible, and very likely in the hands of a skilful teacher, that these tasks will facilitate the development of musical skills and understanding.

The use of the computer and musical keyboard in this way perpetuates musical concepts that have their roots in European music of the mid-eighteenth century. Tonal music is a well-established tradition but has been challenged at various points by composers, working with and without new technologies, in fundamental ways as well as through the expanding access we all have to world musical styles and traditions. Chanan describes the possible influences of new technology in the breakdown of tonality in the early twentieth century like this:

Is it an accident that over the same period as the introduction of the new technology of reproduction, music experienced a revolution in its every aspect? That figures like Debussy, Schoenberg, Berg, Webern, Bartok and Stravinsky turned it inside out and upside down, which not only left it utterly transformed but also became paradigmatic for the whole modernist movement? I hardly want to suggest that technology was the sufficient cause of this transformation, but neither is it neutral, or merely secondary to aesthetic and spiritual processes. (Chanan 1994, p. 16)

For many of those composers named above the 'tools' of composition were the same as for previous generations, yet the wider sociological, technological and cultural changes within which they worked fundamentally affected their practice. Yet, musical development cannot be described by reference to just one culture – within a wider consideration of global musical practice, the 'musical traffic' (Swanwick 1988, p. 110) runs in every conceivable direction. Swanwick lists geographical poles of musical traffic as well as transference between stylistic genres. One could add to this the deconstruction and re-contextualization of musical materials across boundaries of time and place via the internet and through the development and use of recording and sampling mediums. So the prioritization of certain musical qualities or attributes from a Western perspective has always been seen to be questionable by others. Our music education system needs to acknowledge this more readily.

This is important because music teachers have significant power in determining what counts as music within the classroom (Young 1971, Swanwick 1988). The shifting of power between formal and informal influences in the music curriculum (Green 2001) can lead to a fracturing of students' musical experiences inside and outside the classroom. Curriculum content and teaching style within music needs to react and respond to wider artistic and aesthetic issues. The linking of a computer with a 'piano-type' keyboard, however, hinders a re-conceptualization, pre-empting discussion and argument about new ways forward. The interposition of an eighteenth-century piece of technology (i.e. the equal-tempered keyboard) mediates at a fundamental level the type of musical activity in which students can engage. Unfortunately, it also reinforces traditional concepts of success or failure within such an activity. The opportunity for using a computer as a musical instrument has been lost.

The Intrinsic Model

The intrinsic model starts with a piece of ICT and examines it for its inherent musical possibilities. By way of an example, this section will focus on the opportunity of using a standard personal computer as a musical instrument.

Computers with sound-editing or mixing software can facilitate a closer analysis of the micro-phenomena of sound in a way that is impossible to achieve by any other means. Like the skills exhibited by an advanced instrumentalist able to mould and transform an instrument's sound through its highly technical and sophisticated physical interface, users of such pieces of software can quickly get to the very core of sonic material and begin manipulating its structure through simple interfaces.

Electro-acoustic composers produce music in this way. Like all composers, they are fascinated by a sound's inherent potential. The sound itself becomes the source for many new, as yet undiscovered sounds through a process of exploration, a kind of sonic-sculpting via hardware and software interfaces. The impact of the technology, however, goes beyond the practice of composition or performance. It results in a challenge to what constitutes music itself. Wishart (1996) documents many of these ideas at a philosophical level. He quotes the following definitions for 'music', from:

Music is sounds, sounds around us whether we're in or out of concert halls. (Wishart 1996, p. 5 quoting Schaefer 1969, p. 1) to:

> Computer-composed music involves composition, that is note-selection. (Wishart 1996, p. 6 quoting Hiller 1981, p. 7)

The first of these definitions is too broad, Wishart suggests, to be any use and the second too narrow to include even the most basic of electro-acoustical processes. His discussion culminates in the assertion that, at a fundamental level, there is no such thing as an *unmusical sound-object* [his italics] (p. 8) and that in the future it might be better for *composers* such as himself to be referred to as *sonic designers or sonic engineers* [his italics] (p. 5). This idea of composition being redefined as sound design or engineering is an interesting one, since it identifies a change in function brought about by the use of new technologies in musical contexts. It was this premise that underpinned the recent Sound2Picture and Sound2Game projects (UCan.tv 2006).

For many students and their parents, musicality is caught up and defined by a notion of music performance and skill, nearly always related to a musical instrument. Ask your students who they think is musical and why? Typically answers may include, 'Oh, William's musical because he can play the drums really well' or 'Julie is really musical – she plays her violin in the county youth orchestra'. These ideas are rooted in traditional beliefs and values linking the production of musical sounds to musical instruments and the skill to play them well. Their assertion in the classroom context has been well documented by many researchers exploring the establishment of students' musical identities through psychological frameworks (Lamont 2002).

The purchase of a musical instrument is only the first step in a long process towards mastery of that instrument and a controlling of its sound to match the prescriptions of a musical score or the strictures of a particular musical genre. Yet, at an advanced level, the ways in which instrumentalists and composers push at the boundaries of an instrument's capabilities, stretching its sound quality to develop new timbres, only goes to show that a musical instrument, as a particular type of technology, is really no more than a 'field of possibilities' (Théberge 1997, p. 187) for exploration and experimentation. Wishart's conception of composition as sonic design, and composers as sonic designers or engineers, implies that there is a whole new range of skills and processes that students can adopt as they explore and experiment with the nature and structure of sound directly through hardware and software interfaces. This is where the intrinsic model is focused.

It is clear that several key aspects of musical practice need careful consideration, and perhaps redefinition, as various technologies become more common as educational tools. Teachers need to challenge students' often naïve beliefs about what it is to be musical. Similarly, teachers need to widen their understanding of what constitutes musical composition and performance activity in the light of the changing practices that ICT is bringing to music in its various genres.

To reiterate, ICT can be used as a tool to:

- facilitate models of practice extrinsic to the technology itself
- generate an entirely new model of practice, one that is 'intrinsic' to the technology and that allows for a greater exploration of sound itself.

There is not a simple linear relationship between these models. Rather, teachers and students will traverse the boundaries of creative practice with ICT in many different ways. As they use ICT under the intrinsic model, for example, they will need to draw on experiences from the extrinsic models and other types of musical learning without ICT. To do otherwise is to fracture educational experience on a conceptual misnomer. Imaginative application of principles, models and methods is vital.

How Should we Approach Music Teaching with ICT?

> Music history and the sociology of music are seen as accessible only through the doors and windows of particular musical encounters. For it is only in these encounters that the possibilities exist to transform tones into tunes, tunes into forms and forms into significant life events. (Swanwick 1999, p. 45)

Swanwick's definition of musical encounter is a well-established concept. Its clearest definition is found in *Music, Mind and Education* (Swanwick 1988) where he contrasts the notions of musical instruction with that of musical encounter (pp. 120–38). Swanwick draws on the work of Bernstein (1971) to define instruction and encounter through the concept of framing and classification. Framing is:

> to do with pedagogy, teaching style, with the degree of control that the teacher or student possesses over selection, organization and pacing of what is to be learned. (Swanwick 1988, p. 121)

When musical instruction is characterized by strong framing, the teacher maintains control over the ways in which students learn. Swanwick suggests that weak framing, where most of the control of learning lies with the student, can result in an increased possibility of musical encounter. Linked with the concept of framing is the idea of classification. Classification is:

> to do with the exercise of selection over curriculum content, the way in which certain activities, perhaps 'subjects' are marked out for inclusion in or exclusion from the curriculum. (Swanwick 1988, p. 121)

Strong classification is evidenced when teachers choose and fix rigid boundaries in respect to what music might be studied in the classroom; weak classification gives power to students to decide the curriculum content.

Swanwick goes on to give a number of the permutations of classification and framing. These can be shown on a simple graph, in Figure 12.1.

Within effective music teaching with ICT there will be a need for instruction, both musical and technological, for example, when new technologies are introduced for the first time. Then a degree of familiarization relating to their use and musical potential will be necessary. In most cases, this can be done speedily, allowing students the opportunity to explore the hardware or software for themselves once general guidelines have been put in place. On one occasion within the Reflecting Others project (Savage and Challis 2002), this introductory instructional phase was allowed to continue for too long. The explanation of a complex piece of video-editing software was too detailed and lengthy and, although students were fascinated by the potential of the software and seemed keen to explore it for themselves, their chance to move from a position of strong classification and strong framing (teacher-led presentation of specific features of the software) to any other position on the graph was limited (Figure 12.2).

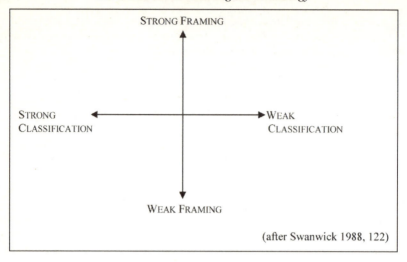

Figure 12.1

In a previous project (Savage and Challis 2001), students were introduced to the workings of a basic sound processor. These sessions were conducted using a variety of approaches. By adopting a position of strong classification and framing, the teacher chose which features of the sound processor to introduce to the class, doing so in a presentational style that allowed students little chance to explore the processor's other features. After this short presentation, however, students were allowed to take away a sound processor and microphone and, within a small-group context, explore both the demonstrated aspects of the sound processor and a range of other features that were easily discovered. This was a move towards weaker framing and, although

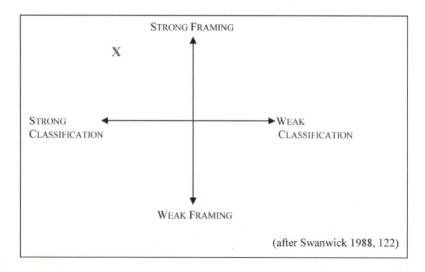

Figure 12.2

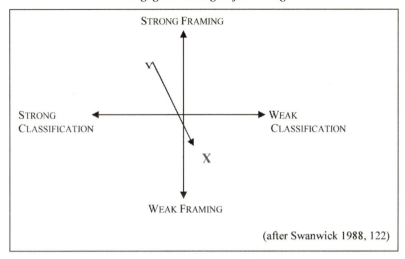

(after Swanwick 1988, 122)

Figure 12.3

the classification level remained high, it did reduce slightly as students discovered new areas of knowledge for themselves.

More significant moves between classification and framing occurred when students began to use ICT within compositional tasks. In the Dunwich Revisted project (Savage and Challis 2001) the use of support documentation played a crucial role. The Dunwich Project: Sound Generation Sheet (Appendix A) is one example. Within this part of the project students had to use a range of ICT to help in the production of basic sound ideas. Although the task was clearly defined, the ways in which students worked, the resources they chose to use and, most importantly, decisions relating to

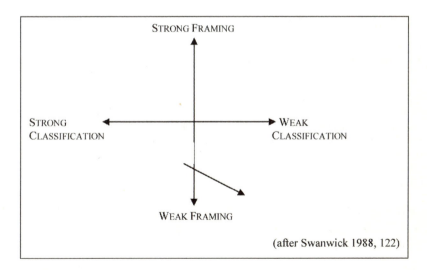

(after Swanwick 1988, 122)

Figure 12.4

the actual material of the musical composition (its selection, manipulation, sequencing and structuring) were within their control. An example of the resulting work can be seen in the planning that students did for their composition work. This represents a significant shift into areas of weak classification and framing (Figure 12.4). Although the suggested way of working through the compositional process was clearly defined, there was flexibility within it to allow students to choose their musical ideas and develop their individual and group-working practices.

Doorways to Musical Encounters with ICT

> Finding a 'doorway in' is an analogy [sic metaphor] designed to help teachers plan instruction to enable students to truly develop a structural understanding of music – an understanding that will empower their ability to listen to, perform and create music, and enrich their capacity to understand what the music expresses. (Wiggins 2003)

The metaphor of doorways is helpful in considering how to increase the possibility of our students experiencing 'musical encounters' through the effective use of ICT. The following section will focus on these metaphors of encounter and doorways to consider how aspects of pedagogy and curriculum design are affected by the introduction of ICT in the music classroom.

In your Planning, Allow for Flexibility and Movement Between Categories

First, it is important to allow for and expect flexible movement between various classification and framing combinations during the course of individual lessons and throughout a scheme of work. Being too strong or weak in any one area for too long will lead to imbalances, and student learning may be inhibited. The most successful moments in the use of ICT in music education are when moves between strong and weak classification and framing are effected smoothly and in a way that does not disrupt students' perceptions of the teaching style or approach that has been adopted.

ICT can be a Helpful Differentiating Tool to Facilitate Inclusion

Secondly, when using ICT in music education it is important to be aware that an individual student's experiences of pedagogical approaches will often be very different to what might have been expected or planned. For example, the supposed freedom of a weakly framed and classified composition task could be intended as beneficial, liberating and a creative opportunity, but for some students the very freedom of the task could become the problem. The need for additional support or instruction (a move towards stronger framing but not classification) would be important in order to complete the task effectively.

Moves Towards Intrinsic Approaches to ICT are Helped by Carefully Worded Learning Objectives

Thirdly, ICT presents increased opportunities for musical encounters when teachers are confident to present learning objectives in a way that allows for major shifts in classification and framing. Wiggins' work in this area is particularly fascinating. Her metaphor of a 'doorway in' to musical encounter captures the essence of the point. The teacher's role is to phrase particular learning objectives in such a way that the particular doorway will capture students' imaginations and cause them to pass through it into a realm of creative possibilities:

> It is an image to help teachers choose music from which to teach, and create lessons that will maximize student understanding of the music and of the ways in which music operates. (Wiggins 2003)

So at one level within this metaphor there is an element of strong classification. But the nature of the creative process allows them to make vital choices about the essence or materials of music:

> The very nature of the creative process necessitates the manipulation of all the elements of music. Students cannot create a work without making decisions about virtually all of the structural elements. (Wiggins 2003)

The Use of ICT will Redefine What Counts as Music

Wiggins' beliefs about the careful selection of musical content and diligent planning are central to effective music teaching. Certain models of classification may, however, need redefining as teachers and students discover the creative potential of new technologies. While it may be perfectly legitimate to use ICT to reinforce existing musical styles and practices, in the intrinsic model students can use ICT to produce music of an eclectic style, defined not by their teacher's pre-classification of musical content but by their own investigation, selection and manipulation of new sound sources. As far as practically and theoretically possible, they can be given the opportunity to explore new musical landscapes through an ICT compositional doorway.

The Efficiency of ICT

ICT allows students to generate, explore and refine musical ideas with a speed of discovery beyond that achieved by conventional approaches. This is undoubtedly a motivational factor for students. They will almost certainly produce too many musical ideas and will have to be taught the value of editing, synthesizing and combining ideas – an important part of many composers' compositional processes (Savage 2005). Breadth of discovery needs to be matched by a depth of enquiry and engagement with sound materials.

ICT will Demand New Approaches to Assessment

One of the largest changes brought about through the use of ICT in the music classroom is in relation to the procedures for assessing students' work. The key point relates to classification and framing. The use of different pieces of ICT can compensate for what might seem like weak framing or classification from a teaching perspective. A vital part of assessment involves recognizing the classificatory or framing effect of ICT on the students' creative work and discussing with the students its effect on their working process with the piece of technology (Savage 2002).

ICT Helps in the Teaching of Music in an Integrated Way

Finally, the use of ICT should facilitate a teaching style that allows for the integration of the curriculum elements of performing, composing, listening and appraising. This is the most important theme in the National Curriculum documentation. Central to this is the demand to 'ensure that listening, applying knowledge and understanding, are developed through the interrelated skills of performing, composing and appraising' (DfEE 1999, p. 20).

Conclusion

> The development of computer technology has suggested to many that the computer can become a technology of unparalleled importance in the arts. What does such a vision imply for the creation of school programmes in the arts? What does a computer allow students to do with images that other technologies don't, and what might such a resource mean for the development of cognitive skills? (Eisner 2002, p. 41)

Eisner's challenge to art educators translates to music educators with equal relevance and force. Yet, although important decisions will need to be made about the future purpose and practice of music education in light of this technological revolution, for many the focus, until now, has been elsewhere:

> For many schools the main focus of activity following installation of networked ICT infrastructure was on teaching ICT skills. Cross-curricular use of ICT is difficult for secondary schools to achieve because ICT has traditionally been a specialist subject for GCSE. *A major shift in culture and established practice is involved in the introduction of ICT within subject teaching.* [my italics] (DfES 2002, p. 19)

Eisner's comments about the potential and challenge of the computer come in a chapter entitled 'Visions and Versions of Arts Education', which seeks to describe some of the common aims and content of arts education programmes prevalent in schools today. While he states clearly that there is no 'sacrosanct vision of the aims of arts education' and that 'examples of diversity abound' (Eisner 2002, p. 25), his summary of the five principles of arts education can be useful starting points to explain the application of new technologies to the music curriculum.

1. Music education should give pride of place to what is distinctive about contemporary musical practice

The use of ICT, in both intrinsic and extrinsic models, addresses a range of musical and technological skills that widen the opportunity for students to engage in music beyond music education's traditional approaches. For this reason, if nothing else, ICT should continue to have a central role in music teaching and learning.

2. Music education programmes should try to foster the growth of musical intelligence

Ability in art is assigned to talent; ability in 'intellectual subjects' is assigned to intelligence. (Eisner 2002, p. 43)

Intelligence takes many forms. The use of ICT exhibits particular forms of artistic and musical intelligence within the cultural context of the classroom. Intelligent evaluation and reflection on the process of creation should be a common theme in all musical work with new technologies. Intelligence belongs to music just as much as to any other part of the curriculum.

3. Music education programmes with ICT should teach how to create and experience the aesthetic

Eisner's suggestion is that within curriculum development the arts 'can, and probably in most situations will, be addressed in an integrated fashion' (Eisner 2002, pp. 43-4). Sound2Picture showed that sound design allowed students to jointly consider aspects of visual and musical significance and investigate their relationships within the digital medium. Within the digital medium, students have another opportunity to create and experience the aesthetic if music teachers are willing to broaden their approaches and, on occasions, work through an integrated model of arts education.

4. Music education should help students recognize what is personal, distinctive and unique about themselves

Personal responses are central to all arts education. A student's personal response to a piece of music, a song or a movie is the starting point for their own creative work. Creating educational situations in which students can imbue their personality, character and creative spirit is the key for teachers. The curriculum framework of creative ideas for the use of ICT in the classroom is as important, if not more, than the pieces of technology themselves. ICT is just another creative tool (albeit a very powerful one).

5. Art education programmes should make special efforts to enable students to secure aesthetic forms of experience in everyday life

Each subject studied in schools affords the student a distinctive window or frame through which the world can be viewed. (Eisner 2002, p. 45)

Eisner draws attention to the larger issues that arts educators hope to address, namely facilitating in students an appreciation of the wider world as a rich source of meaning when viewed within an aesthetic frame of reference. While this is a lofty ideal to which no single curriculum resource or teaching approach can claim exclusive rights, the creative use of ICT can help educators achieve this end.

Finally, there is a strong argument for teachers to respond to the natural pull of digital technologies towards the digital arts (Sefton-Green 1999). The creative use of ICT can, and perhaps should, resituate musical practices within the world of the digital arts. An integrated arts or multimedia approach to musical performance and composition with ICT may engage and motivate students more successfully, facilitate the development of their creative skills and bring about a greater sense of personal aesthetic awareness. Perhaps this is where the future of music education lies?

References

Bernstein, B. (1971), 'On the Classification and Framing of Knowledge', in M. Young (ed.), *Knowledge and Control*. London: Macmillan.

Cage, J. (1968), *Silence*. Cambridge, Massachusetts: M.I.T.

Chanan, M. (1994), *Musica Practica: The social practice of Western Music from Gregorian Chant to Postmodernism*. London and New York: Verso.

Department for Education and Employment (DfEE) (1999), *National Curriculum for Music 2000*. London: DfEE.

Department for Education and Skills (DfES) (2002), *Pupils' and Teachers' Perceptions of ICT in the Home, School and Community*. London: DfES.

Eisner, E. (2002), *The Arts and the Creation of Mind*. New Haven and London: Yale University Press.

Green, L. (2001), *How Popular Musicians Learn: A way ahead for music education*. Aldershot: Ashgate.

Lamont, A. (2002), 'Musical identities and the school environment', in R. Macdonald, D. Hargreaves and D. Miell (eds), *Musical Identities*. Oxford: Oxford University Press, pp. 41–59.

QCA (2005), *Futures: Meeting the challenge (Forces for change, point 2)*. Available at www.qca.org.uk.

Savage, J. (2002), 'New models for creative practice with music technologies', in NAME, *How Are You Doing? Learning and assessment in music*. Matlock: NAME, pp. 38–44.

Savage, J. (2005), 'Working towards a theory for music technologies in the classroom: How students engage with and organize sounds with new technologies'. *British Journal of Music Education*, 22(2), 167–80.

Savage, J. and Challis, M. (2001), 'Dunwich revisited: collaborative composition and performance with new technologies'. *British Journal of Music Education*, 18(2), 139–49.

Savage, J. and Challis, M. (2002), 'A digital arts curriculum? Practical ways forward'. *Music Education Research*, 4(1), 7–24.

Sefton-Green, J. (ed.) (1999), *Young People, Creativity and New Technologies: The challenge of the digital arts*. London: Routledge.

Swanwick, K. (1988), *Music, Mind and Education*. London: Routledge.

Swanwick, K. (1999), *Teaching Music Musically*. London: Routledge.

Teacher Training Agency (TTA) (1999a), *The Use of Information and Communications Technology in Subject Teaching: Identification of training needs – Secondary Music*. London: TTA.

Teacher Training Agency (TTA) (1999b), *Using Information and Communications Technology to meet teaching objectives in secondary music*. London: TTA.

Théberge, P. (1997), *Any Sound You Can Imagine: Making music/consuming technology*. London: Wesleyan University Press.

UCan.tv (2006) www.ucan.tv. Accessed on 17 November 2006.

Wiggins, J. (2003), Handout from the East Anglian Researchers (EARS) meeting at Homerton College, University of Cambridge.

Wishart, T. (1996), *On Sonic Art*. Amsterdam: Harwood Academic Publishers.

Young, M. (ed.) (1971), *Knowledge and Control*. London: Collier-Macmillan.

Appendix A: Dunwich Revisited Sound Generation Sheet

You have a number of things to help you with this stage of the project:

- your notes from the listening lesson and subsequent homework
- the sheet of notes we compiled from our class discussion
- your memory of Mr Challis' composition with its sounds, atmospheres and emotions
- the sound ideas sheet summarizing the results of the homework task
- the thoughts and ideas of other classes doing the project on the display boards.

Your task is to begin to create appropriate sounds that could be used in the Dunwich piece to be performed at Snape on 7 March 2000. Basically, we need two types of sounds:

a. sounds which can be used to represent the natural setting of Dunwich (prior to the town being established and after its gradual erosion)
b. sound which can be used to represent the hustle and bustle of a busy town, social interaction, etc.

We have got four sources from which these sounds can be generated:

- traditional instruments
- voices
- recorded sounds from different environments
- computer-generated sounds.

In your groups:

1. Choose an idea for which you would like to try and produce a sound.
2. Experiment with your chosen sound sources (instruments, voices, samples, etc) and with any technology (sound processors, keyboard, computer, etc).
3. Don't worry too much about the length of your sounds – short sounds can be repeated, longer sounds can be reduced in length if necessary.
4. When you are happy with the sounds being produced, document your work on a 'Planning Sheet' contained in the box at the front of the classroom. Fill this in very carefully, answering all the questions on the sheet in plenty of detail.
5. Be sure to think about the atmosphere, mood and emotion of the sounds being produced. There should always be a purpose for the type of sounds being produced.
6. Record your sounds on the Minidisc player and give the track a title (ask Mr Savage for help if required). Fill in the title of the track on the 'Planning Sheet' (this is vitally important).

Chapter 13

New Forms of Composition, and How to Enable Them

Ambrose Field

Today, we are at a point in musical history unlike any other. More people than ever before have access to tools which can record, shape and structure music. The humble personal computer has reached a state of maturity, and even the most basic systems are now capable of audio manipulation. There are probably more personal computers in the contemporary musical world than pianos – yet what are the consequences of all these developments for the teaching of music technology?

This chapter seeks to identify how *access* to technology has caused an explosion of innovation in music. Since this innovation has been rooted in contemporary cultural developments, teaching and informing new generations of young people about the achievements of their own culture might enable music to become more relevant to greater numbers of people. The chapter will assess several creative strategies which have made computers truly unique tools for musicians, rather than speed-enhanced duplications of existing technologies or methods. Finally, it will propose that consideration needs to be given to changing the way we currently teach and examine music technology.

Electronic music, an area which currently depends largely on the instrumental capabilities of computer systems, has a chequered history. Due to high costs, initial experiments in the 1950s and 1960s using technology to process sound and re-structure music were conducted in radio studios and institutions that already possessed significant resources. Inaccessibility limited the deployment of technology, since composers wishing to explore studio resources would need to have obtained a residency from an institution. It is easy to see why, given these costs and logistical complications, electronic music has not played a greater part in traditional school music teaching.

There is, however, no longer the need to hire a studio and the 'cost-of-entry' to electronic music is the price of a computer. Furthermore, many exciting new musics depend on technology for their existence. Yet, as increasing numbers of people gain access to computer music systems, both inside and outside of school, we need to formulate an educational methodology that can assist them in taking their new art form further.

The chapter that follows argues that music technology should first and foremost be about the music that it enables, and that strategies which inspire creativity should be sought in preference to a skills-oriented curriculum. Although a degree of techno-logical literacy is undoubtedly required, this chapter proposes that it is not the skills themselves that are important, but how they are acquired. It is proposed that the acquisition of skills should come, in the first instance, through their practical application on musical projects and that curricula should be changed to reflect a more individually creative approach.

What Can Be Accomplished with Music Technology?

In the past, computers and the electronic music studio have allowed musicians to be both composers and listeners. Performance as an activity in music technology tended to involve replaying pre-composed tapes over loudspeakers to an audience, prompting Boulez (1986, p. 201) to comment that listening to electronic music in concert bore a 'resemblance to a crematorium ceremony, and [that he found] the absence of action a rehibitory vice'. Yet, due to the computing power revolution of recent years, enabling the real-time production of digital music, people with computers can now be performers too. With our National Curriculum placing much emphasis on *performing*, we need to urgently address the problem of what constitutes 'performance' with computers.

The basis for any performance lies in the delivery of musical raw material modified by human interpretation. As such, computing systems can excel in performance environments, enabling control over a work to be exerted on a wide variety of levels ranging from microscale changes in an internal sonic parameter through to real-time shifts in the broader structuring of a work. The basic strategies for live performance with electro-acoustic media are reviewed by McNutt (2003, pp. 297-304), who is careful to point out that the possible solutions to contemporary performance problems are musical, rather than technological.

Currently, the main issue is that the physical activity of performing with computers doesn't *look like* performance in the sense that instrumental or vocal performance does. Although the performance activities may be occurring, if we can't see them, it is easy to question their existence. Kohut (1985, pp.108-9) points out that musical performance is as much about theatre and personal *expression* as it is about musicality. With laptops, it is difficult to establish if there is any theatre going on behind an upwardly-angled open lid. Should this be a problem? As technology has re-defined the role and capabilities of musical presentation, two types of technological performer have emerged: those who stick to purist musical values and see no need to provide technology for visual benefit (a new methodology), and those who go to great lengths to *show* the audience their working (an approach based on existing notions of performance practice). Skilled electronic music performers tend to create innovative answers.

The artist MR76ix (Skam Records 2005) uses a highly visible array of performance technology, ranging from keyboards to live control surfaces. Freeform (Skam Records 2005) employs a huge range of live control systems, currently including sound modifying technologies based on sensing the position of his hands. He also projects a video presentation based on the images captured by a camera attached to his hands. Ramon Bauer (Mego 2005) employs specially created real-time video graphic displays by Tina Frank (Mego 2005) which work alongside his music. Although we can see Bauer working away in concert, we are given a visual presentation that directly complements the dynamic nature of his music. There is, however, much development work still to be done in providing musicians with a control system that is flexible enough to cope with individual needs, yet applicable enough to be learned, played and mastered.

It would be easy to brand the whole studio as an 'instrument in its own right', instantly legitimising all performance activities that make use of it. Yet, studios, and computers have many functions, some of which are not at all instrumental in nature. Working in a studio will not guarantee sounds that are 'musical'; this term is aesthetically dependent. Out of school, students often generate, organize and manipulate sound as a leisure activity on their own personal computers. But, without knowledge of what structures might be possible, or how others have defined (and broken) forms and genres, creativity can rapidly become self-indulgence.

Technology is now apparent in many aspects of our musical lives, from the creation of music through to its performance and distribution. To help shape the future, educators need to ask what it is that technology can *add* to a musical experience? In contemporary society, technology typically has two roles: it can either help us do *better* what we already do, or it can provide ways of doing new things that *were not possible* before. The former role, largely propagated by post-war optimism for a new world where our daily lives would be free from burden, is certainly appealing – but why is this role so widely applied to the teaching of music technology?

The answer is that innovative thinking is not always necessary to duplicate a process from the past. McLuhan (McLuhan and Fiore 1996, p. 74) shows us that we 'view the future through the rear-view window of the past'. The realizations of orchestral material from a midi box are, without doubt, extremely useful functions of music technology, but they duplicate existing methods for accomplishing the same ends and concern the *mechanics*, rather than the *content*, of music production. While nobody would argue that computers have brought a level of professionalism to classroom notation, it is time to look beyond the useful functions of technology as a time-saving replacement for historical processes to what technology can offer that was not possible to achieve before its inception. The computer is not just a *facilitator*: it is a tool for *enabling* new forms of creativity.

Teaching music technology from a facilitative angle has the additional consequence that computers can be perceived by students as an 'easier' form of music making than playing a traditional instrument. After all, on computers ideas can be tried out in a fraction of the time that it would take to assemble a group of performers with the necessary skills to play the piece accurately. While it may be faster to achieve initial results from computers rather than humans, computers are not substitute acoustic instruments and require a different kind of performance technique. Although a limited level of musical gratification may be achieved in the short term, the longer-term consequences of 'computer as facilitator' are inherently damaging to the perception of music as a discipline in itself. Why should anyone ultimately wish to learn a simulation of music, rather than how to participate in 'real' music-making activities? The speed of musical conception to realization which computers bring can be inspiring (and an important part of the creative process itself), but it is vital that the process of musical creation still has some outside reference and does not become a totally introverted experience. Class peer-evaluation of compositional work in music technology composition assignments becomes immensely important, taking the place of a type of feedback which would normally be received from performers.

In contemporary times, it is difficult to make colloquial stylistic distinctions between the 'popular' and the 'classical', since these connotations of value are no longer tenable: composers of 'classical' works are as likely to incorporate specific devices and musical rhetoric into their structures to sell their product as popular music song writers. At the same time, it is important to recognize that popular music has nurtured new genres which thrive on innovation: for example, the rise of the record label Warp in the 1990s has demonstrated that there is a commercial reality for challenging electronic music which does not conform to accepted norms of structure and sound.

Yet, against a backdrop of such innovation, our music technology GCE A-Level syllabuses still require students to use music technology to 'interpret' Western classical art music. The Edexcel (2003, p. 21) *Music Technology* A-level syllabus currently states:

> Area 2: This area of study is designed to help students gain a broad overview of music from the Western classical tradition ... Students will also recognize ways in which music technology has been used to interpret music from the Western classical tradition, and they will use sequencing or recording to interpret a piece of their own as well as arranging a piece for different forces. This can be achieved through the study of the following suggested works and extracts. JS Bach: Prelude and Fugue No 42, Beethoven [etc.]

This raises serious questions: what, for example, would the musical value of Debussy be when re-orchestrated (interpreted) on electronic virtual instruments? We don't need newly transcribed scores for the 1812 overture, nor does it require re-arranging. Bach doesn't want to be 'switched on' (anymore). Such examples serve to demonstrate that if we are setting and assessing tasks similar to this for music technology students, we are looking only at technological skills and not necessarily musical understanding. Furthermore, the larger, more problematic issues of cultural relevance and the incompatibility of this style of syllabus with some of the most unique and creative uses of technology employed by composers today, need to be given consideration.

The number of students opting to study music in school is in decline, as demonstrated by Lamont *et al.* (2003, pp. 229–41). They analyse this situation and ask: why it is that our in-school experience of music is becoming out of sync with the realities of the musical world outside of school? Although important in all aspects of music making, this question is particularly incisive in the world of music technology. A large portion of music listened to (and produced) by young people is made with music technology – so why is it not studied?

The argument that follows is multi-faceted. First, the accessibility of technology has changed the expectations of what a music education might be. Technology, for many, has now provided access to the musical processes of organizing, manipulating, editing and auditioning materials, at a price which is vastly lower than it was in previous generations. With easy assess to the means to manipulate sonic material itself, newcomers to composition face the primary challenge of *what to do with their own materials* rather than *how to go about making music*. Due to the small 'time-to-feedback' mentioned earlier in this chapter, technology actively encourages experimentation. This promotes the view that it *is possible* to make interesting music by trying out as many possibilities and combinations of material as time allows. Coupled with the desire of young people to be experimental, it is only natural for them to feel considerably empowered by this experience. This begs the question that if young people's relationship with technology is in some way inherently educational, then what role does music technology have in school?

Cain (2004, pp. 215–21) demonstrates clearly that teaching music technology techniques would largely duplicate what students know already from private experience, since many have access to relevant software at home. Instead, we perhaps need to help students develop the materials that they already have on their personal computers, and assist them in knowing the context their work inhabits so that their own forms of musical enquiry can become more focused.

Also it is important that music technology is deployed as a discipline in its own right, and not simply as a route to understanding other aspects of music making, or a bisected combination of science and art. In order to achieve this, it is essential to look carefully at the *music* in music technology. In the last ten years or so, a whole repertoire of musical activity has grown up which would not have been possible without access to technology. It will be argued here that this repertoire should be addressed directly, rather than attempting to apply music technology to process historical musics. This will have the effect of creating less *cultural distance* between the student and the syllabus and will satisfy some of the criteria that Lamont *et al.* identify as being necessary to stimulate greater interest in class music (2003).

As a means to tackle the problem of contemporary repertoire, this chapter offers a few starting points. It should be noted that these examples are just that – examples. The discipline of music technology is too young to identify iconic figures just yet, though we can highlight key contributors of the day. By taking a systemized approach based on views of how technology has enabled the innovation of selected musical parameters, it is hoped that educators will look for musical advances that have been brought about by technology and, importantly, be open to change. The stability of historical musical genres (Baroque, Classical, Neoclassical, etc.) has dissolved today, in that *change* (as a process) is more important in defining musical style than stability. This is, perhaps, a consequence of the ease of and speed in which technology can cross genre boundaries, coupled with a contemporary culture where hybridized thinking (Bryman 2004, p. 57) is the norm.

Seven Strategies to Enable Creativity, Based on Contemporary Repertoire

The argument thus far has been for the re-establishment of *music technology* as a discipline centred around music. The section that follows provides some strategies for analyzing the repertoire of musicians working with technology, exemplifying ideas resulting from new ways of thinking about the role of technology. It is hoped that these will serve as starting points for creative enquiry and individual work.

Creative Strategy One: Exploring Timescale with Technology

Computer systems have no intrinsic concept of duration, other than perhaps an inner awareness of the capacity of their storage systems. Time on a computer does not flow at 30 inches per second, as it did on analogue tape. It is difficult to obtain a *single* viewpoint of time passing since, with contemporary software, there is the facility to zoom-in to the microscale details of a composition or to view an entire work, both in the same visual space.

This freedom to work at any end of the temporal territory with equal attention to detail is perhaps a relatively new experience in musical history – traditionally the musical parameters tend to change relative to the timescale on which you view a work. If, for example, one looks at a piece on a longer-term scale, one can gain a view of structure, tonality (non-tonality or atonality) and their corresponding articulative processes. Looking on a shorter-term scale, the constituent parts of these processes, the individual notes, harmonies, rows, clusters or rhythms (depending, of course on genre) can be observed. Although there is nothing to stop composers employing a hierarchical view of their music structures in computer music, musicians can now experience a new structural freedom with the possibility of seeing and developing materials on a variety of timescales simultaneously and zooming between them at the touch of a button.

As a result, musical elements that once had a notion of timescale factored into them become less defining in terms of how a work can be organized. Consequently, composers working with computers can make changes normally reserved for the microscale (such as the millisecond alteration of a duration) to a whole work. Short-term musical processes, such as harmonic, timbral or rhythmic evolution, are now free from their traditional (human) timescale implications. A computer can make the smooth transition of pitch over a semitone last three hours: a string player might have considerable difficulty with this task which would be second nature on a short timescale. Rhythm becomes timbre if speeded-up to extreme rates (as originally compositionally experimented with by Stockhausen (see Ernst 1977, pp. 30–4), and even something as benign as reverberation or room ambience can become an interesting texture when original durations are modified.

The music of Richard Chartier (12k/Line Records 2005) explores these timescale parameters. In addition to issuing recordings, Chartier performs his pieces live, currently from a laptop computer system. His work is built using looped and extended sounds (largely free of associations of 1960's early loop experiments, such as phasing, flanging and other looping cliché), which have intricately crafted internal motion within the sounds themselves. The longer, extended timescale of works such as *Archival 1992* (12k/Line) have the interesting effect of allowing listeners to focus on the smallest details in the sounds. Chartier is keen to avoid the formulaic in music, and has striven for a fresh, new soundworld:

> particular aspects of the work get translated into formulas ... You add your sounds as the variables into a formula and boom – you have your drum and bass track, you have your microsound track, you have your indie rock track. It just becomes more evident in electronic music because of the speed in which work can be made with the use of certain software. (Chartier, in Sherburne 2002, p. 175)

Computers have changed our views of musical time: this creative strategy asks how can ideas of timescale be explored further with technology?

Creative Strategy Two: Computers Bring Access to Sounds of the World

Computers are not partisan to musical material, and display a Cagean openness to the types of sound sources which can be manipulated. The electronic manipulation of environmental sound is, of course, nothing new: it was Pierre Schaeffer's desire to find a new legitimacy for the genre of Musique Concrete which he discovered (Schaeffer 1966). In creating the lowest common denominator or unit building block of sound, the 'sonic object' (Schaeffer 1966, p. 417), Schaeffer had effectively invented the electro-acoustic equivalent of the note. Furthermore, his 'reduced listening' strategy (Schaeffer 1966, p. 113), asking composers and listeners to free themselves from any extra-musical implications a sound might have and concentrate their attention on timbre, presents an unfortunate problem, since it is precisely for their contextual reasons that using outside, real-world sounds in musical compositions can be so attractive.

Composer Francisco Lopez (2006) employs detailed outside recordings in his music, often presenting them clearly to an audience without additional sonic complication from materials which are contextually unrelated (i.e. he has considerable compositional discipline in selecting his raw materials). Lopez unites this purist approach with an element of Schaeffer's original thinking, asking the audience to listen to his work blindfolded so that the listener's attention can remain focused on the sonic experience, and the imagination can be set free.

Rather than requiring an audience to listen to the internal rhythms already present in an environmental recording, Mira Calix (Warp) has skilfully used technology to reprocess her sounds so that they fit her own rhythmic and structural ideas. Sounds similar to those made by insects form an enveloping texture in the track 'flicker' (Calix, 2003). They provide the forward motion for the piece, yet fit precisely with their surrounding materials.

The editing facilities available to composers on computer systems that permit the re-ordering of materials also permit a great degree of selectivity in the choice of pitch and timbre. The consequence of this technical openness is that an aesthetic of infinite sonic possibilities is easy to imagine. Yet, although the idea of computers bringing access to a limitless palette of sound is attractive, it is utopian at the present time. Once a sound is processed by a computer, it will inevitably start to take on the sound of that process itself. There will come a point where, instead of sounding unique, a sound will only retain the characteristics of the software which processed it. While this process can be used creatively to make pieces, there are still only a finite number of ways to process sound on a computer. It is not surprising that some of the most original compositional strategies mentioned in this chapter are distinctive due to their highly controlled and often deliberately constrained application of computer processes.

Strategy two asks whether sounds need to remain true to their sources, and how we might compositionally organize materials recorded from the outside world.

Creative Strategy Three: Any Input Stimulus Can Create a Composition

To a computer, the world is simply data where a compositional technique looks no different internally to a digital phone book. Just as computers show no sonic aesthetics, so they are indifferent to the stimuli that can be used to create musical works. Given computers in a networked world, it is possible to use information from anywhere as a starting point for a piece, or in some cases even its complete realization. The decision as to where the line lies between assigning responsibility to the computer for the deployment of a particular process and retaining human control is a personal one for composers.

To illustrate by way of example, *Gullibloon* (Gullibloon 2005), a project set up by members of the band Farmersmanual (Mego 2005), takes data directly from real-time internet traffic then maps it directly onto a sonic composition. The world's datastream passing by their computers is responsible for the time-order of sonic events, as well as the timbres generated. Importantly, their publicity information contains no particular *aesthetic* implications about their work: this is a process of sonification to which you are required to bring your own perception. Farmersmanual are careful not to fall into the trap of believing that external stimuli have directly equivalent musical counter-parts. There is, for instance, no musical form that directly represents internet data: we can only make a musical form that is a metaphor for internet data. In this way, the construction of metaphors and mappings for non-musical stimuli in algorithmic composition is little different from organizing abstract and creative thoughts about a work in 'free' composition. No composition can truly be 'free' as there are always limits and constraints which define style and genre. The difference in the compositional process is the degree of formality with which the ideas are encoded.

Strategy three asks educators to explore the processes by which external, extramusical stimuli may be mapped directly into the musical domain using technological systems.

Creative Strategy Four: Music Can Comment on Life, and Other Music

Computers allow composers to incorporate musical material from secondary sources with unprecedented ease. As predicted by Roland Barthes' text *Image–Music–text* (1977), technological empowerment has been accompanied by a change in the value placed on authorship in society – from the iconic to the nearly irrelevant. Importantly, Bathes also suggested that in contemporary society the perceivers of an art form have become the authors. This idea in itself has had considerable artistic implications. John Oswald's *Plunderphonics* album, instantly banned for copyright violation, was perhaps one of the first works by composers who produce new compositions out of existing recorded material (discussed by Cutler in Emmerson 2000, p. 87). There is probably not a single original note of Oswald's in his entire *Plunderphonics*. The album, however, is constructed in an original way which shows the previously existing material in a new light (a process of *transcontextuality* (Field, in Emmerson 2000, p. 50) is taking place). Stravinsky's *Rite of Spring* is adapted in contemporary Hollywood film-score style to contain only the most dynamically active and percussive passages, and Beethoven's 7th *Symphony* in Oswald's treatment sounds like the introduction to a TV western. James Brown (perhaps one of the most sampled artists himself) is given space in a track where all his personal mannerisms and asides come to the fore as musical features.

Oswald's work was ahead of its technological time, although many of the works might be sonically different if they were realized on today's systems. *People Like Us (PLU)* (2006) has updated Oswald's original ideas from the 1970s and given the idea of 'sampling' a new context. Instead of using contemporary controversial and iconic music, *PLU* revisits the public information films and lounge music of the 1950s and 1960s, intercutting original material in such a way that the end result has considerable meaning for today's society in the mind of the perceiver. *PLU* presents the whole process of making music with computers in the film *We Edit Life*, where a lab-designed robot is assigned musicality, and even the accompanying textures loop round in an 'imperfect' way, creating stutters and glitches at the points where the music has been edited.

Looking at the transference of ideas on a higher level, this contemporary freedom to access music from different traditions, genres and parts of the world has resulted in the construction of new musical styles which utilize elements from other, pre-existing styles as their building blocks. Importantly, this practice is different from the idea of *fusion* in jazz, since the constituent styles are not normally presented to the audience as discrete parts which have been 'fused together'. Instead, they take on a new meaning as a result of the new musical surroundings into which they are injected. Computer technology has assisted composers in making this integration possible, due to the precision with which the raw materials of a piece can be forged. Talvin Singh (1998), for example, uses instruments and the gestural language of Raga forms from Indian music within a drum and bass context, yet the result is neither Indian nor drum and bass but rather something entirely new.

The educational power of this type of *transcontextual* thinking is that it makes local culture available as a source of creative inspiration. This could prove profitable in creating compositional assignments which reflect and respect the environment of students, yet stretch their thinking in new directions. It should be noted, however, that this type of creativity does not, and should not, attempt to use local cultural values simply as a 'way in' to some other music or value system. Transcontextual thinking presents each idea as unique, allowing new forms to result from the sum of the parts.

Almost as Marshall McLuhan predicted (McLuhan and Fiore 1997), society has become increasingly globalized and as a result, probably due to the human need to establish a definite identity, localized musical genres and attitudes have begun to emerge. With musical style evolving on a local level, and the ability of individuals to own recording labels (due to the dramatic decrease in distribution and duplication costs), contemporary music exhibits more stylistic diversity than ever before. The artists presented here have accomplished their borrowings in a manner that shows considerable originality. It may be the case that as new material is generated, there will always be someone, enabled by a computer, who wishes to comment upon it. It is the purpose of strategy four to ask: without plagiarism, is it possible to make something new out of something old (or even, vice versa!). Can technology assist us in defining our personal space in 'life'?

Creative Strategy Five: Computers Don't Have to Make Things Sound Perfect

Much commercial sound software has an in-built quest of progress towards a future ideal of perfection. The majority of computer sound-processing tools – such as equalizers, compressors and noise-reduction systems – have at their core the idea that the user employs them in order to obtain 'better' results. But what is 'better'?

Only our ears, and the cannon of music to which we have been exposed, can define a reference point; and it is precisely for this reason that new forms of music have grown up to challenge accepted perceptions of a future digital nirvana by using sounds which technology is supposed to produce 'badly' or whilst failing. In reality, these types of sounds are now more commonly produced by custom sound-treatment software, where a degree of control can be exerted over the process of 'failure'. Destroy-Fx's (2005) free software 'Buffer Over-ride', for example, gives the impression of a problematically looped chunk of sound.

The term 'post-digital' music was coined by composer Kim Cascone (2000, p. 12), who has written extensively on music which leaves behind the aesthetics, structures and apparent perfection of contemporary technology. Moving quickly from its inception in 'glitch' music (Cascone 2000, p. 15) (a 'glitch' is the sound produced by digital-sampled sound missing out a step, causing a short error), post-digital music today is concerned with subverting the ideals of technology in the search for broader forms of artistic expression.

Post-digital ideas are explored by composers such as Merzbow (Mego 2005), who employs huge noise (not pitched) textures to create intricate soundscapes. Hegarty (2001, p. 193) is keen to stress that Merzbow is not simply being reactionary:

> But noise is not just 'good' to music's 'bad'. . . Noise is that which was excluded . . . the exclusion is not just one enacted by music, but by the development of systems and structures of meaning.

Effectively, post-digital music gives educators a means for enquiring into what can be accomplished with the musical material others reject, from the level of individual sounds (glitches, clicks) through to the manipulation of textures and material types traditionally deemed inappropriate for composition (such as pure 'white noise'). The result of this strategy is a practical understanding of the basic nature of musical structure; in particular, the way that structure does not necessarily have to be linked to the materials contained within it.

Strategy five asks: what can technology bring to the relationship between structure and material? What makes one sound usable, and another 'throwaway' or inappropriate?

Creative Strategy Six: New Approaches to Rhythm

So far, this chapter has looked at ways in which technology has been able to add new directions to musical creativity that were difficult to implement before modern computer technology arrived. Computer systems by virtue of their precise nature, should be effective as tools for rhythmic production and manipulation. Early systems, however, were a little too perfect: Roland's famous TR series of 'beat boxes' played in time on each and every beat. Although this is clearly not how real drummers perform (adding 'feel' by regularly delaying or, less commonly, advancing parts of the groove), a plethora of electronic music styles aimed initially at the club dance market began to evolve, making full use of their mechanistic precision. These aesthetic developments are well documented in Toop (1995).

In music, as in science, each action tends to have an equal and opposite reaction. With the freedom to design customized sound processing, and the ability to deploy rhythm programming over a timescale far longer than the two-bars (or 'sixteen steps') of the original drum machines of the 1980s and 1990s, composers in popular electronic music genres began to investigate what would happen if rhythm became unpredictable. Would the results still be danceable if percussion lines in 7/8, 9/8 or 5/4 time could be set against structures in a decidedly traditional 4/4 meter, and does it matter if they are not?

Autechre (Warp 2005) have been prime exponents in the exploration of the possibilities of computer-manipulated rhythmic structures. Their album *Draft 7.30* (Autechre 2003) contains few danceable (in a traditional sense) rhythms, yet the pieces presented have a rhythmic drive which still functions in a way analogous to the presence of a regular beat. This is achieved by grouping irregular rhythmic constructions systematically together (particularly evident in the track entitled 'IV VV IV VV VIII', accomplished in a manner of which Messiaen might have been proud). Autechre have also been effective in evolving the remit of percussion sounds: *Draft 7.30* presents a huge array of carefully processed materials, from the dry, post-digital distorted beats of track 3, entitled '6IE.CR', to sumptuously evocative harmonic textures in track 9, entitled 'V-proc'.

Strategy six asks whether technology can help us re-interpret the well-established quantities of rhythm and pitch. Can technology provide us with a new means of expressing these musical fundamentals?

Creative Strategy Seven: New Approaches to Form

New approaches to musical form have arisen out of the computers' ability to control time precisely (or 'precisely randomly') on very small timescales. To achieve a high degree of precision on a micro timescale, however, it is often necessary to take the compositional process of working with the material on the computer into an out-of-real state, devoting one's attention to small details of the music which can be tweaked and refined at will. The limits of real-time computer performance (and human thought) can be transcended by preparing sonic materials 'off-line', that is to say working on processed sounds which will be cast into their final form later in the compositional process. This approach sounds time-consuming, but it is also liberating in that even the smallest parameter of sound can be sculpted, re-arranged, re-positioned and controlled within a musical work. Composers have not been slow to adopt new ways of designing sonic detail, and this has had consequences for the larger-scale forms which they articulate.

Squarepusher's track 'Boneville Occident' on the album *Go plastic!* (Squarepusher 1998) starts by delivering a funky bass riff and a regular drum and bass percussion pattern. Then, as the music progresses, the structure begins to change: the bass riff is wildly extended and sonic micro-surgery is performed on the drums, dislocating beats, reprocessing their sounds, yet still preserving the rhythmic direction of the track. The piece is sectional in nature, each section re-designing the complexity presented by its predecessor. Importantly, the structure of this piece articulates its contents in a clear and direct way: Squarepusher almost invites his audience to make comparisons of the musical material that he has micro-edited by setting it against itself in a battle of sonic opposition. Squarepusher demonstrates that it is possible to solve one of the persistent problems in new music which is: will the public respond to complexity? Leigh Landy (1994) postulates that new music has become too complex, and that there is a need for new forms of education to assist people in understanding it. Squarepusher's work, on the other hand, presents the audience with a view of intricate inner-compositional workings stripped of the necessity for anyone to be equipped with historical or rhetorical baggage in order to feel part of the experience.

Strategy seven asks educators to think of the implications that technology has for the formal design of works. Why use forms from the past, when perhaps new forms are better suited in articulating new materials? Why do sounds have to repeat? Must all materials develop? Computer technology has removed a vale of imprecision from the compositional process: with appropriate time and material it should be possible to control structures and sounds so that they match our compositional intentions well.

Conclusion

This chapter has proposed seven strategies, based on the music people are currently making with technology, which could contribute to enabling creativity in our music technology teaching and syllabus design. These starting points are not age- or ability-specific. Nor do they constitute a repertoire prescription, since educators are encouraged to review alternative and new material that follows similar processes.

Rather, it is proposed that by making music technology more culturally relevant, avoiding dry technical skill teaching, and by demonstrating the musical achievements of young people currently working with technology, we can begin to rethink this subject area as a discipline in its own right.

References

Adobe (2005), http://www.adobe.com.

Barthes, R. (1977), *Image-Music-Text*. London: Fontana Press. (Trans. S. Heath).

Baudrillard, J. (1994), *Simulacra and Simulation*. Michigan: University of Michigan Press. (Trans. S. Glasser).

Born, G. (1995), *Rationalizing Culture*. Berkeley: University of California Press.

Boulez, P. (1986), *Orientations*. London: Faber and Faber.

Bryman, A. (2004), *The Disneyization of Society*. London: Sage.

Cain, T. (2004), 'Theory, technology, and the music curriculum'. *British Journal of Music Education*, 21(2), 215–21.

Cascone, K. (2000), 'The aesthetics of failure: "post-digital" tendencies in contemporary computer music'. *Computer Music Journal*, 24(4), 12–18.

Cloonan, M. (2005), 'What is Popular Music Studies? Some Observations'. *British Journal of Music Education*, 22(1), 77–93.

Cook, N. (1987), *A Guide to Musical Analysis*. London: Dent and Sons.

Destroy-FX (2005), http://www.smartelectronix.com/destroyfx.

Doornbusch, P. (2002), 'Composer's views on mapping in algorithmic composition'. *Organised Sound*, 7(2), 145–56.

Edexcel (2003), *Advanced Subsidiary GCE in Music Technology (8511), Advanced GCE in Music Technology (9511):* Specification. London: Edexcel Foundation.

Emmerson, S. (1994), 'Live' versus 'Real-time'. *Contemporary Music Review*, 10(2), 95–101.

Emmerson, S. (ed.) (2000), *Music, Electronic Media and Culture*. London: Ashgate.

Endrich, A. (1994), *Professional Computer Music System User Guide*. York: Composers Desktop Project.

Ernst, D. (1977), *The Evolution of Electronic Music*. New York: Schirmer.

Gullibloon (2005), https://gullibloon.org.

Hegarty, P. (2001), 'Merzbow and the end of natural sound'. *Organised Sound*, 6(3), 193–200

IRCAM (2005), http://www.ircam.fr/.

Kohut, D. (1985), *Musical Performance: Learning Theory and Pedagogy*. Englewood: Prentice-Hall.

Lamont, A., Hargreaves, D.J., Marshall A. and Tarrant, M. (2003), 'Young people's music in and out of school'. *British Journal of Music Education*, 20(3), 229–41.

Landy, L. (1994), ' "The something to hold on to factor" in timbral composition'. *Contemporary Music Review*, 10(2), 49–60.

Landy, L. (2001), 'From algorithmic jukeboxes to zero-time synthesis: A potential A–Z of music in tomorrow's world'. *Organised Sound*, 6(2), 91–96.

Lopez, F. (2006). http://www.franciscolopez.net/ Accessed in November 2006.

McLuhan, M. and Fiore, Q. (1996), *The Medium is the Massage*. San Francisco: Hardwired.

McLuhan, M. and Fiore, Q. (1997), *War and Piece in the Global Village*. San Francisco: Hardwired.

McNutt, E. (2003), 'Performing electroacoustic music: a wider view of interactivity'. *Organised Sound,* 8(3), 297–304.

Mego (2005), http://www.mego.at.

Mix (2005), *Professional Audio and Music Production,* 29(4). USA: Primedia Publishing.

Nattiez, J.-J. (1990), *Music and Discourse: Toward a semiology of music.* Princeton: Princeton University Press.

People Like Us (2006). http://www.peoplelikeus.org/. Accessed in November 2006.

Roads, C. (1996), *The Computer Music Tutorial.* Massachusetts: Massachusetts Institute of Technology Press.

Rodgers, T. (2003), 'On the process and aesthetics of sampling in electronic music production'. *Organised Sound,* 8(3), 313–20.

Schaeffer, P. (1966), *Traite des Objects Musicaux.* Paris: Editions du Seuil.

Sherburne, P. (2002), '12k, between 2 points'. *Organised Sound,* 7(1), 171–6.

Skam Records (2005), http://www.skam.co.uk.

Swanwick, K. (1979), *A Basis for Music Education.* London: Routledge.

Toop, D. (1995), *Ocean of Sound: Aether talk, ambient sound and imaginary worlds.* London: Serpent's Tail.

Warp Records (2005), http://www.warprecords.com.

Discography

Autechre (2003), *Draft 7.30.* Warp Records Ltd, London. WARPCD111.

Chartier, R. (2004), *Archival 1992.* 12k/Line records, New York.

Mira Calix (2003), *Skimskitta.* Warp Records Ltd, London. WARPCD104.

Squarepusher (1998), *Go plastic*! Warp Records Ltd, London. WARPCD 85.

Talvin Singh (1998), *Ok.* Island Record Ltd, London. CID8075.

Selected Free Internet Software Resources

These sites are correct at the time of publication: internet addresses may change.

www.kvr-audio.com/
kvr hosts a database of most new music software. You can search and select only the free items, of which there are many.

audacity.sourceforge.net/
Completely free multitrack sound editor and manipulator. For PC and Mac.

www.kreatives.org/kristal/
Kristal is a cubase-like sound editor and multitrack. For PC only, version 1 is free for education.

www.smartelectronix.com
Excellent vst plugins for sonic manipulation. Most are free, some are low cost.

Chapter 14

Music Education and Training: ICT, Innovation and Curriculum Reform

Richard Hodges

Introduction

This chapter examines the changing nature of the relationship between secondary school music and associated further and higher education opportunities. In particular, it focuses on recent years and study related to music technology.

The increasing importance of vocational study in post-16 education, fostered by the widening participation agenda, is beginning to have a profound effect on music curricula. The increased focus on skill-based activity with relevance to employability has encouraged a diversification of the music curriculum, alongside a rise in the number of further and higher education institutions providing programmes in popular music, music technology, music production and commercial music. Furthermore, ICT-based post-16 music education seems increasingly reliant on skill-based study with a clear focus on 'training'.

This is very different from more traditionally structured examination courses that place greater emphasis on conceptual understanding and application, consequently relating more directly to conventional notions of 'education' rather than 'training'. The challenge facing school educators is to consider the extent to which this diversification of post-16 music education will influence music study in secondary schools, particularly with respect to curriculum reform for 14–19 year olds.

Problems of Exclusivity

Although the advent of the GCSE examination in the 1980s presented an opportunity to encourage more students to study music in schools as an examination subject, Bray (2000) notes that students have preferred art and drama as creative option choices at GCSE over music. Given the comparatively low uptake in GCSE music, he postulates that music's inclusion as a national curriculum subject may be threatened in the future. Bray goes so far as to consider 'what is the point in including the subject [music] if 93 per cent do not want to carry on with it?' (2000, p. 88). The issue is that school-based music teaching should prepare a majority of young people to be able to engage with an examination course that appropriately reflects class-based achievement, recognizing that many young people do not have instrumental lessons and involvement with extra-curricular activity which might support academic class-based study.

Wright (2002) provides further evidence for the notion that music GCSE courses have been perceived as exclusive, rather than inclusive. She examined students' perceptions of the GCSE music examination and concluded that a majority of school students view music as elitist. Reasons given for this attitude are the dislocation of school-based study with the popular music industry and contemporary youth culture. It is disturbing for Wright to suggest that 'the battle is being lost in schools in this country to make music a subject in which the majority of 14-year-old students feel they have a chance to succeed' (2002, p. 228). More recently, the Qualifications and Curriculum Authority (QCA) have also commented on the low numbers taking GCSE music compared with other arts subjects (2004b, p. 22). Some slight increase is evident (from 8 per cent in 2001 to 9 per cent in 2003), but the issue highlighted by research identifies a number of school students committed to music activity who choose not to follow a qualification course. As educators, can we sustain a curriculum which sees examination music as a study for a small minority?

Beginnings of Reform

The publication of the *Final Report of the Working Group on 14–19 Reform* in October 2004 (DfES 2004) articulated a number of proposals for radical reform of educational provision for school and college students aged 14 to 19. The Working Group recognized the need to develop a new framework to 'make the system more transparent and easier to understand for learners, universities and employers' (p. 18). Consequently, at the core of the proposed amendments was an intention to arrive at an integrated qualification system that could potentially serve the needs of all school and college students and provide each student with a 'diploma' qualification reflective of their educational achievement. The Working Group proposed to link the Diploma levels to existing National Qualification Framework (NQF) levels.

From a musical perspective, any proposed reform of the music curriculum offers an opportunity for music educationalists to develop music curricula that are relevant to a majority of today's young people. The Working Group proposals recognized ICT as a core component in the template for the proposed diploma, and the development of ICT-based music curricula offers opportunities for delivering music education to many more school and college students. Music educationalists need to embrace such innovations, and develop a curriculum that does not continue to fail a majority of students who see accredited academic music study as inappropriate to their needs and aspirations.

Since coursework is seen as a major contributor to the assessment burden, the Working Group proposed that the coursework burden at GCSE should be reduced. Most importantly, they have questioned the very basis of the current structure, where academic 'stretch' is provided by additional subjects at the same level. For years differentiation has been determined by the comparison of overall quantitative and qualitative achievements of candidates. This notion is now challenged by recent proposals. The intention is to embrace 'broader programmes, more varied learning and assessment styles and the possibility of moving faster to a higher level, rather than simply doing more subjects' (DfES 2004, p. 86), although such simplification may impact negatively by marginalizing music study even further. Doing fewer subjects could mean that opportunities for music study may be reduced at both Level 2 and Level 3.

The curriculum 2000 reforms have successfully developed A-level music provision, providing programmes of study applicable to a broader cohort of students. The current AS and A-level music and music technology examinations allow some flexibility in configuring units with optional material. The QCA (2004a, p. 15) points to the encouraging 88 per cent rise in student numbers since the introduction of the AS and A-level music examination. Despite this success, there is a long-term question mark over the sustainability of the A-level music technology examination as it is deemed uneconomical. The examining group's proposal to withdraw the examination from the current portfolio has met with considerable disdain. One of the reasons given for rationalization is the QCA's insistence that every assessment area has to be tested at both AS and A2 (Mansell 2006). This reasoning seems somewhat short-sighted since the Working Group on 14–19 reform has suggested dropping the number of A-level units studied from six to four, thus reducing the 'weight and prescription of the assessment criteria' (DfES 2004, p. 89).

Clearly, there is recognition of perceived over-assessment as part of the current system, although this is concomitant with unitization of elements. One of the dangers of unitized curricula is that school and college students start to see education as a series of hurdles, and become more concerned with the next hurdle than attempting to embrace wider issues associated with broad-based education in a subject. There is often a reluctance to embrace aspects of study that may not be assessed and, consequentially, reducing the number of units may diminish engagement with certain aspects of a subject. Nevertheless, with 11.6 million unit entries in 2004 (GCSE, AS, A2, GNVQ, VCE, AEA) and £60 million spent on examiners and moderators that 'could be redirected to institutions' (DfES 2004, p. 86), there is a strong political will to rationalize the system.

Rationalization of Provision

The Tomlinson Working Group proposals were considered too radical to be implemented in full in the following White Paper of February 2005 (DfES 2005). Despite advice from Ofsted, the QCA and the Secondary Heads Association to adopt the Tomlinson proposals in full, the Government insisted on the retention of A-levels and GCSEs. Nevertheless, the White Paper established that significant rationalization of the qualification framework will be achieved over the next few years. A new GCSE diploma will be awarded to students who achieve 5 A*–C GCSEs that include English and mathematics. Furthermore, the plethora of vocational qualifications (over 3,500) will be replaced by 14 specialized diplomas – and the 'Creative and Media' Diploma in particular will embrace music elements as appropriate. Thus it is clear that the White Paper seeks to simplify the existing system and rationalize the diverse range of qualifications currently available to the 14–19 age group. Although existing qualifications remain in name, the White Paper continues the movement towards this objective of a single overarching qualifications framework, embracing both 'vocational' and 'academic' elements.

Within a unitized music curriculum, not all modules or units will necessarily share an equal balance of practical and theoretical work. In fact, it is possible that each unit will concentrate on a particular aspect of study. For instance, music performance is an activity in its own right and the current specifications (such as A-level, BTEC Nationals) recognize this. Separation of theory and practice in modular structures can, however, be problematic. An inherent danger in providing maximum flexibility for school and college students is that they may shy away from modules that they perceive as more difficult with respect to their previous levels of experience. More theoretical modules, for example, may be perceived as a greater intellectual challenge and less attractive than units largely concerned with practical activities supported by technological equipment.

In a market-driven system, if some units do not recruit well, managerial pressure will inevitably seek to abandon them in favour of more attractive modules that have greater economic viability. This can lead to an imbalance in the curriculum. Consequently, an integrated approach ensuring that practical activities are supported by appropriate theoretical underpinning is likely to be most successful in engaging school and college students. Further education provision has a long history of practical training, and music curricula in FE colleges have centred on an experiential model that integrates theory and practice, with considerable student involvement. The BTEC national provision is based on a unitary model, and each music-related qualification shares a common framework of core and optional units. Modular structures are now also widespread in higher education; and shared module provision, across related programmes of study, enhances efficient delivery while providing considerable flexibility.

One important issue concerning post-16 provision is that of funding. Hyland and Merrill (2003, p. 15) note that the significant growth in FE college provision since incorporation in 1992 has not been matched by commensurate increases in funding. Consequently, colleges have faced an economic imperative to maximize efficient delivery of the curriculum. Unitized delivery has allowed colleges to have the flexibility to combine groups of students pursuing the same unit or module as part of different academic awards, thereby significantly reducing costs. Schools have been slower to accept the economic reality of maximizing income in relation to costs.

Since it has long been recognized that small sixth-form classes are subsidized by other subjects, music educationalists need to ensure that more students embrace examinable music study. In discussing viability of group sizes in Year 10, for example, one senior manager of a town comprehensive acknowledged that it was necessary to run a music option with only three students, conceding the need to subsidize this from other areas (Davies *et al.* 2003, p. 490). Such subsidization of the curriculum is not sustainable in the longer term. Educationalists need to appreciate the economic advantage that flexible unitized music provision can offer in encouraging opportunities for innovative curriculum development in music education.

Widening and Increasing Participation

The government is vigorously driving forward a commitment to widening and increasing participation in the FE and HE sectors. One key aim of widening participation is to address the social inclusion agenda by increasing involvement from under-represented groups. Greater participation in education and training is seen by the government as essential to economic prosperity. The 14–19 curriculum should 'raise the levels of achievement of all young people in both general and vocational qualifications and increase participation in post-16 education and training, including higher education' (DfES 2002, p. 8). The 14–19 Education and Skills White Paper (DfES 2005, p. 4) articulates the intention 'to transform secondary and post-secondary education so that all young people achieve and continue in learning until at least the age of 18'. The White Paper makes it clear that despite a number of successful reforms to date, far-reaching change is needed to improve the UK's low international position in post-16 participation in education and training (DfES 2005, p. 10).

The government is nevertheless committed to strengthening the engagement of 14–

16 year olds in relevant skill-based vocationally-oriented training. An extra £10 million has been earmarked to increase the participation of 14–16 year olds in programmes of study that offer 'a significant work focus of up to two days a week, with intensive advice and support' (DfES 2006). The government also wishes to see greater participation in HE, and has established a target of 50 per cent of 18–30 year olds being able to enter higher education by 2010 (DfES 2002, p. 10).

It might be imagined that an increase in participation would generate more learners in the educational system and consequentially more growth for music study. The 14–19 Education and Skills White Paper (2005, p. 81) makes it clear, however, that no more teachers in schools are required for the proposed reforms since the next few years will see a significant reduction in the overall number of 14–19 year olds in England. Some additional teaching and support staff are predicted in the FE sector to match the growth of vocational courses. Denholm and Macleod (2003) have reviewed the potential for growth in post-16 participation in the learning and skills sector in line with changes in the demographic profile of the population. One interesting conclusion they draw from their analysis is that an improvement in GCSE performance might lead to increased participation at Levels 3 and 4, resulting in declining participation in vocational learning leading to a consequent rise in academic provision. This would have precisely the opposite effect to that desired by the policy-makers looking for increased participation in vocational provision.

ICT and Assessment Issues

Within the expansion of opportunity proposed by 14–19 curriculum reform, ICT is seen as a key element of curriculum provision. There is official recognition that ICT may eventually not need to be discretely specified as it becomes embedded in all curriculum subjects (DfES 2003a, p. 20). ICT should be an enabler, facilitator and support appropriate curriculum activities rather than dictating methods, approaches and learning experiences. Although this notion of subject-based embedding is now commonly accepted and understood, it could be argued that a curriculum activity such as music technology or music production, which has technology at its very core, is best served by embracing the technology wholeheartedly on its own terms. Our assessment processes need to recognize the importance of the technology itself and that those outcomes related to musical literacy or artistic-based musical composition activity may sometimes function as secondary objectives. A skills-based view acknowledges that demonstrating skills in using equipment may be as valid as any eventual artistic by-product resulting from the process of engagement.

This raises a fundamental assessment issue: are we seeking to validate the product of artistic endeavour or to evaluate the understanding revealed by the student in the pursuit of a recognized activity? If a student demonstrates understanding of a computer-based music recording system, and attempts to emulate a professional recording using a range of post-production processes in relation to mixing, do we evaluate the production qualities of the artefact, the musical quality of the artefact or the conceptual understanding of processes employed, with or without direct reference to the artefact itself?

Our position as assessor will have a bearing on the eventual mark or level descriptor we can ascribe to the artefact and/or conceptual process. With so many learning outcomes written in terms of an activity in unitized curricula, we need to be clear about our position in relation to music ICT. Does the technology support the musical activity, or does the musical activity support technological understanding, and precisely what skills and knowledge are being developed by the learning experience?

These questions address the issue of whether all curriculum-based music activity should have a musical outcome which must be viewed as the primary focus for assessment. With modularized study that encompasses diverse learning experiences, it may be appropriate to re-evaluate our conceptions of subject-based curricula.

Expansion of Subject Boundaries

A number of commentators have expressed doubts about the adoption of ICT in the curriculum, particularly with respect to notions of subject study. Loveless (2004), for example, has questioned the extent to which ICT impacts on the curriculum, particularly with respect to subject domains. ICT may serve as a unifying factor in curriculum design, bringing together discrete subject areas, but how will that impact on organization and delivery in subject-specific, school-based learning environments?

Following on from a research project with teachers exploring multimedia software in two schools, Ellis and Long (2004) have identified three potential issues with respect to multimedia applications that inhibit the exploitation of ICT. First, there appears to be a disjunction between the practices of school and popular culture. This is apparent in much of the academic study of music in schools, which seems remote from the social and cultural experiences of children. Secondly, and most importantly, the discrete subject organization of secondary school subject provision does not encourage integrated multimodal work. With an academic curriculum linked to examinations which are subject-based, such structural constraints are inevitable. Thirdly, conceptions of subject-based study are fixed within subject boundaries 'rather than evolving in response to lived experience' (Loveless 2004, p. 7). ICT (and IT before it) has always struggled conceptually for a place in the curriculum. Should it be taught as a discrete entity in an integrated manner, or embedded within the educational experience of subject-based study? Obviously, subject-based study best serves the needs of the students with respect to support from subject-specific staff – but this does not necessarily fully exploit the potential of ICT environments.

The Working Group on curriculum reform proposed an 'extended project' that has been embraced by the White Paper (DfES 2005). Such a project would allow each individual learner to 'extend his/her learning in creative and innovative ways' and 'take a variety of forms from an essay to a performance or artefact' (DfES 2004, p. 5). Clearly, adoption of the 'extended project' as part of core learning may blur subject boundaries. The consultation document (QCA 2006) provides some specific examples of how the proposed project might relate to both A-level and the new specialized vocational diplomas. The adoption of the same 'extended project' in both academic and vocational provision will encourage further consolidation across differing modes, and allow considerable flexibility of approach in moving away from subject-based notions of delivery.

An underlying objective here is to seek rationalization through consolidation, but it is important not to underestimate the radical effect that this proposal will have on curriculum delivery and assessment. Specifically, is it appropriate in multimodal project work to evaluate the educational significance of an activity with respect to a single specific subject? Furthermore, would assessment from the perspective of one discrete subject area such as music possibly devalue the project? The 'extended project' does recognize the educational value and administrative efficiency of multimodal and multidisciplinary approaches to the curriculum and addresses the fact that there may not be enough time to embrace all subjects discretely. This raises questions, however, about the subject-based nature of study, which is how most schools presently organize delivery of their curricula.

Impact of Increasing ICT Adoption

There is evidence of increasing use of ICT in music education in recent years. In 2000, nearly three-quarters (70 per cent) of secondary schools acknowledged that they utilized little or no ICT in the music curriculum, while examination of data from the DfES revealed that by 2003 this was only true for a quarter (25 per cent) of secondary schools (2001, 2003b) . Undoubtedly, progress is being made, albeit that ICT would seem to be much better used in GCSE and examination groups than with students in Key Stage 3 (Ofsted 2002). Interestingly, older students often have equipment at home that is used between lessons to support study, and some students involve themselves in additional ICT activity outside timetabled lessons. 'Indeed, it is not uncommon to find good work in schools where students are self-taught as far as music technology is concerned, often supported by an older student with more advanced skills' (Ofsted 2002).

These observations have implications for any curriculum planning in music education. Educators recognize that student-centred activity needs appropriate facilities and dedicated time to maximize educational experience, but this has resource implications, particularly with large numbers. In addition, while student-centred working may be appropriate with older students, too much creative freedom can be ineffective with younger ones. Imison and Taylor (2001, p. 81) comment that 'lower down the school some of the worse music lessons for us have been when students are given total creative freedom'. They recommend that structured approaches which are framed by the teacher avoid the 'blank sheet of paper' problem, where students are left not knowing where to begin.

Despite these findings, there is some evidence to support the notion that good practice exists in music technology in Key Stage 3. Mills and Murray (2000) acknowledge that much of the technology purchased by schools was intended for students in Key Stage 4, but comment on a range of characteristics that support good teaching, drawn from observation of Ofsted Inspectors during visits made in 52 schools. They note that good music lessons were characterized by students engaged in the business of music-making itself, and not distracted by technological issues. They cite a wide range of issues that impede progress, from logistical considerations hindering the task in hand (equipment not being ready, or not fit for purpose) to tasks which did not clearly excite or motivate the students to engage appropriately.

While primary schools are lagging behind secondary schools in adopting ICT in music teaching, DfES data clearly demonstrates that the use of ICT is gradually increasing (DfES 2001, 2003b). In 2003, over half (52 per cent) of primary schools declared that they used little or no ICT in music teaching, although this figure was still an improvement on figures from previous years, such as 96 per cent in 2000.

Sutherland *et al.* (2004) highlight the significance of social interaction and peer review as important factors in effectively embedding ICT in music compositional activity. They observed that although students largely worked in pairs at computers, free interaction with others in the classroom encouraged them to elicit musical ideas and technical expertise from each other. Sunderland *et al.* note that culturally relevant music compositional work can be influential in improving motivation, and also recognize the considerable contribution that out-of-school informal learning can make to ICT (p. 417). Nevertheless, they draw attention to the fact that some students 'frequently come to the classroom with a wealth of knowledge and awareness of styles of music; in many cases exceeding their teacher's knowledge in particular areas' (p. 417). Surely it is not a desirable state of affairs for students to exhibit greater knowledge than their teachers, and for teachers to appear out-of-touch with their students?

Problems with Underlying Conceptual Frameworks

Tim Cain (2004) argues that advances in music technology have undermined the conceptual frameworks that currently support pedagogy in music education. He notes the progressive shift towards students working in pairs or even individually with computers, and recognizes that the role of the teacher is affected by modes of working. He calls for the articulation of a theory of music education that does not appear at odds with current conceptual models. Swanwick's (1979) activities-based C(L)A(S)P model (which embraces Composing, Audition [Listening] and Performance as core musical activities in conjunction with literature studies and skill acquisition) has significantly influenced curriculum development in music and the National Curriculum. Cain sees Swanwick's model as problematic for music ICT, questioning whether the model can provide a descriptive framework that can appropriately classify many computer-based music activities, particularly those that make extensive use of pre-composed material. Cain also questions how we might categorize activities such as recording, mixing and computer-mediated performance.

Yet despite Cain's reservations, it could be argued that Swanwick's model still has relevance to ICT-based learning environments. Interestingly, the C(L)A(S)P model articulates the importance of skill acquisition as a distinct component. Certainly, observational research suggests that more time is spent proportionately in skill acquisition than in other music curriculum activities in the model (compare Swanwick 1996). In primary education, time spent on skill acquisition was nearly 70 per cent, greater than all other music activities put together. In secondary education, skill acquisition accounted for nearly 40 per cent of the time, greater than any other individual activity. Music educationalists need to recognize that ICT skills and competencies may need reinforcement in an educational setting in a similar way to the development of music skills. Consequently, it may not be appropriate to expect all ICT-based music curriculum activity to relate directly to an artistic outcome that is qualitatively assessable in purely musical terms related to compositional or perform-ance activity.

Bruce Cole, too, does not consider the activities model to be helpful in relation to ICT-related music study. Cole states that 'the three components which constitute musical study: listening, performing and composing ... are identified, rather oddly, as separate entries in many examination syllabuses and in the National Curriculum of England and Wales' (Cole 1996, p. 53).

Perhaps the activities model is a little unhelpful in ICT contexts, but the model seeks to recognize the totality of musical experience in that music is conceptualized and created, played and performed, and experienced aurally by an audience. Clearly, some musical activities can embrace more than one area. A performance activity such as improvisation, for example, also embraces elements of composition. As educators, if we are assessing the creativity of the performer in realizing a performance, then does it matter that the performance is not notated or, for that matter, that the performer has little ability to transfer, or transcribe such a performance into conventional staff notation? From a popular music perspective, which is acknowledged as a non-notated form (at least in a traditional sense), there does seem to a problem in addressing notions of musical literacy. Now that sequencers are predominantly concerned with audio processing, conventional notation skills are often redundant from a compositional perspective. ICT has completely removed the need to write music down, at least in a conventional sense, so a curriculum activity centred on a product (such as a recording) may be an exclusive focus of assessment.

Some educationalists would argue that assessment should reveal something of the processes related to conceptual understanding of the product, and I would argue that this greater conceptualization and contextualization is what distinguishes school-based study from study in higher education. One view is that the product of an educational encounter provides appropriate evidence of comprehension and demonstrates the application of skills and knowledge so that an objective assessment can be undertaken. But if we simply try to assess products on their artistic terms we bring our own value judgements into play and adopt a subjective view rather than an objective view of the product. With a curriculum that seeks to equip school and college students for employment, we need to recognize that we should be concerned with developing appropriate skills and competencies, while not losing sight of the need to extend conceptual understanding in broadening the knowledge of students.

ICT and Innovation

As technology has developed over the last 20 years, music curricula have been required to adapt and develop with regard to embracing ICT. Not only have there been calls to include (or embed) ICT, but knowledge of other musics besides Western art music is now expected (Kwami 2001a). Green (2002) has observed a change in secondary school teachers' attitudes towards music. In the survey comparing 1982 with 1998, the most noticeable shifts in attitude were observed in the perception of popular music and world music. Green notes that the widely held perception in 1982 that classical music should occupy the predominant space in the music curriculum did not hold to the same extent in 1998. She identified that one major new factor observed in 1998 was the 'strong practical engagement with popular music, involving composition, improvisation and classroom performance as integrated activities' (2002, p. 28). This integrated approach must surely inform any notions of reform of the music curriculum. ICT can act as an integrating agent in this context.

The reform of the 14–19 curriculum provides an unparalleled opportunity in the history of curriculum development to create a system that allows increasing numbers of school and college students to embrace music as an appropriate curriculum activity. The government recognizes the need for a broad and balanced curriculum to include the study of an arts subject (art and design, music, dance, drama or media arts) beyond the age of 14 (DfES 2005, p. 77). There appears to be an increasing recognition that music study in school needs to be linked to the interests of the wider community outside school and the classroom (Kwami 2001b). An education system that seeks to bring the study of music to more school and college students must be desirable as music plays such an important role in the leisure pursuits of the great majority of the population. Surely, this should be reflected in providing an appropriate school, college or university curriculum as a preparation for life. It has been argued that diversification of the music curriculum is inevitable if educationalists are to continue to develop music curricula that are socially relevant and meaningful.

Curriculum reform has the potential to bring music study to a much broader range of students than at present, and the compulsory 'extended project' proposal may be important in allowing students to pursue music study in the context of the 'core' requirement of ICT. Music educationalists need to be ready to take advantage of the possibilities which curriculum reform will bring, particularly with respect to unitization of the curriculum and a possible move away from subject-based study to integrated multidisciplinary or multimodal project work, that is, towards exploring combinations of audio and video in ICT environments. Something of this approach to subject study is promoted in the QCA document 'Futures: Meeting the Challenge' which postulates the question in relation to curriculum design: 'how can we adequately define future learning needs across subject boundaries?' (QCA 2005).

Conclusion

The study of music in the post-14 curriculum should embrace a diversity of practices, both cultural and technological. Furthermore, music education should be inclusive, and this has been clearly recognized in recent years. The QCA annual music report of 2004 proposes that the 'big challenge ahead for music education is to really ensure that music is for all' (QCA 2004b, p. 25). There is a need for change if the music curriculum is to be relevant and meaningful for a majority of students and students. The QCA also acknowledges that there 'is an increasing recognition that courses need to be more varied to match more closely the particular interests and aptitudes of students' (QCA 2004b, p. 23). This report even suggests that there is a need for a new Key Stage 4 music qualification to revitalize the place of academic music in the curriculum.

The emphasis on skill-based activity, with relevance to employability, has encouraged the diversification of the music curriculum together with new academic programmes in further and higher education institutions. The challenge now facing school music educators is how to respond to this diversification, particularly with respect to 14–19 curriculum reform.

Innovative ICT-based music study offers the opportunity for the academic study of music to have greater social relevance for all school and college students. It is the responsibility of educationalists to ensure that all students have the opportunity to realize their musical interests, abilities and potential, and that the qualification and accreditation systems properly recognize educational achievement in music.

References

Bray, D. (2000), 'An examination of Music GCSE uptake rates'. *British Journal of Music Education*, 17(1), 79–89.

Cain, T. (2004), 'Theory, technology and the music curriculum'. *British Journal of Music Education*, 21(2), 215–21.

Cole, B. (1996), 'MIDI and communality'. *Organised Sound*, 1(1), 51–4.

Davies, P., Adnett, N. and Turnbull, A. (2003), 'Market forces and diversity: some evidence from the 14–19 curriculum'. *Journal of Curriculum Studies*, 35(4), 479–8.

Denholm, J. and Macleod, D. (2003), *Prospects for Growth in Further Education: Interim Report*. London: Learning and Skills Research Centre, November 2003. www.lsneducation.org.uk/user/order.aspx ?code=031891. Accessed on 27 November 2006.

DfES (2001), *Statistics of Education: Survey of Information and Communications Technology in Schools 2001*. London: Department for Education and Skills. www.dfes.gov.uk/rsgateway/DB/SBU/b000296/sb09-2001.pdf. Accessed on 27 November 2006.

DfES (2002), *14-19: Extending Opportunities, Raising Standards: Consultation Document* [Cm5342]. London: Department for Education and Skills.

DfES (2003a), *14-19: Opportunity and Excellence* [0744/2002Main]. London: Department for Education and Skills.

DfES (2003b), *Statistics of Education: Survey of Information and Communications Technology in Schools 2003*. London: Department for Education and Skills. www.dfes.gov.uk/rsgateway/DB/SBU/b000421/bweb05-2003.pdf. *Accessed on 27 November 2006.*

DfES (2004), *14-19 Curriculum and Qualifications Reform: Final Report of the Working Group on 14-19 Reform*. London: Department for Education and Skills. www.dfes.gov.uk/14-19/documents/Final %20Report.pdf. Accessed on 27 November 2006.

DfES (2005), *White Paper 14-19 Education and Skills*. London: Department for Education and Skills. www.dfes.gov.uk/14-19/documents/14-19whitepaper.pdf. Accessed on 27 November 2006.

DfES (2006), *Back in Learning: £10 Million to Boost Participation*. 1 June 2006 Press Notice. London: Department for Education and Skills. www.dfes.gov.uk/pns/DisplayPN.cgi?pn_id=2006_0084. Accessed on 27 November 2006.

Ellis, V. and Long, S. (2004), 'Negotiating Contrad(ICT)ions: teachers and students making multimedia in the secondary school'. *Technology, Pedagogy and Education*, 13(1), 11-27.

Green, L. (2002), 'From the Western Classics to the world: secondary music teachers' changing attitudes in England, 1982 and 1998'. *British Journal of Music Education*, 19(1), 5-30.

Hyland, T. and Merrill, B. (2003), *The Changing Face of Further Education*. London: RoutledgeFarmer.

Imison, T. and Taylor, P. (2001), *Managing ICT in the Secondary School*. Oxford: Heinemann.

Kwami, R. (2001a), 'Music education in and for a pluralist society', in P. Philpott and C. Plummeting (eds), *Issues in Music Teaching*. London: RoutledgeFalmer, pp. 142-55.

Kwami, R. (2001b), 'Music education in a new millennium', in A. Loveless and V. Ellis (eds), *ICT, Pedagogy and the Curriculum*. London: RoutledgeFalmer, pp. 216-28.

Loveless, A. (2004), 'Reshuffling the pack of cards?' *Technology, Pedagogy and Education*, 13(1), 5-9.

Mansell, W. (2006), 'Don't take away our music, Edexcel'. *Times Educational Supplement*, 14 July, p. 5.

Mills, J. and Murray, A. (2000), 'Music Technology inspected: good teaching in Key Stage 3'. *British Journal of Music Education*, 17(2), 129-56.

Ofsted (2002), *ICT in Schools: Effect of Government Initiatives, Secondary Music*.

[HMI 707 June 2002]. London: Office for Standards in Education. www.of-sted.gov.uk/assets/2597.pdf. Accessed on 27 November 2006.

QCA (2004a), *Music: 2002/03 Annual Report on Curriculum and Assessment*. London: Qualifications and Curriculum Authority. www.qca.org.uk/downloads/ 7407_music.pdf. Accessed on 27 November 2006.

QCA (2004b), *Music: 2003/04 Annual Report on Curriculum and Assessment [QCA/ 04/1472]*. London: Qualifications and Curriculum Authority. www.qca.org.uk/ downloads/11921_music_annual_ report_curric_assess_03_04.pdf. Accessed on 27 November 2006.

QCA (2005), *Futures: Meeting the Challenge*. London: Qualifications and Curriculum Authority. www.qca.org.uk/downloads/11493_futures_meeting_the_challen-ge.pdf. Accessed on 27 November 2006.

QCA (2006), *Consultation on the Extended Project (Level 3)*. London: Qualifications and Curriculum Authority. www.qca.org.uk/downloads/qca-06-2705_EP_ background.pdf. Accessed on 27 November 2006.

Sutherland, R., Armstrong, V., Barnes, S., Brawn, R., Breeze, N., Gall, M., Matthewman, S., Olivero, S., Taylor, A., Triggs, P., Wishart, J. and John, P. (2004), 'Transforming teaching and learning: embedding ICT into everyday classroom practices'. *Journal of Computer Assisted Learning*, 20, 413–25.

Swanwick, K. (1979), *A Basis for Music Education*. London: Routledge.

Swanwick, K. (1996), 'The relevance of research for music education', in C. Plummeridge (ed.), *Music Education: Trends and Issues*. London: Institute of Education, University of London, pp. 5–26.

Wright, R. (2002), 'Music for all? Pupils' perceptions of the GCSE Music examination in one South Wales secondary school'. *British Journal of Music Education*, 19(3), 227–41.

Chapter 15

Strategies for Enabling Curriculum Reform: Lessons from Australia, Singapore and Hong Kong

Samuel Leong

Introduction

The global educational challenge today is to enable people to successfully and effectively adapt new knowledge and cope with new situations (UNESCO 1992, Darling-Hammond and Sclan 1996). Many countries have initiated education reforms reforms that emphasized the 'role of knowledge, technology and learning in economic performance' in a global knowledge economy (OECD 1999, p. 1). Such a knowledge economy, also known as the 'information economy', is described in *Australia's Strategic Framework for the Information Economy 2004–2006* as one:

> where information, knowledge and education are major inputs to business and social activity. It is not a separate 'new' economy – it is an economy in which the rapid development and diffusion of ICT-based [information and communication technology] innovation is transforming all sectors and all aspects of society. (Australian Government, 2004, Executive Summary)

Driven by the forces requiring rapid innovation in competitive world markets, today's knowledge economy is enabled by ICT's capacity to search, filter, store, transmit, encapsulate, process and manipulate information. Workers of a knowledge economy are expected to possess ICT literacy: the 'ability to use technology to develop 21st century content knowledge and skills' (Partnership for 21st century Skills 2006, p. 11). This new kind of literacy is considered a key '21st Century skill', together with 'global awareness; civic engagement; financial, economic and business literacy; and learning skills that encompass problem solving, critical thinking, and self-directional skills' (Partnership for 21st Century Skills 2005, p. 15).

Schools are seen to play a critical role in producing a workforce that is highly educated and skilled to support a country's economy. This recognition of education as a key contributor to the economy has led school curricula in many countries to mandate ICT as a central component, with teachers being increasingly expected to infuse ICT into the teaching and learning processes. This chapter examines some of the major developments and strategies related to ICT in the education reform of three countries where the author has worked professionally. Lessons will be drawn from their experiences in enhancing curriculum reform for a technology-infused future.

ICT Policies and Education Reform

The global knowledge economy movement has seen the proliferation of government policy statements on ICT in education. The 1999 *National Goals for Schooling in the Twenty-first Century* articulated the goal of having Australian students become 'confident, creative and productive users of new technologies, particularly information and communication technologies, and [to] understand[ing] the impact of those technologies on society' (MCEETYA 1999, National Goals 1.6). The Ministerial Council for Employment, Education, Training and Youth Affairs (MCEETYA 2000) also endorsed *Learning in an Online World: The School Action Plan for the Information Economy*, declaring that 'all schools will seek to integrate information and communication technologies into their operations, to improve student learning, to offer flexible learning opportunities and to improve the efficiency of their business practices' (MCEETYA 2000, p. 5).

A more recent paper, *Raising the Standards* (DEST 2002), pointed out the need for an information and competency framework for teachers, and acknowledged that teacher education institutions require a number of 'capabilities' in order to be effective in preparing ICT-competent pre-service teachers. These include: leadership and vision in the use of ICT; infrastructure providing appropriate access and technical support; curriculum/programmes that integrate the use of ICT; and partnerships with schools to provide appropriate professional experiences for pre-service teachers (*ibid.*, p. 14).

In 2005, a 'national vision for improving education and training outcomes for all Australians through the ubiquitous use of ICT' was released by the Ministerial Council for Employment, Education, Training and Youth Affairs (MCEETYA 2005). Entitled *Building a Knowledge Culture: An Education and Training Action Plan for the Information Economy 2005–2007*, it aims to create an 'innovative society', ensure that all learners achieve their potential, improve the quality and raise standards of teaching and training, achieve efficiencies through the sharing of resource and expertise, and capitalize on the 'internationalization of education' (*ibid.*, 2005, p. 1).

A 2005-commissioned report to the Australian Capital Territory Department of Education (ACT DET) reviewed 'emerging technologies' directly related to the delivery and enhancement of teaching and learning. The report noted that their use in education settings will require 'visionary leadership' as well as a 'flexible, simple and open digital rights management (DGM) regime that enables and supports sharing and exchange of content rather than blocking or limiting it'. It also found 'general trends' emphasizing 'mobility; interoperability; convergence; divergence; integration; richness of content; security; creativity; interactivity and collaboration; and utilization of open source software as a potential initiative'. These 'emerging technologies' are able to 'reduce the digital divide' and nullify the 'one size fits all' approach to learning as 'multi-modal options and device-independent access will be the norm' (ACT DET 2005, Executive Summary). The Chief Executive of the ACT DET highlighted globalization, the knowledge society, ICT, diversity and equity in the curriculum as the 'key drivers' of curriculum reform in Australia. He asserted that 'curriculum must provide access to knowledge for all' and that teachers are 'integral' to the design, development and delivery of curriculum (Bruniges 2006, p. 5).

The Singapore government's vision and commitment to integrate ICT seamlessly and efficiently into all aspects of government, business and lifestyle, have seen it being ranked first in the world for its propensity to exploit the opportunities offered by ICT by the World Economic Forum (2005). This achievement bears the hallmarks of

Singapore's management style, which is characterized by a multi-sector, synergistic approach.

Singapore's liberalization of the telecommunications sector led to the merger of the Telecommunications Authority of Singapore (TAS) and the National Computer Board (NCB) in 1999. This process commenced in 1997, which was the same year as the launch of the initial 5-year 'Masterplan for IT in Education' and another education reform initiative, 'Thinking Schools, Learning Nation' (see MOE website). These education policies worked in tandem: one addressed hardware and software provision while the other considered pedagogical issues. 'Thinking Schools, Learning Nation' envisioned Singapore as a place where assumptions are challenged, where its citizens seek better ways of doing things through participation, creativity and innovation, and where lifelong learning is encouraged (MOE website, Mission Statement), while the first IT Masterplan saw US$1.2 billion poured into creating ICT-enriched school settings. The investment occurred mainly through the provision of hardware and software and 30–50 hours of professional development courses in IT for every teacher in every school over a year. Its initial provision included a whole-school computer network; a teacher–notebook ratio of 2.1 in every school; and a student-computer ratio for secondary schools and junior colleges of 5.1, with the latter enabling 14 per cent of curriculum time to be used with ICT.

The 'Masterplan 2 for IT in Education in 2002 took a more comprehensive approach to reform, in its considering of the relationship and impact between six key components of the education system. These were:

1   ICT
2   curriculum
3   assessment
4   instruction
5   professional development
6   school culture.

Curriculum design was to take account of new teaching methods made possible by technology, and ICT was to be integrated into the 'a more flexible and dynamic curriculum' (MOE website, Speeches).

Then, on 20 June 2006, Singapore launched the 'iN2015 Masterplan', offering a 'digital future for everyone' and aimed at propelling the nation into 2015 and beyond, bringing 'benefits for the people, businesses and the global community'. The vision was to have ICT become 'intrinsic in the way people live, learn, work and play', thus transforming the city-state into an 'intelligent nation and global city'. The plan will also explore ways to cater for the elderly, less-privileged and people with disability, enabling them to enjoy 'connected and enriched lives for self-improvement and life-long learning' and 'bridge the digital divide and create opportunities for all' (IDA website, 2006).

The Hong Kong government's Education and Manpower Bureau (EMB) launched its first five-year masterplan for ICT in Education in 1998 (EMB 1998). This was, followed by a second five-year plan, which focused on applying ICT as a lever to achieve the goals of the Education Reform (EMB 2004). At the end of the last millennium, the Curriculum Development Council (CDC) conducted a 'holistic review' of the school curriculum and recommended 'guiding principles' in curriculum development to 'meet the challenges of a knowledge-based, interdependent and changing society, as well as globalization, fast technological development, and a competitive economy' (CDC 2001, p. i).

The Education Commission (2000) articulated 'learning for life' and 'learning through life' as 'a new culture of learning and teaching', emphasizing 'learning how to learn', 'integrated learning' and 'integrated and flexible arrangement of learning time' (2000, pp. 60–62). The curriculum reform promoted the infusion of 'generic skills' such as information technology in teaching and learning (CDC 2000, p. 28). The inclusion of IT in the education process was expected to serve 'as a powerful educational tool that can play a catalyst role in the transformation of school education' (EMB 1998, p. 1) and 'transform school education from a largely teacher-centred approach to a more interactive and learner-centred approach' (EMB 2004, Foreword).

The new curriculum framework and learning goals aim to enable students to 'develop independent learning capabilities through developing generic skills, foundation knowledge in eight Key Learning areas, and personal values and attitudes, with learner-centred and whole-person development to stretch the students' potential and four key tasks for promoting learning capabilities: moral and civic education, reading to learn, project learning and information technology for interactive learning' (CDC 2001, p. 5). In order to facilitate 'gradual' change, a 10-year plan in three phases was proposed: 2001/2 to 2005/6 (short term), 2006/7 to 2010/2011 (medium term) and beyond 2011 (longer term) (*ibid.*, p. 12).

It is disappointing that the music and cultural industries were not been given some prominence in the government policy documents related to ICT in education. The contributions of music and culture to a country's economy deserve better recognition, given their prevalence in so many facets of human society. From books and magazines to sound recordings, movies and TV shows, from advertisements and the performing arts (dance, theatre, opera and concerts) to fashion shows, toys and games, ICT and innovations are deeply embedded in the practices of the music and culture industries. Moreover, the creative arts are most suited to achieving the reform goal of getting schools to produce creative and innovative citizens and workers.

ICT in the Schools of Three Countries

Hong Kong

Publishing well-articulated government policies is one thing; getting them efficiently and effectively implemented with longer-term sustainability is a different ball game. The Second International Information Technology in Education Study (SITES M2) – a project of the International Association for the Evaluation of Educational Achievement (IEA) – sought to investigate the innovative characteristics of 'technology-using classrooms most indicative of classrooms of the future in preparing students for challenges of the knowledge society' (SITES M2 website, Report, p. 1). Conducted between 2000 and 2003, 174 case studies from 28 countries, including those in North America, Europe and the Asia Pacific, were collected. They were analysed for interactions between the teacher, students and technology, with classroom innovations contextualized within the broader school, and regional and national policies and strategies.

Hong Kong contributed nine of these cases to the study – three from primary schools, two from junior secondary schools and four from senior secondary schools. These were coordinated by the Centre of Information Technology at the University of

Hong Kong, and were analysed applying six *a priori* key dimensions of curriculum implementation of ICT. The six dimensions were:

(1) curriculum goals
(2) roles played by the teachers
(3) roles of the learners
(4) complexity and sophistication of the ICT used
(5) learning outcomes exhibited
(6) the extent to which the classrooms are connected to the outside world through external participants (SITES M2, Report, p. 4).

The analysis concluded that ICT in the Hong Kong case studies was 'used mainly as a learning and productivity tool', specifically for searching the internet for information and communicating via emails and discussion forums (Law *et al.* 2005, p. 192). All but one of the case teachers had to 'build up the requisite infrastructure and teacher competence by themselves'. The 'support and collaborations' and 'transferability' of the knowledge and expertise gained by them did not extend beyond their individual school perimeters' parameters (*ibid.*, p. 193).

The case studies demonstrated that it will take more than the provision of school computers, a high level of access and connectivity, and basic computer literacy training, for teachers to have ICT successfully integrated into the school curriculum for the purposes of achieving education reform goals. The basic ICT skills acquired by teachers will most likely only be adequate for them to use ICT at a general purpose level and to use software not specifically designed to suit the intended outcomes of their particular curriculum. Law *et al.* (2003) are right in pointing out the importance of choosing the appropriate kinds of ICT tools and resources.

In order for teachers to effectively use ICT to achieve the educational goals for the 21st century, two important criteria have to be satisfied. First of all, teachers have to recognize that the use of ICT tools is not value free and there are often deep pedagogical assumptions embedded in their design and use. This has important implications for the choice of ICT tools and resources in schools as well as in the nature of the professional development provisions for teachers. Another issue relates to design and dissemination of education-specific ICT tools and resources. While the relatively low level of use of specialized ICT tools may imply that there is a lack of availability of such tools, a more important fact probably is that such tools do not 'travel' well. While the general ICT tools like internet, office and multimedia tools are marketed with great vigor, and are dominated by a few key products, there are no education-specific tools and resources that are widely known even within the education circles. The lack of dominant market winners in educational software and tools is not simply a result of the lack of capable marketing agents. More importantly, the adoption of such tools requires changes in the classroom culture and the roles played by teachers and learners. How to market new learning tools in tandem with a new learning culture is a key challenge to education in the information age. (Law *et al.* 2003, p. 6)

Despite the huge investment by the government in setting up the ICT infrastructure for Hong Kong schools since 1998, the Quality Insurance Annual Report 2000/2001 (EMB 2002) found that computers and music software were not accessible in most primary schools. In addition, the report was not satisfied with their knowledge of ICT applications in music teaching. Secondary school music teachers were in need of encouragement to integrate ICT in their teaching, particularly in the area of creativity. Three years later, the Quality Insurance Annual Report 2003/2004 (EMB 2004) noted that Hong Kong schools 'displayed a mediocre performance in their incorporation of IT elements into different subject curricula and the application of IT for interactive learning' (*ibid.*, p. 8).

The state of preparedness of teachers in using ICT in the school curriculum was severely tested when schools had to be closed suddenly during the SARS (Severe Acute Respiratory Syndrome) epidemic in 2003. Hong Kong teachers were confronted with the real need to find new teaching strategies which could fulfil curriculum requirements and provide their students with alternative opportunities to learn away from regular classrooms. It was reported that 'many teachers simply recorded teaching monologues and uploaded them online. Other more innovative teachers set WebQuest activities, but most were unprepared' (Fox 2004, p. 319).

This period witnessed a quickened intensity of the use of ICT in education, with school leadership scrambling to provide the necessary assistance to facilitate continued 'delivery' of learning to students. It also hastened teachers' appreciation of the limitations and potential of ICT tools. It sensitized them to the benefits of guiding students to become independent learners, to set goals in relation to given tasks, to search for and select appropriate information that contributes to achieving the goals, to work collaboratively with peers and teachers, and to evaluate their own progress. Teachers witnessed the power of ICT in facilitating increased interaction and collaboration between learners and teachers as well as between learners and learners. Indeed, they learned to move away from rigid examination-oriented approaches towards assessment modes that considered both process and product in less traditional forms, such as online submission and portfolios. They experienced the benefits of integrating ICT into the learning process and how not to treat ICT as an 'add on' or substitute. They also began to realize the differences between learning via ICT and learning how to use ICT.

A study in 2002, involving 15 primary and 15 secondary school music teachers and over 500 students, found that half of the primary schools did not have computers in their music classrooms and only three had CD players (Ho 2004). Two-thirds of the participating schools had one computer in their music classrooms and three schools had multiple computers for music purposes. About half the teachers believed that 'music technology improves the quality of their teaching practices' (*ibid.*, p. 61), and the majority of students (80 per cent) 'thought music technology could enhance their quality of learning' (*ibid.*, p. 62). Most students thought music technology could motivate them to learn music (90 per cent) and be more creative in music making (80 per cent). However, nearly two-thirds of the students acknowledged the importance of their music teachers in teaching them how to write, perform and compose music.

A larger survey study, involving both music and art teachers from 1,225 schools, was conducted in the summer of 2003 by Cheung and Au (2003) as part of the Alliance for Education Innovations (AEI) project at the Hong Kong Institute of Education. A total of 725 music teachers responded, with over half representing the secondary school sector and over 60 per cent representing the primary school sector. This study found that 84 per cent of music rooms in secondary schools were equipped with computers, while only 51 per cent of primary schools had them. About 40 per cent of schools provided a website for music. It was the perception of about half the music teachers that other music teachers did not often use a computer for teaching, and only 24 per cent of music and art teachers thought that other arts teachers in Hong Kong were proficient in using ICT. Nearly half of the music teachers 'generally agreed' that they had 'mastered the software skills' needed in teaching, and 41 per cent admitted they had 'not mastered the use of hardware related to their teaching' (*ibid.*, p. 55). The hardware and software commonly used in music were found to be: CD/VCD/DVD-ROM, LCD projector, PowerPoint, Internet Explorer, MS Word, soundcards, speakers, MIDI keyboards, Finale and Cakewalk. Towards the close of the five-year period of the ICT Master Plan, many music teachers still seemed to need help in becoming familiar with computer hardware and software.

In a study involving fresh graduate music teachers' perspectives on computer-based music technology in teacher education, Yip (2003) identified 'a need to provide advanced/refresher course in this field for professional development of in-service music teachers and for the enhancement of technology applications in music education' (2003, p. 437).

Indeed more needs to be done to enable music teachers to be more competent and confident in integrating ICT into their music curriculum. For a start, the official music ICT handbook for music teachers, which dates back to the turn of the century, should be updated (Education Department 1999).

Australia

In Australia, a 'strong' need to 'develop the confidence and skills of teachers to integrate ICT in teaching and learning' and 'to address digital divide issues, for example, for indigenous students and students with disabilities' in Australia was recorded in the *Final Report of Asia and the Pacific Seminar-workshop on Educational Technology* (APEID 2004, p. 14). The recent *National Review of School Music Education* (Pascoe *et al.* 2005) found 'a lack of evidence of music technology being deeply embedded in schools particularly when compared with its place in the music industry' despite official music syllabi incorporating opportunities for music technology (*ibid.*, p. 129). It also found 'considerable resistance' to 'alternative teaching methods' in the context of distance learning. Considering the expanse of land and the distribution of remote populations, it was surprising that there were only 'some encouraging, but tentative, evidence of successful teaching using distance learning and electronic delivery' (*ibid.*, p. 126).

The literature indicates that most teachers are not keeping up with their students in terms of new ICT knowledge, and many are teaching what they know rather than what is needed (Brown 2006). This is reflected in the bold *Policy Statement on Computer Literacy* of the Australian Computer Society (2005), which declares that 'while ICT has become embedded into all aspects of our home and work lives, this has not yet been achieved in the nation's class rooms'. The blame may be put on the 'levels of available infrastructure and support within schools, lack of integrated ICT strategies in teaching programs and the capacity of teachers to make meaningful use of technologies in their teaching programs' (*ibid.*, p. 3).

An Australian survey found only one in four secondary music teachers and 11 per cent of primary music teachers indicating that their pre-service teacher education prepared them to use music technology confidently (Leong 1995). Respondents provided 17 perceived benefits of using technology in music teaching and gave 18 reasons for not using technology in their teaching. They cited reasons for non-usage to include costs, space, classroom control and coordination, lack of expertise and confidence, constantly changing technologies, fear that computers would compensate for lack of musical skills, and lack of know-how in integrating technology (*ibid.*, p. 24). With the prevalence of music technology in contemporary lifestyle, it has been suggested that teacher ignorance in this area would adversely affect teaching effectiveness (Dillon 2001). An in-depth study of teacher-education students just before their graduation found most of the participants to possess a high level of competence and confidence with ICT (Finger *et al.* 2004). However, their confidence was confined to a limited range of applications and many had 'no competence with certain applications' (*ibid.* p. 9). The researchers noted the need to ensure that all graduates acquire the necessary competencies and confidence to integrate ICT into their teaching.

Singapore

The commitment and determination to support and implement government policies bore early fruits in Singapore. Soon after Singapore launched its five-year 'Masterplan for IT in Education' in 1997, an innovative project was conceived which embedded ICT in school music. This project had secondary students, aged 14 and 15, working in groups of ten to investigate the manner in which cultural and historical contexts influenced three Singapore songs. It required students to be engaged in music analysis, sound recording and editing, web designing and presenting, as well as conducting to conduct exchanges with peers at a school in the UK via the internet (Chong 1999).

By the end of the implementation period of the five-year 'Masterplan for IT in Education', nearly two-thirds of teachers thought that preparing ICT-based lessons was worthwhile, and nearly 80 per cent of them wanted to explore more ways of integrating ICT into their teaching. Almost all (90 per cent) of the students thought ICT had made learning more interesting, and about 80 per cent believed that ICT had improved their learning and encouraged them to learn beyond their curriculum (Soh 2002).

Three recent projects demonstrate how ICT has been successfully incorporated into Singapore schools: (1) 'Instrumental Karaoke', which had primary school students performing on their instruments, such as recorders, violins and synthesizers (see MOE website); (2) a 'guitar project' which integrated five areas of the junior secondary school curriculum (design and technology, home economics, art, science and music) (see MOE website); and (3) a 'National IT Music, Arrangement and Performance Challenge', organized by a secondary school in conjunction with community organizations, a music education company and a local polytechnic (see MOE website reference). The latter is the first polytechnic in Singapore to offer a three-year Diploma in Music and Audio Technology (in 2005) featuring internship in the music industry. This educational initiative caters for a growing area of need with tremendous employment potential in the South-East Asian and Asia-Pacific regions. It also demonstrates a major paradigm shift from viewing music as leisure/entertainment to valuing music as 'content'. While ICT serves as the 'tools' and education provides the 'process', music is the 'content' created for community sharing, enjoyment and appreciation of culture.

Strategies for Enabling Curriculum Reform

Although technologies in themselves are enabling agents, humans have designed them to increase their ability to control and improve aspects of human living, but we need to be able to make informed decisions with regard to ICT applications in teaching and learning. Due consideration needs to be given to the questions of: why to do, what to do, when to do, where to do and how to do.

While ICT has enabled educational practitioners to 'update' their presentation and transmission modes without altering their pedagogical practices (e.g., from overhead transparencies to PowerPoint displays, from library searches to internet searches), often it is seen merely as a learning and productivity 'tool' for enhancing delivery and access (e.g. email, WebCT, PDF). In some music classrooms, ICT becomes the 'content': as teachers and learners focus on the features and capabilities of hardware (e.g., synthesizers, controllers) and software (e.g., Band-in-a-box, Finale, Musition), while making minimal connection with the more theoretical and performance components of the music programme and student learning outcomes.

Given the speed of technological advances, educational practitioners should be keeping abreast of these new developments and be mindful of the uptake of these technologies by the young. There are now currently tremendous opportunities for adapting teaching methods methods that embrace new ways of engaging learners. This is made possible with the emergence of new technologies such as Multi-User Virtual Environment (MUVE), Podcast, Vodcast (Video on Demand), wikis, VoIP (Voice over Internet Protocol), digital TV, P2P (peer-to-peer) network, RFID (radio frequency identification technology) and Smart Cards.

Curriculum reform involves more than using ICT to help students 'cover' the syllabus and or to be better prepared for tests and examinations. Learning in the knowledge economy is about knowledge construction, knowledge networking, knowledge harvesting, knowledge creation and knowledge reuse. Teaching and learning strategies must create opportunities for these new foci of learning.

We have seen how a range of strategies by governments and education systems in Singapore, Australia and Hong Kong have attempted to transform schools and their practices through the incorporation of ICT with varying levels of success. Many schools have been wired up and networked, fitted with hardware and software, given sets of policies and curriculum guides, as well as staff professional development courses. However, the evidence points to the impotence of policies, rhetoric and equipment in shifting the pedagogical culture of many localities. Such a transformation requires vision and leadership at all levels of the educational food chain. It calls for leadership that dares to replace piecemeal solutions lacking in symbiotic impact and sustainability with a more comprehensive approach to seeking, implementing and enforcing solutions.

Several important lessons can be learned from the education reform experiences of Australia, Singapore and Hong Kong.

1. Vision and Leadership

Governments should adopt a multiple-sector approach, linking education reform to the economic reform and ICT reform agenda. A combination of holistic vision and comprehensive leadership would ensure a more effective and efficient realization of the desired goals, as in the case of Singapore.

2. Symbiosis

The overall impact of reform will be greater when there is proper alignment between strategic plans, vision statements, education infrastructure and organization, school cultures, whole-school operations, teacher education and the continued professional development for leaders. The lack of reform effectiveness in Hong Kong and Australia may be attributed to the non-alignment of actions by the many parts contributing to the whole. Issues such as building designs, rigid scheduling, large classes, an aging teaching population, the high value placed on high-stake examinations, and society's academic expectations, will take more than the capabilities of ICT to resolve.

3. ICT Support and Music Curriculum Reform

It is not common for those with the IT expertise and interest within a school to possess the necessary expertise to support music-specific needs, such as audio and multi-media. Music teachers will need better technological support in order to teach in ways that motivate today's prosumers (Leong 2003). They need to be able, on the creative and innovative aspects of music education, to focus and connect to the real world of music making.

4. Pedagogical Culture

Schools and teachers need to embrace the culture of a 'learning organization', being ever ready for continued changes, self-renewal and self-improvement. The SARS crisis in Hong Kong forced educational practitioners to confront some of the realities and possibilities of ICT and to explore new ways of doing things. New teaching practices, beliefs and thinking should be encouraged through a periodical review of questions relating to the fundamentals of education. Some examples are: should education be ICT-based, -centred, -supported, -enabled? How are these positions different? Should learning be ICT-centred, student-centred, programme-centred, subject-centred, skill-centred, economy-centred, problem-centred? How different is school learning culture from that of e-learning? With high-speed connections and knowledge access, ICT has now enabled teachers to be multi-skilled, and to design new kinds of learning tasks and assessments.

5. Teacher Education and Professional Development

Despite teacher education and professional development being recognized as critical to the effectiveness and 'shelf-life' of teachers, many governments have largely paid only lip-service to enabling those tasked with educating the future workforce. Pre-service teachers these days have to cope with making ends meet while juggling with their education studies. In-service teachers have so much to do in school that they hardly have the time and mental 'space' to keep abreast of new research and technological advances. The teacher education system in Singapore and England are unusual in 'paying' trainee teachers during their period of training. Teachers also need models of effective ICT integration in their particular subjects (see Richards 2005). The school curriculum in a knowledge economy should move beyond a discipline-based and separate-subjects approach to a thematic approach which explores the relationships between subjects (Voogt and Pelgrum 2005).

6. Sustainability

The built-in obsolescence and limited capabilities of mono-application technologies meant that the provision of music technology in schools used to be very expensive. This is no longer the case with the advent of laptop computers, wireless technologies, open-source software and platforms. Space is no longer an issue either, and the creation and manipulation of music can be extended beyond the traditional music technology laboratory or multimedia centre. Finally, learning is no longer confined to schools, computer workstations and dedicated learning spaces. There can now be increased sharing of facilities and expertise between the disciplines as the technologies converge. However, new considerations such as security, confidentiality, interoperability/compatibility, plagiarism and internet protocol issues would need to be addressed by the education sector at large.

7. Music Valued as Cultural Capital

Music holds its place amongst the most loved and saleable 'commodities', classified as 'cultural capital'. The music industry has grown to be a multi-billion dollar industry worldwide, and continues to expand. The preponderance of music in youth culture gives it extra credence for it to be properly valued in today's schools. Students should be well-taught and well-prepared to be cultural creators and workers who contribute significantly to their countries. Besides giving a multitude of benefits for those who learn music, its modern role in the cultural development of a society should be better advocated.

Coda

Driven by the global trend to become knowledge economies, Australia, Singapore and Hong Kong have produced impressive policies with visions and strategies for education reform. Since about 1997, their respective reform goals have been implemented with varying levels of success. The reform experiences of these countries have demonstrated the importance of vision and leadership and the symbiotic impact of multi-sector coordination and collaboration.

Adequate preparation and support for those engaged in the achievement of reform goals is critical; this includes ICT support, teacher training and continuing professional development. The possibilities afforded by emerging technologies for providing new ways of managing and enhancing teaching and learning cannot be ignored. As a potential key contributor to the economy, music's unique place as cultural capital in cultural development and cultural industries should be well-valued by communities. Governments should be proactive in enabling the education sector to sustain its significance in the economy through effective teaching and learning both in schools and lifelong learning.

References

ACT Department of Education and Training (ACT DET) (2005), *Emerging Technologies: A Framework for Thinking. Final Report*. Canberra: education. au.limited. Available online at www.decs.act.gov.au/publicat/publicat.htm. Accessed on 27 July 2006.

Asia Pacific Programme for Educational Innovation and Development (APEID) (2004), *Final Report of Asia and the Pacific Seminar-workshop on Educational Technology, 30 August to 6 September 2004*. Tokyo and Kyoto, Japan. Available online at http://gauge.ugakugei.ac.jp/apeid/apeid04/FinalReport/final_final_report.pdf. Accessed on 30 July 2006.

Australian Computer Society (2005), *Policy Statement on Computer Literacy*. Australia. Available online at www.acs.org.au/publication/acspolicies. htm. Accessed on 27 July 2006.

Australian Government (2004), *Australia's Strategic Framework for the Information Economy 2004-2006*. Canberra: Department of Communications, Information Technology and the Arts.

Brown, A. (1995), 'Digital technology and the study of music'. *International Journal of Music Education*, 25, 14-19.

Brown, A. (1999), 'Music, media and making: humanizing digital media in music education'. *International Journal of Music Education*, 33, 3-9.

Brown, A.R. (2006). *Computers in Music Education: Amplifying Musicality*. New York: Routledge.

Bruniges, M. (2006), 'What is driving curriculum reform in Australia?' *Curriculum Leadership*, 4(25), 1-6.

Cheung, J.W.Y. and Au, E.K.O. (2003), 'The use of information technology in arts education in Hong Kong', in Y.S.C. Chee, N. Law, K.T. Lee, and D. Suthers (eds), *The 'Second Wave' of ICT in Education: From Facilitating Teaching and Learning to Engendering Education Reform. Proceedings of the International Conference on Computers in Education. Hong Kong, China, 2-5 December 2003*. Norfolk, VA: Association for the Advance of Computing in Education (AACE), pp. 53-6.

Chong, S. (1999), 'Weaving a musical web: a music project between a secondary school in Singapore and another in the UK', in D. Forrest and N. de Carmago (eds), *Building Bridges Between Mass Media, Technology and Music Education*. Victoria, Australia: RMIT University, pp. 37-44.

Curriculum Development Council (CDC) (2000), *Learning to Learn: The Way Forward in Curriculum Development. Consultant Document*. Hong Kong: Curriculum Development Council of Hong Kong.

Curriculum Development Council (CDC) (2001), *Learning to Learn: Life-long Learning and Whole-Person Development. The Way Forward in Curriculum Development*. Hong Kong: Curriculum Development Council of Hong Kong.

Darling-Hammond, L. and Sclan, E.L. (1996), 'Who teaches and why: dilemmas of building a profession for twenty-first century schools', in J. Sikula, (ed.),

Handbook of Research of Teacher Education. New York: MacMillan, pp. 67–101.

Department of Education and Training (DE&T). (1998), *Learning Technologies Teacher Capabilities*. Available online at www.sofweb.vic.edu.au/pd/tchcap/tchcap.htm. Accessed on 28 June 2006.

Department of Education, Science and Training (DEST) (2002), *Raising the Standards: A Proposal for the Development of an Information and Communication Technology (ICT) Competency Framework for Teachers*. Available online at http://dets.gov.au/schools/publications/2002/raisingstandards.htm. Accessed on 30 June 2006.

Dillon, S. (2001), The student as maker: an examination of the meaning of music to students in a school and the ways in which we give access to meaningful music education. Unpublished PhD thesis, La Trobe University (Australia).

Education and Manpower Bureau (EMB) (1998), *Information Technology for Learning in a New Era. Five-year Strategy 1998/1999 to 2002/2003*. Hong Kong: Education Commission of the Hong Kong SAR Government.

Education and Manpower Bureau (EMB) (2002), *Annual Report: Quality Insurance Inspection 2001-2002*. Hong Kong: Government Printer.

Education and Manpower Bureau (EMB) (2004), *Information Technology in Education: Way Forward*. Hong Kong: Education Commission of the Hong Kong SAR Government.

Education Commission (EC) (2000), *Learning for Life. Learning Through Life. Reform Proposals for the Education in Hong Kong*. Hong Kong: Education Commission of the Hong Kong SAR Government.

Education Department, Hong Kong. (1999), *The Application of Information Technology in the Teaching of Music: Handbook for Music Teachers 1999*. Hong Kong: Creative Arts and Home Economics Section (Music), Advisory Inspectorate Division.

Finger, G., Lang, W., Proctor, R. and Watson, G. (2004). 'Auditing the ICT experiences of teacher education undergraduates'. *Australian Educational Computing*, 19(1), 3–10. Available online at www.acce.edu.au/journal/journals/AECvol19_1.pdf. Accessed on 2 August 2006.

Fox, R. (2004), 'SARS epidemic: Teachers' experiences using ICTs', in R. Atkinson, C. McBeath, D. Jonas-Dwyer and R. Phillips (eds), *Beyond the comfort zone: Proceedings of the 21st ASCILITE Conference*. Perth, Australia, 5–8 December, pp. 319–27. Available online at www.ascilite.org.au/conferences/perth04/procs/fox.html. Accessed on 30 July 2006.

Ho, W.C. (2004), 'Use of information technology and music learning in the search for quality education'. *British Journal of Educational Technology*, 35(1), 57–67.

Infocomm Development Authority of Singapore (IDA) (2006), *Singapore iN2015 Masterplan Offers a Digital Future for Everyone, 20 June 2006*. Available online at www.ida.gov.sg/idaweb/marketing/infopage.jsp?infopagecategory=&infopageid=I3881&versionid=1. Accessed on 29 July 2006.

Law, N., Kankaanranta, M. and Chow, A. (2005), 'Technology-supported educational innovations in Finland and Hong Kong: A tale of two systems'. *Human Technology*, 1(2), 176–201.

Law, N., Yuen, A., and Chow, A. (2003), Pedagogical Innovations and Use of ICT. Paper presented at the 10th Biennial Conference of the European Association for

Research   on   Learning   and   Instruction,   Padova,   Italy,
26-30 August 2003. Available from SITE M2 website at sitesdatabase.cite.
hku.hk/link/main.asp?in_page=8. Accessed 20 July 2006.

Leong, S. (1995), 'Music technology competency and effective teacher preparation'.
Australian Journal of Music Education, 1995(1), 21-25.

Leong, S. (2003), 'Musicianship in the Age of the Prosumer: the business of cultivating
the planetary musician', in S. Leong (ed.), *Musicianship in the 21ˢᵗ Century:
Issues, Trends and Possibilities*. Sydney, Australia: Australian Music Centre, pp.
151-69.

Ministerial Council for Employment, Education, Training and Youth Affairs
(MCEETYA) (1999), *National Goals for Schooling in the Twenty-first Century*.
Available   online   at   www.mceetya.edu.au/mceetya/nationalgoals/index.htm.
Accessed on 29 July 2006.

Ministerial Council for Employment, Education, Training and Youth Affairs
(MCEETYA) (2000), *Learning in an Online World: The School Action Plan for
the Information Economy*. Adelaide: Education Network Australia. Available
online at www.edna.edu.au/edna/file12665. Accessed on 29 July 2006.

Ministerial Council for Employment, Education, Training and Youth Affairs
(MCEETYA) (2005), *Building a Knowledge Culture: An Education and
Training Action Plan for the Information Economy 2005-2007*. Available
online at aictec.edu.au/aictec/page13.html. Accessed on 29 July 2006.

Ministry of Education website (MOE) (n.d.), *Mission Statement*. Available online at
www.moe.gov.sg/corporate/mission_statement.htm. Accessed on 23 July 2006.

Ministry of Education website (MOE) (n.d.), *Speeches*. Available at http://www.moe.-
gov.sg/speeches/2002/sp24072002.htm. Accessed on 23 July 2006.

Organization for Economic Cooperation and Development (OECD) (1999), *The
Knowledge-based Economy*. Paris: OECD.

Partnership for 21st Century Skills (2005), *Assessment of 21ˢᵗ Century Skills: The
Current Landscape*. Pre-publication draft. Available online at www.21stcentur-
yskills.org/index.php?option=com_content&task=view   &id=131&Itemid=103.
Accessed on 28 July 2006.

Partnership for 21st Century Skills (2006), *Results that Matter: 21ˢᵗ Century Skills and
High School Reform*. Tucson, Arizona: Partnership for 21st century Skills.
Available online at www.21stcenturyskills.org/index.php?option=com_content
&task=blogcategory&id=3&Itemid=64. Accessed on 28 July 2006.

Pascoe, R., Leong, S., MacCallum, J., MacKinlay, E., Marsh, K., Smith, B., Church, T. and
Winterton, A. (2005). *National Review of School Music Education: Augmenting
the Diminished*. Canberra: Australian Government, Department of Education,
Science and Training.

Richards, C. (2005), 'The design of effective ICT-supported learning activities:
exemplary models, changing requirements, and new possibilities'. *Language
Learning and Technology*, 9(1), 60-79.

SITES M2 website. Available online at http://sitesdatabase.cite.hku.hk/online/index.-
asp. Accessed on 20 July 2006.

Soh, V. (2002), 'MP2: The next Masterplan for IT in education'. *Education*,
September–October, 2002, pp. 30-33.

United Nations Educational, Scientific and Cultural Organization (UNESCO) Principal
Regional Office for Asia and the Pacific (1992), *Towards Developing New*

Teacher Competencies in Response to Mega-trends in Curriculum Reforms. Bangkok: UNESCO.

Voogt, J. and Pelgrum, H. (2005), 'ICT and curriculum change'. *Human technology*, 1(2), 157–75.

World Economic Forum (2005), *Networked Readiness Index.* Available online at www.forbes.com/technology/2005/03/09/cx_0309wefranking.html.   Accessed on 25 July 2006.

Yip, L.C.R. (2003), 'Computer-based music technology in teacher education', in L.C.R. Yip, C.C. Leung and W.T. Lau (eds), *Curriculum Innovations in Music.* Hong Kong: Hong Kong Institute of Education, pp. 432–7.

Chapter 16

Creativity and Technology: Critical Agents of Change in the Work and Lives of Music Teachers

Pamela Burnard

Introduction

Change is constant for teachers; it is a process which presses in from many directions and underpins the concept of *teacher development*. The impact of school reform agendas and the interest in raising educational standards is ramified in multiple ways, directly and indirectly, in the personal and professional elements of our work and life (Day *et al.* 2006). While *change agendas* most commonly focus on accountability and raising student attainment, the meanings that we, as teachers, attach to different challenges vary according to the societal, cultural and technological factors framing (and reframing) our work (Anderson 1997, Wubbels and Poppleton 1999).

In our digital age, the situation of childhood and youth cultures in society is changing. The balance between school and family is changing. The relationship between school and home is changing. As a result of these processes, the factors influencing the contexts in which teachers work and live, and how we conceive of teaching and ourselves as teachers, require rich datasets and exclusive focus for teacher development (Fishman *et al.* 2006, Burnard 2006a).

There are new models of how music can be created, experienced and received in society (Savage 2005). The influence of broader social, cultural and technological conditions on music teachers has consequences for practice, and leads to increasing demands in terms of time and commitment (Mills 2005). Secondary school music is at a crossroads. With the conflicting forces of 'underperformance' (Mills 1997), 'the crisis of confidence in secondary school music teaching' (Cox 2002, p. 129) and declining student motivation (Harland *et al.* 2005), many music teachers feel overwhelmed, demotivated and disenfranchized (Baker 2005). To frame change in the music curriculum, secondary music teachers need to think radically about the conditions of new technology and creativity, both enabling and constraining, and consider how the dilemmas of the job can be addressed within collaborative working environments where colleagues learn from each other (Price 2005).

The paragraphs that follow will set the context for the chapter. A two-fold purpose is at work. First, the chapter considers the kinds of challenges associated with school music and the dilemmas of the job of secondary music teaching. Second, in highlighting what is distinctive about the increasing importance of creativity and technology, the chapter argues that secondary music teachers need to not only *learn* from research but also to *engage* in research in order to raise awareness of their own professional development and develop professionally within their working environment.

The argument concludes with a call for new research directions and commitment to the research of new technologies. It looks at the contribution of creativity as an agent of change to improve secondary music teaching and re-evaluates its purpose in terms of reframing the work of music teachers in schools.

Taking Account of the Changing Nature of Secondary School Music

We live in an increasingly technologically mediated world. Our everyday lives are dominated by digital media. We make daily use of compact discs, the internet, iPod MP3 players, iTunes and CD burners. With some 6.3 million MP3 players sold in 2006 in the UK alone, it is no surprise that today we have a digital generation of plugged-in listeners. Yet, while it may feel like we are bombarded with more technology in our lives than ever before, rather it is that we are bombarded with greater access to information, communication and expression through technological innovations.

For teenagers, an iPod is both a social status symbol and an object that shapes their everyday experience of digital–audio–visual environments. The social effect of music chosen for an iPod is particularly important since it represents identity and provides a sign of being 'way cool' (Iemma 2006). Such gadgets offer young people adaptive modes of musical participation, and increased access to music and tools for mediating musical experience. Furthermore, the technologies available can be adapted to constructive learning environments in which the making, experiencing, receiving and creating of music has changed dramatically (Folkestad 2006).

At the interface between home and school, teenagers experience a changing sense of place and belonging. Closing the gap between technology use at home and school preoccupies teacher thinking about *what* should be included in the curriculum, *how* it should be delivered, and *where* in the curriculum it should be positioned (Espeland 2006). The question arises of whether we should be placing technology at the centre of the curriculum (as is presently the policy), or whether it is a better goal to have technology-as-subject or music-technology-as-subject or technologically-mediated musical experiences at the centre?

Underachievement, dropout and negative attitudes to music have been advanced to explain the contested nature of music education. Teachers are pressured to accept that they do not know everything, nor are they the purveyors of all musical knowledge (Pitts 2001). The challenge of technology is to find ways of developing the knowledge about digital music consumption and production brought from the home to school; moving technology from being an 'add-on' to being in the centre, embedded rather than integrated in the secondary music curriculum; employing technology to do more than merely 'serve' tradition; and enabling technology to bring 'real world' experience into the classroom. All of these issues underscore the changing nature of secondary school music (Ofsted 2004, 2006).

Taking Account of the Creativity Agenda

Since 1999, there has been a phenomenal growth in funded projects that employ teams of musicians and other artists to undertake creative production with young people. The increasing importance of creativity in the school curriculum, which aims to embed creativity 'at the heart of young people's personal, educational and career development' (see government report referred to earlier called the Roberts' review), is evident in an unprecedented resurgence of activity in the field of creativity in education. These areas of scholarship reflect a key element of the shifting education policy context and official agenda driving efforts to improve schools.

In England, a creativity agenda has been developing for several years. It has been aided by work in schools and supported by a range of organizations and arts funding agencies including the Department for Culture, Media and Sport (DCMS) and Department for Education and Skills (DfES 2003, 2004), Creative Partnerships (Creative Partnerships/DEMOS 2003; Creative Partnerships 2004a, 2004b) and the National College for School Leadership (NCSL 2004, 2005).

Much of this work is funded through a variety of government departments and influenced by the National Advisory Committee on Creative and Cultural Education's 'definition' of creativity as 'imaginative activity fashioned so as to produce outcomes that are both original and of value' (NACCCE 1999, p. 29). The work of NACCCE led to a four-year development and research project undertaken by the Qualifications and Curriculum Authority (QCA), which sought to enable teachers to find and promote creativity in classrooms with children. It has also led to the development of a policy framework for creativity (QCA 2005a, 2005b).

Many of these projects are funded in partnership with Youth Music (www.youth-music.org.uk) in England, Wales and Scotland (see also Glover and Hoskyns 2006 for reflections on several such projects in rural and urban locations in England). Other government initiatives and arts-funded projects include Musical Futures (see www.musicalfutures.org.uk and/or Price 2005); the Music Manifesto (2006) intended to secure wider musical opportunities for school children (www.musicmanifesto.-co.uk); and BECTA (www.becta.org.uk), which provides links and information on education-related topics and project write-ups.

Creative Partnerships, another government initiative, has foregrounded a well-researched and documented creativity agenda in teaching and learning (www.creative-partnerships.com/projects). Creative Partnership projects report on teachers' capacity for innovation and creativity. In conjunction with Creative Partnerships, the Creativity Action Research Awards (CARA) programme, funded by the DfES, has provided time, space and support for teachers working with artists and mentors to better understand how to help their students be more creative (see CapeUK 2006 and www.creative-partnerships.com/cara).

Recent studies have shown that when *time*, *space* and *interactivity* are coupled with teacher expertise, then creativity and technology are embedded in curriculum development. We have seen that technology frees *time* for creative development through automation. Somekh (2000) and Ruthmann (in press) maintain that digital technologies offer the opportunity to extend the *spaces* for creativity by bringing communities together for collaborative partnerships, for example, between schools and other learning sites at the individual artist, arts organization, school and university levels. Composers, performers, audiences and artists offer teachers new, collaborative kinds of *interactive* practices and extend the *spaces* available for interaction and exhibition. It becomes possible to experiment, be innovative, take risks and close the traditional gap (and relationship!) between the 'inside' and 'outside' school communities of learning (see Ledgard 2006 for a discussion of the work of the Teacher Artist Partnerships (TAP) consortium).

The potential of the internet as a new learning environment has resulted in several organizations developing technology-enhanced learning. The Associated Board, for example, recently launched an innovative free website: www.soundjunction.org.

SoundJunction comprises a set of dynamic tools for exploring, discovering and creating music. The site offers opportunities to link creativity with technology and claims to break the boundaries of conventional music practice.

Another initiative for stimulating creativity with innovative technological practice is Sonic Postcards. This is a national education programme devised and delivered by Sonic Arts Network, which promotes and explores the art of sound via the internet (www.sonicartsnetwork.org). Sonic Arts Network has recently been awarded *The New Statesman* New Media Award 2006 for making the most significant contribution to education through the use of new media technology. Sonic Postcards won the award for helping children learn about new media technology by developing a fun and educational experience. The way Sonic Postcards works is through enabling school students from across the UK to explore and compare their local sound environment by the composition and exchange of sound postcards with other schools via the internet. It illustrates how, when digital technologies intersect with civic life, the impact can affect a small community or an entire nation. This is a promising use of technology which extends rather than reinforces traditional models.

Recent research has shown that new learning environments such as the internet can facilitate the intersection of formal and informal educational settings (Webster and Hickey 2006). The internet has shown itself to be a dynamic teaching tool for exploring, discovering, creating, communicating about and playing in virtual music-making contexts. It provides a mechanism for connecting a network of places, spaces (both physical and symbolic), musical worlds, music makers, generators, performances and productions. In doing so, it enables participation across places and fields through multiple forms of expression. (An example of what this kind of learning environment offers is illustrated by Sonic Postcards.)

Ignite, a programme for exceptional young people in England, funded by the National Endowment for Science, Technology and the Arts (NESTA), offered a combination of residential Creativity Labs (for 10–15 year olds) and Creativity Fellowships, with mentors and creative advisers (for 16–21 year olds). The accounts of the 10–15 year olds highlight the need to overcome fear of failure and feelings of self-consciousness (Burnard 2006b). The kinds of challenges and dilemmas young people face, particularly when working creatively with technology, may affect how those who aspire to excel creatively view themselves in relation to technology use at school (Craft *et al.* 2004).

Each of these organizations presents a shifting amalgam of creativity and technology as vital dimensions in transforming learning and teaching practice. The challenges posed by aiming to embed these in the secondary music curriculum, to meet the musical needs of the learner, are great indeed. The paradox lies in establishing an appropriate organizational climate (i.e. of course structures) in the midst of a policy agenda which sometimes treats teachers like technicians rather than artists, and centrally controls both curriculum content and teacher practice (Craft 2005).

While this rich array of creative opportunities for young people may sound wonderful, it would be false to paint too enthusiastic a picture since it translates into only pockets of innovative practice. Lack of support for the creation of space and time for music does little to achieve widespread implementation of the latest government edicts. How much teachers can do as managers of new technologies depends on what policy-makers can facilitate through new models of educational provision. As Pitts points out:

> Music is a subject that has always had to fight for its place in the school
> timetable, competing with those more 'useful' subjects that have an obvious
> relevance for future employment or social survival. (Pitts 2001, p. 54)

The fact that there still lurks a rigid teacher practice adhering strictly to the
accumulation of musical knowledge in formal sites, in the form of 'given' or
uncontested Western traditionalism, is testament to deep resistance and fear of
change. Indeed, many music teachers feel overwhelmed by struggles for status,
recognition and allocation of resources, with few engaging voluntarily in change
(Baker 2005). The tensions experienced are a consequence of not reflecting closely on
practice, as noted by Schön who offers this observation:

> When a member of a bureaucracy embarks on a course of reflective practice,
> allowing himself to experience confusion and uncertainty, subjecting his frames
> and theories to conscious criticism and change, he may increase his capacity to
> contribute to significant organizational learning, but he also becomes, by the
> same token, a danger to the stable system of rules and procedures within which
> he is expected to deliver his technical expertise. (Schön 1983, p. 328)

Change is risky, destabilizing and bound up in teacher dilemmas. Perhaps this is why
fostering change in professional practice is rarely the result of a single intervention but
rather takes place most effectively when closely related to the factors motivating
teachers to engage in the process in the first place. The rewards that inhere for a
teacher who wants to extend their work and rethink the nature of the profession are
arguably less than the challenges. Teaching is a risky business; collaboration with
colleagues, experimentation and gathering feedback can also be risky processes – so
how are teachers to succeed?

In the current climate of accountability and control, when change happens it is
likely to result from a combination of factors. As the phenomenal growth in funded
teacher development research projects suggests, the grounds of practice are shifting.
Creativity is a locus for change and a significant area for future work by practitioner-
researchers to research, theorize and practise.

Taking Account of the Technology Agenda

The questions of *what* is perceived as possible and *how* best school music can
contribute to nurturing highly motivated secondary school leavers need to be
addressed by seeking to understand young people's views on the nature of music and
technologically mediated music making. A motivation for change is rooted in the
profound need to continually re-set teaching into the broader context of young
people's lives. Knowing how (not whether) to position and deal with technology and
creativity in the curriculum – to create, perform, learn and talk about music in new
ways – is a major challenge (Cain 2004).

One way to begin the process of changing school policies and teacher practices is to
look at the intersection of teacher and student lives (Cox 2002). We need to listen to
young people's views (Rudduck 1999) and look beyond the formal and informal
musical ways of learning in Western societies and cultures (Folkestad 2006). While, on
the one hand, technologically mediated music making can challenge the most

cherished practices of classroom music teachers, on the other hand, it can generate the desire to (and ways in which to) diversify existing pedagogical practice.

Secondary school music teachers are constantly criticized and labelled as less successful than those from other disciplines in terms of adjusting to the extension of learning time as a benefit of new technology. At the same time, music teachers continue to be under-resourced, lacking appropriate technologies and time to think through what technology can offer music education (see, for example, Chapter 15 by Leong). The gap between those schools which have and those which don't have adequate access to new digital technologies (i.e. funding for these technologies) is continuing to grow, while the gap between student engagement and music achievements in-school and out-of-school is also widening. The political and professional imperatives of engaging students more strategically, and of making music education accessible, relevant and motivating (i.e. more 'in synch' with young people's musical needs), reflect the continuing challenges to teacher.

We know that technology is deeply embedded in the contemporary lexicon of young people's musical lives. The internet is their new playground and creates different social rooms for them. Its profound effect is conveyed in what sociologist Margaret Meade calls 'reverse heritage' – children encounter and familiarize themselves with innovations before their parents, and indeed teachers, do – a reversal of the usual hierarchical roles of parent and child and child and teacher.

It appears that many young people are already high-end or consumption-bound users and consumers of music technology, mass media and the production technologies when they come to school. They are often motivated by out-of-school experiences of digital musical cultures. What they bring to school from home and community, key sites in the context of leisure for cultural consumption, offers new challenges to teachers.

It seems that some young people have access to technologies that can download, link, transfer, record, adapt, communicate and exchange musical information. Many have access to a wider range and are listening to more music than ever before. Some are fearless in their willingness to try new things with digital technology, although those who practise consumption rather than production behaviour are not confident users.

We know less about what teachers know and learn regarding technology in practice – and how the knowledge is deployed in practice. Questions arise concerning how the teacher's role changes in different pedagogical contexts, what creative practices enhance effective technology use in the secondary school classroom, what is learned from experience and from students, and how teachers experience being an ongoing learner themselves. In the present policy climate, the dilemma is that there is little that secondary school music teachers can do about government dominance over professional development agendas (in particular given the current obsession with literacy and numeracy targets, and the presumption that educational 'standards' and 'effectiveness' are defined at the primary or elementary phase of schooling). Other limitations to the positioning of technology (and creativity), as associated with secondary school music teaching, are the tensions around developing expressions of policy into practice and documenting innovative practice to make the tacit explicit. The work being developed in Creative Partnerships to offer a cultural and creative entitlement to young people, for example, needs to be brought into articulation with the possibilities and prospects foregrounded for the secondary music curriculum.

Setting New Agendas from Inside the Secondary Music Classroom?

Having identified some of the challenges inherent in secondary school music teachers' translation of policy to practice, the next steps involve setting out an agenda for the professional development of music teachers in relation to what has been learned from research on creativity and technology in secondary school music education. It is hoped that teachers will not only respond and adapt to change but become the authors of change in their own classrooms and in the wider context of their schools. To bring this about the following needs to be done.

1. The imperative of becoming a research-informed and research-based profession needs to be applied. This would enable music teachers to aspire and have the confidence to take control of their professional development agendas within work contexts which were characterized by creativity and technology.
2. The imperative for authoring new agendas needs to be applied. This would enable teachers to address the shifting amalgam of personal and professional change by researching and theorizing about what is educationally worthwhile from within secondary schoool music classrooms.

The following section will explore what is distinctive about the contribution that technology can make to reflection. It will address this in the light of determining the development of practitioner research through a greater awareness of the complexity of the education process and research-based professional development (Hargreaves 1996).

Becoming a Research-informed and Research-based Profession

Research, like teaching, involves the fundamental act of reflection. The arguments for its value and the purposes it serves are reiterated throughout this chapter. We know that real change in values and attitudes, which takes place through professional reflection, leads to more effective practice in teaching (Burnard and Hennessy 2006). If music teaching is to become not just a research-*informed* profession but a research-*based* profession, as thought to be the most enduring and successful way of ensuring progress in high quality musical learning (Hargreaves 1996), then we need a genuine attempt to engage the whole professional community of secondary school music teachers in reflecting on their pedagogical practice. Reflective practice could act as both catalyst and response in creating a new agenda.

When considering how creativity and technology can be positioned in the secondary school music curriculum, we need to have clear understandings. While these understandings may be rooted in all kinds of research, the most important is practitioner research in reflective practice since this is a process whereby teachers look critically not only at their own practice but also at broader educational questions (Burton and Bartlett 2005).

Although teachers are currently under increasing pressure – they have less time and opportunity for professional risk taking, innovation and deep engagement with the principles and tensions between practice and policy (DfES 2004) – as researcher practitioners, it is possible for the teacher to author change from inside the classroom. Teachers can combine observational data with interviews of learners as they interact with and react upon the issues they seek to understand. This is not a pretentious claim because the human capacity for sheer adaptation is as defining of teachers' work as it is of their life histories (Baker 2005). Although music education 'enjoys' the educational potentials of creativity and technology, in order to do so vigorously, teachers need to recognize the *problems* besetting music education as *opportunities* for change.

Teachers need to view the educational experience through the eyes and perspectives of their students. They also need to understand, and trace the roots of, success and failure, motivation and demotivation in both themselves and their students.

Some ideas for practitioner-researchers' classroom enquiries might be:

1   exploring how the real creative use of technological platforms for new media and creative production helps and potentially may inhibit student creativity
2   identifying how this (wired) generation of creative users (along with the technophobic users) differs from other generations (past and future)
3   developing a deep understanding (or 'verstehen') of what the relationship with the technology reveals and conceals about how digital technology and creativity interact to underpin, inform and adapt to new learning environments for learning and teaching music
4   evaluating the affordances (or enabling conditions and limitations) of web-based and e-technology environments for advancing the development of musical creativity (i.e. what technology reveals and conceals as opportunities in creative production or in teaching when blocked by technological rather than musical problems (see Dillon, S. 2006, Heidegger 1977))
5   consulting students (i.e. giving learners a critical and democratic or genuine say) in the acquisition of technologies, about how to use new learning technologies and, indeed, opportunities to create their own learning technologiesand different kinds of technological spaces which enhance collaborative and personal creativity.

If understanding is to be the goal, then future practitioner research needs to involve both teachers and learners. We need much more classroom enquiry into aspects of what is distinctive about views at the level of a) learner and classroom and b) learner and outside-school settings. We need to take into account the institutional and home factors that contribute to learning and thereby to new models of teaching with technologies (as illustrated by Ruthmann, 2006). We need to understand what learners say and do as a consequence of how they interpret the world. Importantly, we need to understand more about experiences, interactions and events from the viewpoints of secondary school students.

Teachers need to aspire to work as practitioner-researchers, engaging creatively with the opportunities for collaborative possibilities offered by technology. University lecturer-researchers can help with mentoring conversations in producing new classroom-based enquiry and the effective use to which academic research may be put by teachers anxious to learn from research findings (see CapeUK 2006).

In the 1970s, Stenhouse (1975) was advocating classrooms as sites for teacher research. Stenhouse (1983) continued to argue that classrooms constitute the best context(s) for researching and constructing understanding. He advocated learning itself as a research process and research as the basis for teaching. As Stenhouse (cited in Rudduck 1999, p. 52) famously said, 'it is teachers who, in the end, will change the world of the school by understanding it'.

Perhaps most significantly, we must question to what ends our potential as music practitioner-researchers may be creating, and can create, new possibilities. To what extent can we raise new agendas for making the secondary school music curriculum relevant? We need to address the key role played by creativity and technology in the secondary school music curriculum and in complementary educational sites. These considerations are the remit for those teaching music in the internet age who want to identify the real creative uses of technology in their music classrooms.

References

Anderson, L.W. (1997), 'The stories teachers tell and what they tell us'. *Teaching and Teacher Education,* 13(1), 131–6.

Baker, D. (2005), Voices in Concert: Life Histories of Peripatetic Music Teachers. Unpublished thesis for Doctor of Philosophy, University of Reading, May 2005.

Burnard, P. (2006a), 'Reflecting on the creativity agenda in education'. *Cambridge Journal of Education,* 36(3), 313–18.

Burnard, P. (2006b), 'The individual and social worlds of children's musical creativity', in G. McPherson (ed), *The Child as Musician: A Handbook of Musical Development.* Oxford: Oxford University Press, pp. 353–74.

Burnard, P. and Hennessy, S. (2006), *Reflective Practices in Arts Education.* Dordrecht: Springer.

Burton, D. and Bartlett, S. (2005), *Practitioner Research for Teachers.* Thousand Oaks, CA: Sage.

Cain, T. (2004), 'Theory, technology and the music curriculum'. *British Journal of Music Education,* 21(2), 215–21.

CapeUK (2006), *Creative Action Research Awards 2: The Handbook.* A programme initiated and commissioned by Creative Partnerships, led and managed by CapeUK. Leeds: Cape UK.

Craft, A. (2005), *Creativity in Schools: Tensions and Dilemmas.* London: Routledge.

Craft, A., Miell, D., Joubert, M., Littleton, K., Murphy, P., Vass, E. and Whitelock, D. (2004), *Final Report for the NESTA's Fellowship Young People Project, Ignite, September, 2004.* London: National Endowment for Science, Technology and the Arts (NESTA).

Cox, G. (2002), *Living Music in Schools 1923-2000: Studies in the History of Music Education in England.* London: Ashgate.

Creative Partnerships (2004a), *Catalyst: This Is How Education Should Be, Isn't It?* London: Creative Partnerships.

Creative Partnerships (2004b), Creative Partnerships Website. Available at: www.creative-partnerships.com/aboutcp/.

Creative Partnerships/DEMOS (2003), Creative Learning. Unpublished working document.

Day, C., Kington, A., Stobart, G. and Sammons, P. (2006), 'The personal and professional selves of teachers: stable and unstable identities'. *British Educational Research Journal,* 32(4), 601–16.

Department for Education and Skills (DfES) (2003), *Excellence and Enjoyment.* London: HMSO.

Department for Education and Skills (DfES) (2004), *Key Stage 3 National Strategy: ICT Across the Curriculum*. London: DfES.

Dillon, T. (2006), *Exploring Young People's Collaborative and Creative Processes Using Keyboard and Computer-based Music Technologies in Formal and Non-formal Settings*. Milton Keynes: The Open University.

Dillon, S. (2006), 'Before the eyes glaze over'. *Music Forum: Music Council of Australia*, 13, 32–3.

Espeland, M. (2006), Symposium papers on Internet-based Music Education in Schools, presented at the International Society of Music Education (ISME) World Conference, Kuala Lumpur, Malaysia, July 2006.

Fishman, W., DiBara, J.A. and Gardner, G. (2006), 'Creativity: Good education against the odds'. *Cambridge Journal of Education*, 36(3), 383–98.

Folkestad, G. (2006), 'Formal and informal learning situations or practices vs. formal and informal ways of learning'. *British Journal of Music Education*, 23(2), 135–46.

Glover, J. and Hoskyns, J. (2006), 'Reflection and evaluation: Tools for learning by arts practitioners', in P. Burnard and S. Hennessy (eds), *Reflective Practices in Arts Education*. Dordrecht, Netherlands: Springer.

Hargreaves, D. (1996), *Teaching as a Research-based Profession: Possibilities and Prospects*. TTA Annual Lecture, April 1996.

Harland, J., Lord, P., Stott, A., Kinder, K., Lamont, E. and Ashworth, K. (2005), *The Arts-education Interface: A Mutual Learning Triangle?* Slough: National Foundation for Educational Research (NFER).

Heidegger, M. (1977), *The Question Concerning Technology and Other Essays*. Translated and with an introduction by William Lovitt. New York: Garland.

Iemma, M. (2006), 'Six ways to iPod, MP3 tools for your classroom'. *Music in Action for Australian Educators*, 4(1), 26–7.

Ledgard, A. (2006), 'Fair Exchange: Shared professional development and reflective action', in P. Burnard and S. Hennessy (eds), *Reflective practices in arts education*. Dordrecht: Springer.

Mills, J. (1997), 'A comparison of the quality of class music teaching in Primary and Secondary Schools in England'. *Bulletin of the Council for Research in Music Education*, 133, 72–6.

Mills, J. (2005), *Music In Schools*. Oxford: Oxford University Press.

Music Manifesto (2006), Details of project available at www.musicmanifesto.co.uk.

National Advisory Committee on Creative and Culture Education (NACCCE) (1999), *All Our Futures: Creativity, Culture and Education*. London: Department for Education and Employment.

National College for School Leadership (NCSL) (2004), *Developing Creativity for Leadership in the Primary School*. Nottingham: NCSL. Available at www.ncsl.org.uk.

National College for School Leadership (NCSL) (2005), Available at www.ncsl.org.uk/index.cfm. Accessed on 22 September 2006.

Ofsted (2004), *Tuning In: Wider Opportunities in Specialist Instrumental Tuition for Pupils in Key Stage 2*. London: Office for Standards in Education.

Ofsted (2006), Inspection reports for schools available at www.ofsted.gov.uk. Accessed on 14 July 2006.

Pitts, S. (2001), 'Whose aesthetics? Public, professional and student perceptions of music education'. *Research Studies in Music Education*, 17, 54–60.

Price, D. (2005), *Transforming Musical Leadership: Shaping Music Education - An Emerging Vision*. London: Musical Futures/Paul Hamlyn Foundation.

Qualifications and Curriculum Authority (QCA) (2005a), *Creativity: Find it, Promote - Promoting students' creative thinking and behaviour across the curriculum at Key Stages 1 and 2 - practical materials for schools*. London: Qualifications and Curriculum Authority.

Qualifications and Curriculum Authority (QCA) (2005b), Available at www.ncaction. org.uk/creativity/about.htm. Last accessed on 8 December 2006.

Rudduck, J. (1999), 'Teacher practice and the student voice', in M. Lang, J. Olson, H. Hansen and W. Bunder (eds), *Changing Schools/Changing Practices: Perspectives on Educational Reform and Teacher Professionalism*. Louvain, Brussels: Garant, pp. 41–54.

Ruthmann, A. (in press), 'The composers' workshop: An emergent approach to composing in the classroom'. *Music Educators Journal*.

Savage, J. (2005), 'Working towards a theory of music technologies in the classroom: how students engage with and organize sounds with new technologies'. *British Journal of Music Education*, 22(2), 167–80.

Schön, D.A. (1983), *The Reflective Practitioner: How Professionals Think in Action*. London: Avebury.

Scott, D. and Usher, D. (2004), *Researching Education: Data, Methods and Theory in Educational Enquiry*. London: Continuum.

Somekh, B. (2000), 'New technology and learning: policy and practice in the UK, 1980–2019'. *Education and Information Technologies*, 5(1), 19–37.

Stenhouse, L. (1975), *An Introduction to Curriculum Research and Development*. London: Heinemann.

Stenhouse, L. (1983), *Authority, Education and Emancipation*. London: Heinemann.

Webster, P. and Hickey, M. (2006), 'Computers and technology', in G. McPherson (ed.), *The Child as Musician: A Handbook of Musical Development*. Oxford: Oxford University Press, pp. 375–96.

Wubbels, T. and Poppleton, P. (1999), 'Knowledge about change and its effects on teachers?', in M. Lang, J. Olson, H. Hansen and W. Bunder (eds), *Changing Schools/Changing Practices: Perspectives on Educational Reform and Teacher Professionalism*. Louvain, Brussels: Garant, pp. 149–56.

Contributors

ALEX BAXTER became interested in music technology at the age of 15. After following conventional courses in music to post-16 level, he studied electronic music at the University of Hertfordshire. He specialized in acoustic and electro-acoustic composition and sound recording, developing an interest in music software design before training to teach music in secondary schools. He is now in his second year of teaching and is in charge of music technology at Windsor Boys' School.

ANDREW R. BROWN is an associate professor in music and sound at the Queensland University of Technology in the Faculty of Creative Industries, and the Digital Media program manager for the Australasian CRC for Interaction Design (ACID). Andrew's expertise is in technologies that support creativity, algorithmic music and art, and the philosophy of technology. His current research focuses on adaptive music for computational arts and interactive entertainment. He is an active computer musician and a builder of software tools for dynamic content creation.

PAMELA BURNARD is a senior lecturer in Music and Arts Education in the Faculty of Education at the University of Cambridge, UK. She coordinates and lectures on the MPhil in Educational Research and the MPhil in Arts, Culture and Education courses. Her research interests include creativity, creative learning and teaching, musical creativity, artists and educational partnerships. She is co-convener of 'BERA: SIG Creativity in Education' and serves on numerous editorial boards one of which is a new *Journal of Music, Technology and Education*.

MIKE CHALLIS is a freelance composer and educator who utilizes technology to enable composition in a variety of situations. He has worked with schools, prisons and community groups. Mike has a long association with Westbridge Pupil Referral Unit in Ipswich. His other education projects include A Digital Portrait; Reflecting Others; and A Cultural Mirror for Aldeburgh Education; and Berio Fusion for BBC 21CC. Mike's personal electro-acoustic works include 'Arboretum', 'Right Foot Lower than the Left' and 'Garden' and his installations include 'Bladderwrack' on Aldeburgh beach and 'Jets', at the Faster than Sound event for the 2006 Aldeburgh festival. Mike lectures at the University of East Anglia, Norwich and is in the process of completing a PhD in collaborative composition.

LOUISE COOPER studied for her Postgraduate Certificate in Education at Cambridge University, where she was also an undergraduate on the music course. After achieving her Certificate in Education, she taught English to Junior High School students in Matsuyama City, Japan, before working as a music teacher at St. George's College,

Weybridge, where she is currently employed. Other interests, alongside the use of music technology, are musical theatre, early music and gamelan.

SERENA CROFT is a full-time director of music at a comprehensive school in Suffolk for students in the age range 13–18 years. She studied at Foyle and Londonderry College in Northern Ireland, before moving to Wales to complete a music degree at The Royal Welsh College of Music and Drama. Further study at Cambridge University led to her present career in music education. Whilst pursuing a career in the classroom, she was awarded a Masters Degree in Education (Jesus College, Cambridge) specializing in the benefits of music technology as an aid to composition. Subsequent research interests have been in the development of music technology in the music curriculum, with the aim of developing a greater general interest in music by providing a motivational learning environment.

STEVE DILLON is a senior lecturer in Music and Sound at Queensland University of Technology in the Faculty of Creative Industries. He is internationally recognized as a leading researcher in the field of positive effects of school and community music programs, particularly on at-risk youth. He is the director of the 'save to DISC' (Documenting Innovation in Sound Communities) research network. He supervises a cohort of postgraduate students; and collaborates with a team of international researchers who examine and document relationships between music, meaning, and health and well-being research utilizing digital technology.

TERESA DILLON is an artist, researcher and director. Her main interests include the use and role of existing and emerging technologies within live performance and interaction, particularly in public, site-specific and educational contexts. In 1996 Teresa established Polar Produce. She currently directs and produces in collaboration with others under the company name. She also works as a freelance artist, producer and researcher for various organizations such as the BBC and Becta. Prior to focusing on Polar Produce, Teresa worked for Futurelab, UK, where she developed new digital prototypes and future ideas for learning. Teresa holds a PhD from the Open University, UK, where her worked addressed the creative collaborative process involved in making music. She has published on the subjects of collaborative creativity, music, digital arts, open source and designing new media.

AMBROSE FIELD is senior lecturer and chair of Graduate Studies in Music at the University of York. His professional work as a musician has gained many international awards, most notably at the Prix Ars Electronica – the largest digital arts and contemporary media awards in Europe. His work is released on a number of commercial CDs and is broadcast frequently on BBC Radio 3. The *Guardian* recently highlighted *Storm!*, Field's 2006 studio album (Sargasso SCD28054), as a 'riveting, futuristic action-pic'.

JOHN FINNEY is senior lecturer in Music Education in the Faculty of Education, University of Cambridge, UK. His research is focused on understanding the ways in which young people can contribute to the transformation of music education, through taking on both leadership roles within the classroom and through their untapped potential to research and critique music educational practices. The publication *Rebuilding Engagement Through the Arts: Responding to Disaffected Students,* authored with Richard Hickman, Morag Morrison, Bill Nicholl and Jean Rudduck (2005), presents innovative research in the field of 'student voice'.

RICHARD HODGES followed study at the Royal College of Music with ten years' teaching in secondary schools in London. His postgraduate studies in music education at London University initially fostered his interest in ICT. He became senior lecturer in music at Derbyshire College of Higher Education in 1988, developing provision in music technology on BEd, MEd and Postgraduate Certificate in Education programmes. He became subject leader in music at the University of Derby in 1993, and developed the BA (Hons) Popular Music with Music Technology degree that commenced in 1996. Since 2001, he has been primary subject area leader in Performing Arts Technology at the University of Derby, developing degree provision in live event technology, multimedia technology, music production, music technology and popular music.

KEVIN JENNINGS is a musician, teacher and music educator. As a classical guitarist he has performed widely in both Ireland and Europe giving solo recitals, chamber music and concerto performances, television and radio broadcasts. He has over 20 years of experience in music education, including a variety of school appointments, most recently as Head of Fine and Performing Arts, Holy Names High School, Oakland, California. He has worked with many children's orchestras, choirs and other performing groups and has been extensively involved in children's music theatre. He is currently a research fellow at the Centre for Research in IT in Education (CRITE) at Trinity College, Dublin where he investigates the application of technology to music learning and teaching, with a particular interest in non-standard graphical interfaces and their role in facilitating learner and teacher reflection.

SAMUEL LEONG is head of the Department of Creative Arts and Physical Education at the Hong Kong Institute of Education. A native of Singapore, he was co-director of the Australian National Review of School Music Education and director of Music Education at the University of Western Australia, before moving to Hong Kong at the end of 2005. His current research projects are in the areas of i-learning, assessment and curriculum reform.

S. ALEX RUTHMANN is assistant professor of Music Education at Indiana State University in Terre Haute, Indiana where he teaches courses in music education technology, general music methods, introduction to music education and research. Prior to this he taught technology-infused general music at a middle school in Michigan. His research interests include collaborative music learning, composing curriculum and pedagogy, and music education technology. He also serves on the advisory board for the Center for Applied Research in Musical Understanding and the editorial board for the *International Journal of Music Education: Practice*.

HANNAH QUINN is a secondary school music teacher currently working at an international school in Beijing. She has worked in various state schools in the UK and completed her Postgraduate Certificate in Education at Cambridge University in 2004. Trained as a classical musician, Hannah discovered music technology in her teenage years – a discovery which was to inform her musical life from then onwards. Particular interests involve developing composition and performance techniques, both electronically and acoustically, with her students and accessing the wealth of musicianship they bring with them to school each day.

JONATHAN SAVAGE is a senior lecturer in Music Education at the Institute of Education, Manchester Metropolitan University and Visiting Research Fellow at the Royal Northern College of Music. Until 2001 he was Head of Music at Debenham High

School, a comprehensive school for 11-16 year olds in rural Suffolk in the east of England. His main research interests lie in the field of developing innovative uses of new technologies within education. He is managing director of UCan.tv, a not-for-profit company that produces innovative interactive educational resources.

FREDERICK A. SEDDON is currently a researcher at the Dipartimento di Scienze dell'Educazione, Universita' degli studi di Padova where he conducts research for the research project *'Nuove tecnologie e processi ideativi e compositivi nell'educazione musicale'*. He formerly worked as a research fellow at the Open University, in the UK, an instrumental tutor and head of music in a secondary school. His PhD (completed in 2001 at Keele University, UK) investigated adolescent computer-based composition in relation to instrumental experience. He is a member of the editorial board of the *British Journal of Music Education*.

Glossary

ABRSM
Associated Board of the Royal Schools of Music

affordance
A term commonly used to describe the features of an object that indicate how the user should interact with that object, e.g. buttons afford pushing, chairs afford sitting down.

algorithm
A step-by-step procedure for problem-solving or creating.

Apple iMac
An all-in-one desktop computer designed and made by Apple where the central processing unit (CPU) and monitor are combined in one enclosure.

Assessment for Learning (AfL)
Using evidence and dialogue to identify where students are in their learning, where they need to go and how best to get there.

Band-in-a-Box
Band-in-a-Box is an intelligent, automatic accompaniment software program.

bit-rates
The amount of bits (or data) transmitted per second.

blog
A blog is a special type of website that displays information as an online journal or diary. Most blogs consist of short entries, which may also include links to other websites, pictures, and other multimedia content, as 'posts' that are often displayed in reverse chronological order. A feature common to most blogs is the ability for readers to add their own comments to individual posts, enabling the possibility for collaborative online conversations. Popular free blog websites are Blogger.com, LiveJournal.com, WordPress.com and Xanga.com.

Bluetooth
A computing and telecommunication industry specification that enables compatible devices to interconnect wirelessly over a short distance.

bpm
A measure of tempo in beats per minute.

bricolage
From the French-language verb *bricoler*, meaning 'to tinker' or 'to fiddle about'.

broadband
Broadband refers to a method of transmitting large amounts of data (voice, video, sound image, etc) at a higher frequency than normal telephony networks.

Cathedral
Cathedral is an on-going interactive work of music and art designed specifically for the web by media artist Nora Farrell and composer William Duckworth.

chatting
Another term for MCing (see below).

ChucK
ChucK is an audio programming language for real-time synthesis, composition and performance.

CoAudicle
CoAudicle is a collaborative live coding environment that presents a graphical interface to ChucK.

code jamming
Writing software collaboratively, especially in a performance or time-limited context.

constant comparative method
An analysis procedure for the qualitative analysis of text based on 'Grounded Theory', introduced by Lincoln and Guba in 1985.

Continuator
The Continuator software enables real-time musical interaction with a system that mimics music played into it.

cross-fade
Action of fading down one sound source and bringing in another.

cross-fader (noun)
Key feature on a DJ mixer that allows you to fade down one channel and fade up the other using only one fader.

Cyberjazz
A site that allows real-time MIDI instrument connections to perform simultaneously, enabling collaborative musical interactions on the internet.

decks
Turntables/record players that play vinyl records and incorporate speed changing facilities and rapid start/stop facilities.

DGM (digital rights management)
A term that refers to any of the technologies used to control and restrict digital data or hardware access and usage; sometimes confused with copy protection and technical protection measures.

dongle
A device that plugs into a port of a computer (often USB) that adds certain capabilities to the object the device is plugged into.

drum and bass
Genre of music characterized by the use of heavy drum beats and a strong bass-line with a tempo of around 165 bpm.

DrumSteps
A software application enabling the user to create percussion music by positioning steps, ladders and other graphical elements on the screen and causing animated balls to bounce off these static objects.

eJay
eJay is a CD-ROM music program, which allows your PC to become a basic editing studio. It contains pre-recorded vocal and instrumental samples that allow users to compose, arrange, edit and record music in dance, rave and hip-hop styles and input their own samples. See http://www.ejay-uk.com/

e-learning
Network-enabled transfer of skills and knowledge, including applications and processes in web-based learning, computer-based learning and virtual classrooms.

emceeing or MCing
Generic term for when anyone speaks over a beat.

e-learning environments
'Virtual' environments for exchanging, discussing, evaluating and developing the contents of computer files without having to be in the same physical space or time.

electro-acoustic
Music created with electronic technologies which may or not include acoustic, instrumental, environmental and computer-generated sounds.

electro-acoustic composition
Pre-recorded, synthesized and processed sounds are used to create music which is free from traditional rhythms and melodies. Spatial characteristics of sound are often explored.

electronic music instrument
An instrument whose sound source is generated digitally rather than acoustically, i.e synthesizers and signal processors.

electronica
In the 1990s, this term was used to describe experimental music that used predominantly electronic production techniques. This term has now been coined to describe a wider variety of genres such as big-beat, trip-hop, dub and even Madonna.

ethernet
The most common set of computer networking technologies, hardware and software protocols, for establishing a network between computing devices. The technology upon which the internet is built.

flanging
Like phasing, but the audio within the second copy is subject to variable delay. The result often sounds like a jumbo-jet taking off.

formal instrumental music training (FIMT)
A term first used by F.A. Seddon in his MSc dissertation in 1996 to define instrumental lessons received by students participating in his research study.

garage
Genre of music which, in the UK, describes a largely London-based electronic music style that usually runs at a tempo of around 135 bpm.

generative music
Music that is determined by computer-based algorithms or asynchronous tape loops. The resulting music evolves over time and cannot be repeated.

Glasbead
Microsoft Windows software that presents a multi-user collaborative musical interface allowing players to manipulate and exchange sound sample files and create a myriad of soundscapes and rhythmic musical sequences.

graphical interface
A graphical interface (GI) or graphical user interface (GUI) is a method of representing information and interacting with a computer through the direct manipulation of graphical images (icons, menu item, animation, etc.) in addition to text.

graphical musical software applications
Software that facilitates musical interaction and composition by presenting graphical representations of musical objects which may be manipulated to achieve various musical effects.

grime
A musical offshoot of UK garage music developed in East London at the beginning of the twenty-first century.

Hyperscore
A software application that enables users to compose extended pieces of music by creating short musical fragments or motives and combining these by drawing coloured lines.

iMovie
Apple's easy-to-use video-editing software.

infrared connectivity technology
Wire-free communication and data transfer via an infrared port/dongle. Infrared devices usually have to be lined-up to enable data transmission. Infrared is a red light that humans cannot see.

Interconnected Musical Networks (IMNs)
IMNs are flexible, distributed and networked computer music systems, which allow players to independently share and shape each others' music in real-time (Teresa Dillon's chapter, Weinberg 2005).

interfaces
The point of interaction between a human and a computer is commonly called a user interface. Interfaces may be physical (a mouse or joystick) or graphical. Graphical user interfaces (GUI) accept input via physical devices, such as a computer keyboard or mouse, and provide articulated graphical output on the computer monitor.

inversion
A musical term used to indicate which note of a chord is heard in the bass. Also used to indicate a musical operation consisting of turning a pair of notes upside-down, so that the higher-pitched note becomes the lower and vice versa.

Impromptu
Impromptu is a Mac OSX programming environment for composers, sound artists, VJs and graphic artists with an interest in live or interactive programming.

iPod
iPod refers to a brand of portable digital audio players, though which users can access, listen and view various multimedia (music, images, film) while on the move. For example, refer to the Apple iPod, http://www.apple.com/itunes/.

jam2jam
jam2jam is an application which generates music that you can control while it plays. Even better, you can connect via a network with others who have jam2jam to jointly control the music. You can jam just like a band, but without the need for complex instrumental skills.

Kabuki
A form of Japanese musical theatre involving elaborate costume and stylized movements.

kinaesthetic drawing
Creating a line or gesture on the computer screen by making an intuitive physical gesture with the mouse.

a learning community
An approach to classroom organization whereby all students are involved in decision-making and collaborative teaching and learning.

looping
The practice of repeating a sound indefinitely.

MC
Master of ceremonies or Mic controller. The MC generally MCs live while a DJ mixes the tunes.

meta-level control
The ability to manipulate parameters that, in turn, affect one or more other parameters within a hierarchical control structure.

MIDI
(Musical Instrument Digital Interface). A standard protocol introduced in 1983 to facilitate the interchange of musical information between musical instruments, synthesizers and computers.

midi box
A synthesizer, controllable by computer.

MIDI files
Music files saved on computer that can be accessed and played by a variety of music software programs.

MIDI set-up

A music technology system incorporating a computer and electronic MIDI instruments.

motives

Short musical fragments or ideas which form the basis for composition in the Hyperscore interface.

MP3

'MPEG-1 Audio Layer-3'. A technology and format for compressing a sound sequence into a very small file whilst preserving its original level of sound quality.

Multi-User Virtual Environment (MUVE)

'A shared space available online where learners can interact, communicate, and build knowledge' (Murfin 2001, pp. 406–7). MUVEs support asynchronous and/or synchronous communication through tools such as discussion boards, text-based chats, audio chats, file transfer, file and application sharing, and even the emulation of everyday actions such as giving and taking objects (through avatars – or on-screen personalities). Visually, they can range from 2D graphics, or video, to 3D immersive environments. Some MUVEs allow users to build their own virtual environments or worlds (Murfin 2001). Examples of different types of MUVEs include the following: Activeworlds (www.activeworlds.com), Tapped-in (www.tappedin.org), MUDs (Multi-User Domains/Dungeons) and MOOs (MUD, Object Oriented).

musical chat

The sending of musical snippets between users over the internet, in a similar way to text chat that sends text messages.

musical co-construction

Musical co-construction is the reciprocal process through which individuals co-create and develop a shared musical understanding, while simultaneously acknowledging their individual musical differences (see Teresa Dillon's chapter, Dillon 2006).

musical loops

Small 'rifs' or musical phrases pre-recorded and saved that can be manipulated and repeated within certain music software programs.

music sequencing computer programs

Computer software programs that facilitate the recording of music as MIDI and audio files in a multi-track environment.

Musit Interactive

A Norwegian music-sequencing software program from which previously saved music and text files can be emailed between students thus creating a specific music e-learning environment.

National Curriculum Level Descriptors

Statements that indicate the type and range of performance which students working at a particular level should demonstrate.

networked improvisation

Semi-prepared real-time musical interaction over a computer network.

notation systems
Symbolic systems which are used to represent musical entities or sounds. The most prevalent such system is western staff-notation. Other notation systems include solfege, tonic sol-fa and various tablature systems, along with the kinds of computer-based systems referred to here.

OSC
An acronym for Open Sound Control. A protocol for communication among multimedia devices over an ethernet network.

on-line collaborative tools
On-line collaborative tools are any of a set of technologies and websites that enable people to easily collaborate with each other on the internet. Blogs, wikis, podcasts and social networking sites are all examples of these technologies. Currently, many online collaborative tools such as blogs and wikis utilize text-based collaboration. However, recent developments in internet technologies are enabling people to collaborate directly using audio and video through technologies such as Skype and iChat and websites such as YackPack.com and Twitter.com.

panning
The placement of sound(s) within the stereo field.

parametric data
Information about the state or value of algorithm settings.

phasing
An audio effect caused by playing a second copy of the same material with a slight delay. In 'flanging', the audio is subject to variable delay. The result can reveal interesting inner patterns within the original material.

piano-roll notation
A music notation system common in computer software applications, where notes are indicated by horizontal rectangular shaded regions.

PitchWeb
One of the virtual instruments designed for William Duckworth's Cathedral site to allow listeners to play together online.

podcast
A method of publishing files, usually audio ones, on the internet. Users can subscribe and receive new files automatically, usually at no cost.

post-digital music
Music which moves beyond the mere application of technology into areas such as testing the boundaries of what is expressively possible with digital systems.

P2P (peer-to-peer) network A type of internet network which allows two or more groups of computer users in the same networking program to directly access files from each other's hard drives.

Quoth
Quoth is a dynamic interactive system for creating collaborative narrative structures in real time. The major use of Quoth so far has been for musical livecoding.

range
The complete set of notes and intervals from the highest to the lowest notes, ie. from C1 to C6. In jam2jam this would focus on a scale that formed the style algorithm and extends over three octaves.

raw audio data
Refers to digital audio data recorded without compression.

Reason
A complete virtual music studio software, developed by Propellerheads.

RFID (radio frequency identification technology)
A wireless system using a smart tag with a microchip transmitter embedded in it. Enables identification and tracking of objects without direct contact.

ritornello
Ritornello is a form of musical structure, rooted in the Baroque genres of the concerto and opera, in which melodic and harmonic materials return again and again in the course of the movement. An example of a ritornello is Vivaldi's 'Four Seasons'.

sample
A small segment from an audio recording which is copied and possibly edited for use in a new recording.

sequenced keyboards
In addition to the basic keyboard functionality and design, sequenced keyboards have various pre-set features such as metronomes, rhythmic backings, 'automatic' harmony and demonstration sequences, which vary depending on whether the keys are 'full size', like a piano, or more touch sensitive.

sequencer
A computer music-sequencer is a piece of software that enables sequential recording and subsequent mixing and editing of musical tracks or voices.

sketch window
The window in Hyperscore in which musical motives or ideas are combined to create a composition.

Smart Cards
A credit-card sized gadget with built-in microprocessor, which serves as a 'stored value' card or holds information about the cardholder. www.merchantseek.com/glossary.htm

social networking sites
Social networking sites are a new class of websites designed to bring together people of similar interests online. Users of these websites create a personal online profile which can be personalized with streaming music and video, images, links to websites, and common interest groups. These sites often include an embedded blog where users can update their circle of friends through posts about current events and topics of interest. MySpace.com and Facebook.com are two popular sites among secondary- and teritary-level students.

software synthesizers
The Software synthesizers utilize the sound files normally contained within keyboard

synthesizers. By detaching the sound files from the musical keyboard and installing them in a computer, the sounds of several different keyboard synthesizers may be played by a generic keyboard linked to the computer that has the software-synthesizer sound files installed.

'spit over'
A term similar to 'rapping'.

standard staff notation
A music notation system comprising a staff or stave consisting of five horizontal lines on which note symbols are placed to indicate pitch and rhythm.

stroke
A line drawn in the Hyperscore sketch window, the effect of which is to both repeat and manipulate the pitch content of an associated musical motif.

symbolic form
The concrete depiction of an otherwise abstract structure. In this context, the visual representation of sound or musical structure.

shuffle
In music, a swung note or shuffle note is the rhythmic device in which the duration of the initial note in a pair is augmented and that of the second is diminished.

SuperCollider
An environment for programming real-time audio synthesis, music composition or performance.

text chat-boxes
Fields (areas) within software applications where the user can type alphanumeric characters (text).

Theremin
An electronic instrument from the early twentieth century that produces a simple monophonic tone controlled by a user moving their hands around two antennas, one controlling pitch the other loudness.

Tonic sol-fa
A system of musical notation based on relationships between tones in a key. Instead of graphical symbols, pitches are indicated by written syllables (e.g. do, re, mi, fa, sol, la, ti, do) or their abbreviations (d, r, m, f, s, l, t, d). 'Do' is chosen to be the tonic of whatever key is being used (thus the terminology 'moveable Do').

TopLap
A community of livecode performers, mostly musicians. Also refers to the website through which this community communicate.

union
The combination of two or more entities or groups.

Vodcast (Video on Demand)
A term used to describe technologies that enable users to select pre-encoded video content from a central source for viewing at any time on a television or computer screen.

VoIP (Voice over Internet Protocol)
Refers to the technology that enables the digital transmission of voice information over a data network via the internet. Calls made are usually cheaper since it bypasses traditional telephone services.

Vox pop
A name given to a jam2jam algorithm which draws from rap and hip hop musical styles.

.wav files
'Waveform Audio'. A common audio file format developed by Microsoft and IBM.

WebQuest   Refers to an activity used in education where information gathered by students is mostly obtained from the World Wide Web.

wikis
Usually refers to a web program allowing multiple users of a web forum to add and edit content.

wireless hand-held computer
A hand-held computer is a portable computer, also known as a pocket PC or personal digital assistant (PDA), that is small enough to be held in one's hand or pocket. The iPAQ, developed by Hewlett Packard, is one form of wireless hand-held computers that can be connected without wires to other devices via a broadband connection.

wireless media
Refers to media (images, sounds, video, etc.) that are transferred via wireless telecommunication devices and networks in which electromagnetic waves (rather than some form of wire) carry the signal over part of, or the entire, communication path.

Index